When God Steps In

THE AMAZING STORY OF ACRE GOSPEL MISSION

When God Steps In - The Amazing Story of Acre Gospel Mission
© Copyright 2001 Victor Maxwell

ISBN 1 84030 106 6

Ambassador Publications
a division of
Ambassador Productions Ltd.
Providence House
Ardenlee Street,
Belfast,
BT6 8QJ
Northern Ireland
www.ambassador-productions.com

Emerald House
427 Wade Hampton Blvd.
Greenville
SC 29609, USA
www.emeraldhouse.com

When God Steps In

THE AMAZING STORY OF ACRE GOSPEL MISSION

by
Victor Maxwell

AMBASSADOR

BELFAST, NORTHERN IRELAND
GREENVILLE, USA

CONTENTS

Chapter One
FROM EAST TO WEST *7*

Chapter Two
AT HOME IN THE GREEN HELL *17*

Chapter Three
TWO ARE BETTER THAN ONE *30*

Chapter Four
FACING NEW FRONTIERS *42*

Chapter Five
WHAT SHALL WE CALL THE MISSION? *65*

Chapter Six
WILL YOU NOT COME BACK AGAIN? *81*

Chapter Seven
REINFORCEMENTS NOW APPEARING *92*

Chapter Eight
GREAT DOORS SWING ON SMALL HINGES *105*

Chapter Nine
LET ME BURN OUT *120*

Chapter Ten
FAITH TAKES A STEP BACK *136*

Chapter Eleven
UP AGAINST IT *149*

Chapter Twelve
NEW THRESHOLDS *162*

Chapter Thirteen
WHAT NEXT? *180*

Chapter Fourteen
HEAVENLY RESOURCES *197*

Chapter Fifteen
PUSHED INTO EUROPE *217*

Chapter Sixteen
A GATEWAY AT THE MARKET *233*

Chapter Seventeen
OUT ON A LIMB *242*

Chapter Eighteen
HEAVENLY TREASURES *248*

Chapter Nineteen
A ROYAL AUDIENCE *258*

Chapter One

FROM EAST TO WEST

Captain George Gracey, a young man wearing wire rimmed spectacles and standing more than six feet tall, was a gaunt figure as he stood erect against a mud splattered wall. The crumpled and unkempt uniform of this brave Ulster man gave evidence of the rough treatment he had received at the hands of his captors, the ruthless Bolsheviks. Now he stared down the barrels of their guns. Ironically, he felt more pity for his executioners than panic for himself. He was not only sure that soon he would be with Christ, but he also believed that God had been in control of the circumstances that had brought him to this precarious moment.

Prior to the outbreak of the Great War George Gracey had been a missionary in Urfa, Turkey since 1904. During the course of the war Captain Gracey had been enlisted as an Intelligence Staff Officer for the British Military Mission. He was fluent in Turkish, Russian and Armenian. With his multi-lingual skills he was assigned to be a member of an American military relief expedition to the Caucasus to assist over two hundred thousand Armenians who had fled from Turkey to Russia in 1915. Single handedly he had rallied large

numbers of Armenian and Russian soldiers to hold positions that
had been deserted by revolutionary Bolsheviks during the Great War.

His courageous troops had fought bravely under his leadership
even though they were sandwiched between the forces of the German
Kaiser on the West and the followers of Vladimir Lenin to the East.
After one fierce battle Captain Gracey was taken prisoner by the
Bolsheviks at Vladikavkaz. He survived a four month trek to Moscow
through deep snow during the severe Russian winter of 1917 when
many other prisoners fell victim to the cold or a bullet put them out
of their misery.

In the Russian capital Captain George Gracey was sentenced to
be executed by a firing squad for alleged crimes against Lenin's
new revolution. He was reprieved at the last moment when he lined
up with others to be shot. This was now the second time he faced a
firing squad.

The Captain's mind was filled with thoughts and prayers for his
family back in Britain as he faced the moment of certain death. He
was sure that his body would soon fall in a heap where he now stood
but was equally certain that in that same moment he would be with
Christ. Peace filled his heart as he committed himself to his Saviour
whom he had trusted many years earlier. He still believed that God
was in control of his circumstances.

Just when it seemed he would fall victim to a Russian bullet, the
firing squad was again commanded to disband and Captain Gracey
was returned to the prison compound. *Why this torture? Are they
brainwashing me?* He wrestled in his mind.

The reason for his reprieve soon became evident. Authorities in
Turkey had offered $10,000 for the capture of the Ulster man. Rather
than have him handed over to the Turks, the Bolsheviks struck a
deal with Britain and Captain Gracey was repatriated to his homeland.

Following the end of the war he was deservedly awarded the
Distinguished Service Order by King George V for bravery on the
field of battle. After such a distinguished military career Captain
Gracey dedicated the rest of his life to Christian work. He never
ceased to testify of his conversion to Christ and how God preserved
and gave him peace in desperate and dangerous circumstances. He

travelled widely as an advocate of Christian minorities and soon became the General Secretary of Save the Children Fund.

One of the first places the war hero visited on his return to Ulster was Argyle Place Presbyterian Church where he held a group of young men spellbound telling of his conversion and how he had proved God in the most hostile circumstances. Not only were the young men greatly impressed by the striking appearance of the tall officer, but the message he delivered touched their hearts. At the end of the meeting Captain Gracey knelt beside a teenager by the name of William McComb and led him to faith in Jesus Christ.

William McComb, better known as Willie, was a Belfast lad who, like most other boys of his time, left school at fourteen years of age. He gained employment at Ireland's, a Linen Merchant on May Street in Belfast's city centre. Even though he was still an immature Christian Willie was not embarrassed to take his stand as a Christian both at work and at the Northumberland Street Mission Hall where he began to attend.

Although he worked long hours Willie seldom missed a meeting at the Mission Hall and soon became greatly involved in its weekly activities. Within a short while, it was evident to all that the young man's zeal for Christian work was supplemented with an ability to preach. This did not escape the attention of the leadership at Argyle Place Presbyterian Church.

Very soon Willie was given the responsibility of leading the work at the Hall and spearheading the Mission's open-air witness on the Shankill Road. It was an era of great evangelistic passion in Belfast and especially in the Shankill district. Dr. Hugh Montgomery was at the height of his ministry at nearby Shankill Mission and had invited the Ulster evangelist W. P. Nicholson to conduct evangelistic meetings in a tent on the Shankill Road. There was a sense of revival abroad as hundreds of people were converted in the area. Some hardened drunkards forsook the local pubs to attend West Belfast's many mission halls or churches.

On Saturday afternoons throughout the winter and during the long evenings of the summer, Willie McComb and a group of other zealous young people sang and testified of the Lord Jesus to all and sundry in the densely populated Shankill community. Not only did thousands hear the gospel from these young people, but scores were led to personal faith in Jesus Christ. Among those led to faith in Jesus Christ were Willie's own brother and sister, Joe and Sabina McComb.

The Saturday night rally was a special feature of Northumberland Street Mission and the hall was packed to capacity with both young and old for a good night of singing and Christian fellowship. It was in this meeting that Willie shone with his good sense of humour wisely balanced with his evident devotion to Jesus Christ and passion for lost souls.

There also was great missionary interest and sacrificial giving by the friends at Northumberland Street Hall. They not only gave their finances, but gave themselves to the Lord and His work. During the twenties and thirties eighteen members of Northumberland Street Hall became missionaries in various parts of the world. These included Joe Wright, Violet McGrath, Mollie Harvey, Fred Wright, Maimie Christie (later Maimie became Joe Wright's wife), Joe McComb, Margaret McKnight and Willie McComb, all of whom formed the backbone of the young people's fellowship at the Hall.

Significantly Willie McComb was the first of this formidable band of brave young Christians to step out and become a missionary to a foreign land. All of the others followed and served God distinguishably in many lands around the world.

One night Willie was with a group of young Christians who were all greatly challenged when they heard a young Royal Air Force officer testify of how God had called him to the Amazon region of Brazil. Lieutenant Fenton Hall, who hailed from County Donegal and had a distinguished career in the Royal Air Force, was a striking figure, a man of exceptional physique and fine Christian character. At six feet and four inches tall it was not surprising that Fenton Hall had been a heavyweight boxing champion in the Royal Air Force. It was his devotion to Jesus Christ and the work of worldwide evangelization that touched Willie McComb and caused him at the end of the meeting to surrender his life fully to the Saviour.

It was just eighteen months after Fenton Hall sailed to Brazil that news came through that the young airman had passed into the presence of his Lord on Christmas Day, 1924. While engaged in pioneer missionary work on the River Pindaré Fenton Hall had succumbed to a bout of dysentery and died. This report not only startled the youthful McComb, it brought home to him how perilous and sacrificial it could be to follow in the footsteps of this worthy servant of God.

Notwithstanding the sacrifice and danger of serving God in Brazil's Amazon, Willie McComb felt the constraint of God upon his life. He announced to the leadership of the Mission Hall that he was offering himself for missionary work. Although his own family expressed their concern that he was giving up his career, most people were not surprised, for they had perceived that God's hand was upon the young man's life.

In 1924 Willie left the shores of his native Ulster for the first time to embark on a course of study and training at the Missionary Training Colony at Upper Norwood, London. This was not a theological college. It was practical missionary training for a group of men who were housed in army huts which had been discarded after the First World War. Mr. Geoffrey Buxton, who was respectfully known as "BG" to his students, was not only the founder of the Training Colony, but was also known as the Camp Commandant.

The training was rigorous and austere. The day began at six o'clock with the beating of a loud gong. All students were obliged to engage in physical exercise with a quick run around the camp in all sorts of weather. This was followed by a mandatory cold shower, even on the cold winter mornings, after which the students retreated to their billets for personal devotions. Only after two hours was breakfast contemplated and this was provided by the students who were assigned to cook on that day. Throughout the rest of morning the students attended classes to study the Scriptures while the afternoon was taken up learning practical skills.

The colony offered a nine month course, but during two months of summer the students, dressed in khaki shirts and shorts, trekked with a gospel cart through the urban areas of Ireland or Scotland. All this was designed to produce pioneer missionaries who were prepared to face forbidding conditions on foreign fields.

Willie McComb embraced the opportunity to learn as much as he could. However, the lasting memory of the Training Colony for him was the camaraderie and fellowship he enjoyed with other dedicated young men some of whom later became martyrs for the cause of Christ in distant lands. The deep spirituality and dedication of BG made a lasting impression on Willie's life. The two men became firm friends and corresponded with each other for decades.

The ten month's training in Upper Norwood led Willie to feel the need to enroll for a course at London's Hospital for Tropical Diseases. There he learned the rudiments of tropical medicine and hygiene, dentistry and minor surgery. He also learned how to use a microscope for which he developed a lifelong interest. These skills proved to be invaluable tools in later years both as aids to Willie's ministry and for his personal well-being and that of his family.

While pursuing the course at the Tropical Hospital Willie applied to the Worldwide Evangelization Crusade which had its headquarters in nearby Norwood. Since its inception the Crusade had made two principal advances which were known as Heart of Africa Mission and Heart of Amazonia Mission. It was for the latter that Willie made application and was duly accepted.

Family, friends and many people from the Northumberland Street Mission Hall gathered at the Belfast docks in November 1925 to bid farewell to the young missionary. Among those at the quayside was Margaret McKnight who shared William's missionary commitment and with whom William had struck up a romantic friendship which both had agreed to keep secret. While others shook Willie's hand and assured him of their prayers and support, Margaret gave him a special lingering embrace in spite of their romance supposedly being secret. They were both aware of the special bond that would blend their lives together for future service.

After Willie tore himself away from the hugs and handshakes of family and friends, he hurried up the gangway as some out of the crowd called, "We'll be praying for you, Willie."

Willie shouted back, "Remember McComb's Big Loaf." This was in reference to a maxim displayed on the side of the delivery carts used by McComb's Bakeries, one of Belfast's leading confectioners. Willie exploited the slogan to his advantage and insisted to his friends, "When you see the slogan McComb's Big Loaf, remember to pray for Willie McComb in the Amazon."

As the steamer pulled out into Belfast Lough, Willie stood with other passengers at the stern of the vessel while the assembled crowd waved and sang "Take the Name of Jesus with You," and other hymns and choruses until the ship sailed beyond the bend of the river.

In Liverpool Willie was joined by two former colleagues from the Missionary Training Colony. Like Willie, Pat Symes and George Sharpe who both came from Australia, were also accepted as missionary recruits for the Heart of Amazonia Mission. Mr. Norman Grubb wrote of the three new missionary candidates:

> When people at home become careless and indifferent to the needs of the lost, Amazonia loses the battle and it becomes more difficult to fight. Who knows to what sacrificial living these brethren may be called? Let us get into prayer for them right away.

The great Booth Line Steamer, *The Hildebrand*, maneuvered its way out of the River Mersey on 17th November 1925. From the third class deck of this passenger liner Willie McComb viewed the receding skyline of Liverpool. The city was enveloped in a blanket of noxious clouds created by the rising smoke from a myriad of terraced houses and pollutants from the city's great industrial plants.

The gentle sea breeze rustled through Willie's hair while the sway and heave of the ship entering the Irish Sea seemed to cradle his thoughts as they drifted to the family, friends and sweetheart he had left behind in the busy factories and mills of Belfast.

The young man found it amusing and strange as he pondered the events that had singled him out from many of his peers to leave his native shores and head for distant Brazil as a missionary. God had wonderfully supplied his need. He had been able to purchase his equipment from the Army and Navy Stores in London. Three steel trunks in the hold of the ship and a kit bag in his cabin contained all the supplies which the Mission considered necessary for five years in the tropics. Like his two colleagues he paid the great sum of £14 for the voyage from Liverpool to Belem at the mouth of the great Amazon River.

Willie was soon wakened out of his musing and reminiscing by a cacophony of sounds created by the Portuguese passengers who had arrived on deck and had begun to assemble their deck chairs in the most advantageous locations. Never shy about meeting new people, Willie and his missionary colleagues joined a few other English speaking passengers and Portuguese travellers as Marcos, the Brazilian steward, arrived calling "Meelk, caffee, butarr, sugarr."

Willie bought a cup of coffee, but it was much stronger than any he had ever tasted. He added sugar and pretended to enjoy it and realised this was only one of the many changes he would have get used to. Many hurdles lay ahead of Willie a major one of which was that of a new language. Willie listened intently to the Portuguese passengers engage freely in conversation with Marcos and wondered how he was ever going to learn Portuguese. However, this was all in front of him.

Marcos was again in attendance to the three missionary candidates and other passengers he had befriended when they sat at the long white tables in the ship's dining room. Small bowls of clear water were placed at each setting on the table. After giving thanks to God for the food, Willie and his two missionary friends decided to down the bowls of water before their hot meal arrived. They were somewhat embarrassed later when Marcos served drinking water in proper tumblers. It was only then they realised that the water they had drunk from the glass bowls had been provided for finger washing at the end of the meal.

After the first day at sea there was little activity in the dining room. Earlier in the day the *SS Hildebrand* had run into a violent storm in the Bay of Biscay and the great ship plowed her way through waves more than fifty feet high. The sea washed across the ship's bow and spray soaked all the decks on the great vessel. Like other passengers Willie McComb felt more secure lying in a horizontal position, but even then, the heaving and swaying of the boat became so fierce that he began to question if the vessel would survive the storm.

Willie remembered that the prophet Jonah also suffered in a storm because of his disobedience and his mind began to flood with doubts and questions about the decision he had made to volunteer as a missionary to the Amazon jungles. *Have I made the wrong decision? Am I in the wrong place?*

Although he was feeling squeamish as he lay on his bunk bed, Willie reached for his Bible and began reading at Mark 10, his designated reading for that day. When he came to verse twenty-nine, Willie startled the other passengers in the cabin when he suddenly shouted a profound, "Praise the Lord."

This verse gave God's answer to the wavering doubts that troubled the young man's heart; "And Jesus answered and said, 'Verily I say unto you, There is no man that hath left house, or brethren, or sisters, or father, or mother, or wife, or children, or lands, for my sake, and the gospel's, But he shall receive an hundred fold now in this time, houses, and brethren, and sisters, and mothers, and children, and lands, with persecutions; and in the world to come eternal life.'"

These words so encouraged and assured Willie McComb that he never again doubted that God had called him to be a missionary in Brazil. Even though the ship continued to be tossed on the shifty waters of the ocean, Willie steadied his hand and wrote in the margin of his Bible at Mark 10:29, 30 what David Livingstone had written in his Bible sixty years earlier, "The words of a Gentleman of the highest order."

This timely reassurance became an anchor for this young missionary as he faced the rigors of the life that awaited him in a region that was commonly called "The Green Hell."

After some hours the steamship rode out the violent storm and headed down the coast of the Iberian Peninsula to Lisbon. Following a day at anchor in Portugal, the ship continued its voyage across the Atlantic, taking two weeks to reach the East Coast of South America.

Willie and the other passengers awoke one morning to find that although there was no land in sight, the ocean water had changed from its usual aqua marine to a muddy brown tone. They were already engulfed in the waters of the Amazon seventy miles from shore.

Willie and the passengers watched from the deck as the ship's pilot steadily guided the vessel through the narrows of the Amazon delta. The awesome primeval Amazon forest spread out before them like a never-ending green carpet yielding an awesome welcome to the three new missionaries.

Chapter Two

AT HOME IN THE GREEN HELL

The *Hildebrand* finally docked at the city of Belem, the capital of Pará State. This city later became the location for the headquarters of the Heart of Amazonia Mission. The arrival of the three new missionaries increased the missionary personnel of the Heart of Amazonia Mission to fourteen international workers.

The sights, sounds and smells of the New World fascinated Willie McComb and his colleagues. Dressed in white linen suits despite the intense heat and humidity, they explored the tree-lined avenues and sampled many tropical fruits of which they had never even heard. However, these young men had not left their homes to travel in Brazil as tourists. Willie McComb and his colleagues had a longing to learn Portuguese so that soon they could communicate to Brazilians the story of the love of God in Jesus Christ.

The leadership in Brazil divided the work into two regions, East Amazonia and the Heart of Amazonia. Before Willie headed deeper into the Amazon region he was separated from his travelling companions, Pat Symes and George Sharpe, who were designated to the East Brazil Field while Willie was sent to Manaus, one thousand miles farther up the Amazon.

Mr. Kenneth Grubb, Alex Hutchinson and Charles Knight welcomed Willie at the floating dock in Manaus. Almost immediately he engaged in language study with a view of communicating with the people in Portuguese and eventually evangelizing some of the unreached Indian tribes of the Amazonas region.

As Willie continued his language study, a steady influx of missionary personnel began to arrive in the needy Amazon region. Just four months after his arrival, Willie's friend, Joe Wright from Northumberland Street Mission Hall in Belfast, also arrived in Manaus as one of the latest recruits of the Mission. Two years later Willie's own brother, Joe McComb, also joined the growing missionary force in the Amazon. In early 1934 Joe Wright's brother Fred, fired by the challenge of his brother's letters, dedicated his life to serve the Lord in Brazil. Like Willie and Joe, all these new missionaries had attended B. G. Buxton's Missionary Training Colony at Upper Norwood. Two years after his arrival Fred Wright and two of his colleagues, Australian Fred Roberts and Tasmanian Fred Dawson, were martyred for the cause of Christ by the Kayapó Indians on the River Xingú. The challenging story of the "Three Freds" inspired many other young people to offer themselves for missionary service.

After several months of language study Willie rehearsed his expanding vocabulary with local Brazilians and he, along with Joe Wright, joined other missionaries in evangelizing West Indian workers who had their left their islands to find jobs in Manaus.

A report in the *Worldwide* (The WEC's magazine) of October 1926 gave a report of Willie's activities and progress with language study:

> We have had times of revival at the West Indian Church. About four weeks ago we gave a message on "He that winneth souls is wise." We were very conscious of the Holy Spirit's presence in the meeting. The following Tuesday, one of the West Indians sent a messenger asking us to call at her home. When we got there a few others had gathered. We had no sooner entered the house when one of them suggested a word of prayer, which was rather

a shock to us. After this they began individually to pour out confession after confession — lack of love for souls, hatred toward other fellow Christians and such like. They then began to tell of how they had been inspired to make a new start.

One dear soul spent two whole days visiting all the West Indians that she knew. Another printed little notices of the meetings and had them delivered to their homes. The result was wonderful. The following Sunday we had between twenty-five to thirty people present. We have started a midweek service which is attended by some fifteen professing Christians.

The small open-air meeting we started a few weeks ago has been blessed to many. At this meeting we have good opportunity to practise the language.

Once Willie was somewhat proficient with the language, Pastor Gomes, who although a Brazilian, had an evident measure of Indian blood running through his veins, shared his burden with Willie how he planned to reach the Jauaperí Indians. Gomes pastored a small Baptist church in Manaus which the new missionaries attended. Willie felt this was his opportunity to be involved in reaching these remote people. He joined Pastor Gomes in planning to travel up the River Negro with a small party of Christian men. They borrowed a thirty-foot long river boat for the trip.

These Jauaperí Indians had already killed nine men and one woman just six months before this expedition started. Conscious of possible dangers, the party of men packed not only rations and equipment for the trip, but also rifles and sufficient ammunition for personal protection and to hunt game in the forest.

In his book *Into a Large Place*, Willie McComb gave a witty account of his first journey to make contact with the Jauaperí Indians.

Our trip to Moura, the town opposite the mouth of the River Jauaperí, took nine days travel. Our time in the town gave us a fresh vision of the spiritual needs of the people. Meetings were held nightly, in the homes. One was amazed and saddened to discover how few knew anything about the gospel.

The hospitality of these river dwellers is legendary. In almost every home at which we stopped we were given a meal. It was in one of these homes that I was introduced to monkey meat under rather amusing circumstances. We were seated at a large table having the midday meal when a boy, opposite to where I was sitting, picked from his plate a hand, complete with nails and began to eat around it. It was only then that I became aware I had been eating monkey. This became one of our most common dishes while working with the Indians.

Moura was a beautiful little town with a facade of huge rocks and an emerald-green background. The rocks, including those under the water, are covered with deeply carved hieroglyphics. Their origin is unknown.

During our two days stay an election was in progress. This brought many men and women from the interior, presenting us an ideal opportunity for the distribution of Gospels and tracts. A few days after the election we replenished our food supplies and made general preparation for the final stage of the journey.

The River Negro opposite Moura is almost fifteen miles wide and can be dangerous to small craft. We heard the sad story of a complete family of seven who were drowned in a storm just opposite the town. We planned to leave early morning, but as strong winds were blowing we were advised not to travel. Eager to get on our way, we ignored the advice.

We had not travelled far when it became evident that we were in for a rough journey. The waves were five or six feet high. The two canoes on tow soon became waterlogged. Anything not securely tied down rolled around the deck.

My little dog Pongo was violently sick. As the waves hit us broadside there was a danger of the launch somersaulting in the water. It certainly looked top-heavy.

I was at the wheel. Gomes was at his wits' end. He was taking three kinds of remedies for nerves and now he really needed them.

Eventually, as the situation deteriorated, he entered the cabin and closed the door, I presumed to pray. With one hand firmly holding an iron support and the other holding the wheel I began to sing at the top of my voice: "Master the tempest is raging." The consciousness of His presence infused courage.

For several hours we zigzagged across this wide expanse until we arrived in the calm waters of the Jauaperí. Gomes emerged from the cabin with a profound "Graças a Deus" - Thanks be to God.

We decided to spend the night near the mouth of the river. The following day we set off, bright and early, into the unknown. What a thrilling experience to find oneself in the territory of the Amazonian Indian. The river was narrow. The thick jungle came down to the water's edge and in some places it was impenetrable. The suspense can be imagined as we travelled on and on up river. We were fearful that an arrow might, at any moment, come whizzing from the forest.

It was an unforgettable experience when, on rounding a bend on the river, we saw in the distance a naked Indian standing on the bank of the river, complete with bow and arrows. Suddenly, he was accompanied by a dozen other warriors armed in the same manner. The natural instinct was to reverse the motor and make a hasty retreat. Instead we ran the launch ashore, disembarked and were soon surrounded by these naked sons of the forest, each one slapping on his chest and shouting.

"Yacanoo-moray" is what they cried. We had no idea what this meant but took the risk of accompanying them with the same gesture and trying to utter the same phrase. This proved to be in order, as we eventually discovered that it meant "good friend."

Without invitation they invaded the launch and helped

themselves to anything that might be of use to them, including much of our food. "Yacanoo-moray" indeed.

A good supply of clothing, collected by Pastor Gomes for the Indians, soon disappeared. I also lost my best palm beach jacket which was not intended to be available for charity.

We were faced with the problem of not knowing the language. Every method possible was used to express friendship. My only musical instrument was a mouth-organ and realizing that music charms the savage breast, I began to play it. While still playing the mouth organ I put my arm through that of the big chief and marched him up and down the sandy beach. Apparently this was acceptable, as all the other Indians soon followed in a duck file and were almost overcome with laughter. This was a real breakthrough and made us feel at home with them. Unfortunately, I had to hand over my mouth-organ to the chief.

We spent several weeks with this group and others who came to join them. Most of them were very primitive, using bone for their arrow heads and shaping their bows with pigs' teeth.

Each night we had meetings in Portuguese, which seemed to amuse them very much. They tried to join in the singing. One of the first phrases they caught was "Jesus morreu na cruz."—Jesus died on the cross. They showed a certain reverence when we sang and pointed to the sky.

It gave me a thrill when I discovered the Jauaperí words for "What is this?"—"Ambee-a-nee." The Indians were quick to observe this discovery and gave every possible help in securing an initial vocabulary.

Before leaving Manaus we had made plans to be joined by two of our missionary colleagues, Charlie Knight and Joe Wright, about a month after our departure. As they did not arrive when expected, we continued our journey to our objective, the River Alalahu, an affluent off the River Jauaperí.

Each day we pinned notices on prominent trees to assure our expected missionary friends that we were still alive and were pressing on up river. After six weeks on the river food supplies were running low. Each day we found it necessary to spend a few hours fishing. Gomes proved to be an expert at this. His method of finding turtles' eggs intrigued me. At a sandy beach he would stop the launch, cut a suitable branch and with this he would prod the sand as he marched along. When the treasure was found, he would dig with his hand and produce fifteen to thirty eggs. The clue was a little dent in the sand, at the water's edge, caused by the turtle's tail as it re-entered the river.

On one occasion we took our small canoe into a large lake. We were well armed with harpoon and fishing gear. Gomes was convinced that this was the habitat of the cow-fish (Manatee), known as "the whale of the Amazon." Also, here we saw the world's largest freshwater scaled fish, the Piraracú.

We had not gone far when the uncanny stillness of the lake was disturbed by a noise. It was caused by the appearing of a dark grey object on the calm surface. This was the moment to travel fast but with as little noise as possible. Gomes knew that the cow-fish would repeat the movement and come to the surface every ten or fifteen yards. We travelled alongside. When it emerged within striking distance, the shot by Gomes was well and truly aimed. Five hundred pounds of wounded cow-fish, at the end of a harpoon line can be dangerous to the occupant of a small canoe. It could make a dash for the cover of fallen trees along the margin of the lake. This would cause the line to entangle. The large mammal could also dive into the deep water causing the canoe to overturn.

Transporting this seven-foot manatee behind our canoe was slow business and getting it on to land was a Herculean task. I had heard that this mammal had three types of flesh, similar to that of cow, pig and fish, which I verified when I dissected it. Most of the meat was cut into large slabs and spread on nearby rocks to be dried in the sun. This provided food rations for several weeks.

With an ample supply of food, we decided to make the final push to the River Alalahu. Arriving one afternoon about 3.00 p.m., we decided to anchor opposite the mouth of the river and enter the waterway next morning at dawn. We had been informed that three years previously at this spot the Indians had killed four men and a woman, and the year before our arrival they had wrecked a launch similar to ours. As we travelled up this beautiful river we were conscious of the danger of an attack any moment.

Eventually we arrived at the first rapids—an awe-inspiring sight. Gomes, aware of the unreliability of our motor, decided to anchor below the rapids while we studied the possibility of a channel through. We found a suitable opening about ten feet wide. In our small canoe, with Gomes controlling the outboard motor at full speed and me in the prow paddling with the utmost effort, inch by inch we got through this fast-flowing body of water into a calm part of the river. We continued on our travel until we came to yet more rapids with huge rocks scattered across the river. We could see immediately that it would be unwise to attempt a passage through.

One of these massive rocks, in the centre of the river, was known locally as A Rocha Criminosa—The Criminal Rock. Another craft had been wrecked at the same rapids in recent times. Those who could swim reached land from where they could view the scene of the disaster. To their horror they saw one of their companions who was unable to swim, sitting on this huge rock and calling for help. For fear of an attack from the Indians they left the scene with the call for help in their ears. The man was never seen again.

It was with sad hearts that we turned our canoe and left the scene. One of the famous explorer, Shackleton's, most trying expeditions was termed "a glorious failure."

This was how we felt about our trip. Indian work can be most frustrating.

On our return journey we had several meetings, some with as many as thirty men present. Most were hearing the Gospel for the first time and gave the utmost attention to the Word.

We arrived in Manaus about 8.00 a.m. on Easter Monday. One of the first persons we met was Charlie Knight, working at his launch in the harbour. The first news he gave us was that the boat in which he and Joe Wright had been travelling in the hope of joining us on the River Jauaperí had overturned in a storm and that all the baggage, including more than two dozen letters for me had gone to the bottom of the river.

While crossing the River Negro, almost opposite Manaus, they had run into a tropical storm. To avoid the danger of being swamped they had made for an island in the centre of the river. This proved to be covered with twenty feet of water, with only the tops of the trees showing. While travelling through these, the propeller had become entangled in the undergrowth and remained fixed. The canoe had been unable to ride the waves and was soon swamped. My colleagues had spent the afternoon and night sitting on the top of the trees.

When daylight broke, they discovered that the canoe was stuck in shallow water. They descended from their perch and with much effort they were enabled to re-float the canoe. With two boards they made improvised paddles which enabled them to return to Manaus.

Thus ended Expedition Jauaperí.

Some time later Willie McComb and Joe Wright set out for the River Jauaperí again in a small canoe to visit the Indians they had contacted. However, as they made their way up the mighty River Negro they got swamped during a sudden storm. Practically everything they possessed was lost except the canoe, the Elto motor. Willie McComb told the story in the *Worldwide*.

Joe Wright and I, said good-bye to the brethren at about three o'clock in the afternoon. We started the Elto and got under way for the River Jauaperí. Our canoe was only about twenty feet long but we were well loaded with foodstuff, kerosene and supplies which brother Gomes had asked us to take up to him.

We got across the River Negro safely and were ascending the river near a submerged island when we encountered a slight swell and began to take on water. The tops of the trees of the island were showing and I thought if I could get to the other side of these we should have at least some protection from the wind and swell. In putting the thought into action, the propeller got caught in some undergrowth and we were unable to release her. We were broadsided on to the swell as the water continued to enter. In just a few seconds, the canoe was swamped. I shouted to Joe to jump for it, then we swam to a nearby tree and climbed into its branches.

We watched helplessly as most of our possessions flowed downstream in the strong current. Thankfully, we were able to rescue a paddle which we would need later.

We were at a very lonely spot, far from land, seated in the branches of a rotten tree only a few feet above the water with swarms of ants crawling all over us and biting for all they were worth. We were in this predicament from 4.00 p.m. until 10.00 a.m. the next day.

About 7 o'clock in the evening, one of the worst storms Manaus has had for some time broke on us. The rain was terrific and the cold wind seemed to cut one to the bone. The tree was swaying with the wind and we expected it to crash and throw us into the water any minute. How we prayed that the Lord would keep that tree from breaking. Praise God it held.

We survived an awful night cramped up in the branches of this tree bruised and scratched all over and feeling very sore. We had prayed together many times during the night and felt the presence of the Lord. Although the situation was very serious, we could not help laughing when we considered the other side of the affair. We thought if B. G. from the Missionary Training Colony could see two former Colonists in undervests and pants stuck up in a tree, he would have had something to say to us. We really felt we had been shipwrecked.

When morning came, we asked each other how were we to get safely to land. In vain we scanned the horizon for the sign of a passing canoe or vessel. We knew that to spend another night like the last one would just about finish us. The only way possible was to float our canoe. We had already tried to do this once or twice but due to the awning we had put on to protect us from the sun and rain we, found it impossible. The only alternative was to knock off this covering, since we had no tools, we had to use our bare hands.

We were in the deep water for three hours pulling at the covering while being scratched with thorns and suffering bruising and bites all over our bodies. Finally, Joe dived into the water to secure a rope on to the Elto motor. Both of us then hoisted the motor out of the water and tied it to a tree. Again Joe submerged into the river to secure the illfated canoe.

Together we dived into the river six times before finally bringing the craft to the surface. We then jerked the canoe to tip out some water and with our remaining strength started to bail out with our hands. With most of the water out, we ripped up a floor board to steer the craft and made some progress with the rescued paddle. We finally returned to civilization in an empty boat, except for a pathetic Elto motor and ourselves, grateful to be alive.

In the middle of 1927, Willie received an unexpected but important visit from two friends he had never met before. At the time he had no idea how they would influence his future in such a profound way. Willie explained in another witty letter:

A missionary colleague and I were housed in a little room just eight feet square and the rafters one foot above our heads. In this small room we cooked our meals on a pocket Primus stove and studied Portuguese in over 90 degree weather. We killed mosquitoes by the hundreds and slept to the tune of rats parading along our hammock strings.

While poring over my Portuguese grammar, I was suddenly summoned by the clapping of hands of someone outside the small dwelling. They were obviously seeking admittance. Looking up, I was confronted by a stocky little Brazilian man with a bright cheery face. He was one of two intrepid colporteurs from the British and Foreign Bible Society and he had just returned from a prolonged journey of three months to the Territory of Acre.

His account of his journey to the remote area had left such an impression on my mind and heart that was never erased. The colporteurs spoke of a large district with a population of approximately one hundred thousand souls practically untouched by missionary effort. Because the Acre Territory was over two thousand miles from the mouth of the Amazon, the cost of living was extremely high and consequently it was a neglected mission field.

Our smiling friend told of how they had sold all their Scriptures but that there were still many hungry souls groping in the darkness without the light of the gospel of Christ. Then he added, "There are no missionaries there."

Although Willie McComb and his colleague were touched with the colporteurs' reports, they had other commitments which prohibited them from responding to the challenge immediately. It was somewhat frustrating for Willie that he could not go where he felt missionaries were needed most, but he accepted that this was not God's time for him to go to the Acre.

After working with the Jauaperí for two years, Willie joined his brother Joe McComb and Joe Wright in a team of missionaries who concentrated efforts on the Maué Indians of the lower Amazon near to Santarem. Among these indigenous Indians, they found great spiritual hunger and had great satisfaction in leading many of them to Jesus Christ. However, after another two years of living with these nomadic people, the work was still very much at an embryonic stage. There was much painstaking travel, learning their language and trying to communicate fluently to them the message of the Saviour's love.

These first missionary trips were typical of many other journeys that Willie McComb made as a bachelor on various tributaries of the Amazon. He and his missionary colleagues endeavoured to reach other well-known Indian tribes. The Parintintin, the Pirahun and the Maué Indians were of special focus at that time and as a result of their pioneer work, doors swung open for the evangelization of these neglected tribes.

However, having served the Lord for five years in these remote areas, Willie McComb was more than ever convinced that he needed a wife to help and encourage him in this work.

Chapter Three

TWO ARE BETTER THAN ONE

People who have challenging goals generally find great meaning in life. To reach these objectives, such people must not only aim for the target, but also keep on going toward their goal even while they help others along the way. Perhaps it was aiming and going for goals that summed up Margaret McKnight's early life.

As a teenager Margaret had been led to faith in Jesus Christ by the well-known gypsy evangelist, Pat Smith, who during the early twenties conducted evangelistic missions all over Ulster. Soon after her conversion she made her friends among other young people at the Northumberland Street Mission Hall. As a result of her association with the Hall her early Christian life was greatly influenced by the missionary and evangelistic fervour which prevailed on the Shankill Road.

She not only admired Willie McComb's ability to lead the meetings and preach, but there was also something about him that attracted her to him like metal to a magnet. It was to Margaret's surprise and delight that she discovered that his magnetic field was also zoning in on her. Soon casual conversations developed into more personal exchanges until the young couple started their secret romance.

Not long after Willie McComb left for Brazil in 1925, Margaret began her nurse's training at the Belfast City Hospital. This was followed by a six-month midwifery course at nearby Malone Place. Throughout her training Margaret never lost sight of the goal. She felt her life was reserved for the Lord's work. Her relationship with Willie McComb sharpened her focus on Brazil.

Margaret's zeal to win souls began long before she arrived on the distant mission field. During W. P. Nicholson's evangelistic campaign at the Shankill Mission in Belfast in the early twenties, Margaret endeavoured to take her friends from work to hear Ulster's dynamic preacher. One of those friends was Mollie Harvey who was converted as a result of Margaret's personal persuasion to attend the Nicholson meetings. Mollie would play an important role in Margaret's life in later years.

Following the nursing and midwifery training Margaret enrolled at Redcliffe Bible School. It was a school designed mainly for the training of lady missionaries. Throughout all this time, letters were exchanged in which both Willie and Margaret contemplated uniting their lives in marriage to serve the Lord in Amazonia. There was one major obstacle which stood in the way of planning a marriage at home, or even in Brazil in the near future. The mission had a strict code which prohibited a serving missionary from marrying a person who had not been accepted by the mission or who had not served the probationary period of two years on the field.

Willie and Margaret felt they had embarked on a life of sacrifice and self denial to serve the Lord, therefore, without questioning, they accepted these conditions as part of the price they had to pay to serve God together. The delay meant their courtship was not only chiefly conducted by correspondence, but it was also prolonged to more than five years to comply with the Mission's policy.

Mail from Northern Ireland to Brazil was slow to arrive, especially to the Amazon region. Nevertheless, for intrepid missionaries, news from a far country was always welcome and refreshing no matter how late it was. No letters encouraged Willie McComb more than the correspondence from Margaret McKnight. She not only circulated the latest news from Brazil to their friends at Northumberland Street, but Margaret also kept Willie informed of her latest plans in preparing to join him in the work in the Amazon. Of course those letters were peppered and spiced up with all the things that sweethearts write to each other. Five years of absence only made their hearts grow fonder for each other and confirmed their plans for marriage.

Margaret applied to the Worldwide Evangelization Crusade and was accepted for work in Amazonia. Late in 1929 Margaret sailed for Brazil following the same route Willie had taken four years earlier. When she arrived in Brazil, Margaret was designated to the East Amazonia sector of the Mission. This decision was taken to keep her and Willie at a respectable distance from each other. Open courtship between missionary couples on the field was greatly discouraged.

Five years of pioneer work in the Amazon seemed to fly in for Willie McComb. In spite of the Amazon's inhospitable reputation which had been greatly sensationalized by the disappearance of the famous explorer Dr. Fawcett, Willie McComb loved his work and the people. However, repeated bouts of dysentery and falling victim to other fevers took a toll on Willie's body. For these reasons he was glad of a welcomed furlough early in 1930. On the other hand, he was disappointed by the irony that now that Margaret had arrived in Brazil he was leaving her to go home to Northern Ireland. Life seems cruel at times.

Before he left for home, Willie spent a few weeks in Belem where he was able to be with Margaret. He tried to encourage her to keep focused on language study while he was on furlough and then when the two-year probationary period was completed, they would marry on his return to Brazil.

All too soon the few weeks with Margaret rushed by and again they were parted for more than a year. The same ocean he had traversed five years earlier on his way to Brazil was crossed again in the opposite direction on another Booth Line Steamer, *The Denis.*

Waiting at the Belfast quayside for the early morning arrival of the boat from Liverpool was Willie McComb's family. They were glad to see him even though he looked somewhat emaciated from the rigours of life in the tropics.

Soon after renewing acquaintance with friends at the Northumberland Street Mission and Argyle Place Presbyterian Church, Willie embarked on a busy round of meetings all over Ulster. He was a spirited, humourous and enthusiastic speaker, and his zest endeared him to the Christian public. It also insured he was frequently in demand to speak at conventions and church meetings and even to the Belfast Rotary Club. Here is a magazine report of one of those meetings:

> A few weeks ago there were two articles in the press concerning two great disasters. One was the R101 Air Ship disaster in which forty-four people died. That article concluded by saying that those lives had been lost in pioneering aviation work. Those in authority were not daunted by this setback in their work, but all the more determined to go forward in mastering the air.
>
> The other account was that of two missionaries who had been murdered in China. Those in authority had called on all missionaries to withdraw from those dangerous parts. May God give us more and more the spirit of the airmen to continue our pioneer work and not that of those who withdraw in time of danger. We feel that we need and want nothing less than the Spirit of God to carry the gospel to the millions of souls who are without Christ.
>
> We all realize that pioneering work is not a picnic. No doubt there are some here who have been readers of the *Christian Herald* for the last fifty years. Two years ago there appeared on the front page a picture entitled "Pioneering with the Gospel in Brazil." I was in the middle of the picture wearing a colossal sun helmet, Bishop's collar and trousers with a crease on which you could have cut your finger (much laughter followed). That is the impression some people at home have of pioneering work. Don't you believe it! In reality I wore a half-crown (13 pence) pair of trousers with no crease, a little sweater and

a 2d (1pence) hat (more laughter). Still we rejoice that God has given us the privilege of carrying the gospel.

Now I want to give you my first and last impressions of the Red Indians. I think you always remember the beginning of a venture and the end of it. I remember when I first went out and the last scenes before I left.

(Here followed a little "Irish muddle" which caused great mirth, but which endeared the speaker to his audience. The easy way in which he got out of it appealed to everyone, and because they appreciated his sense of humour, they completely opened their hearts to him. When the solemn message followed it went deep down into their hearts and made a lasting impression on all present. The meeting tonight absolutely confirmed what was said to me some days ago, 'When Mr. McComb speaks about the Red Indians he draws your heart right out towards them.' Indeed this is true.)

Among the Maués we spent a considerable time visiting their villages. We travelled for many weeks and reached sixteen villages. When we got to those villages, we told the story of Jesus Christ and His glory. Night after night the Indians gathered around to listen to the story of Jesus and His love. They implored us to stay and teach them. "Won't someone come to help us?" they asked.

This was my last picture of those Indians. We had come to say good-bye, and on the last night we taught them a little chorus in Portuguese, something to impress the gospel story on their hearts. Sadly, they did not know what they were singing; they did not realize what it meant.

The next morning it was time to head off. We went down to the beach at the river's edge, a beautiful sandy beach with the clear river flowing by and the green forest as a background. Every man, woman and child came down to see us off. They stood around and sang the same chorus we had taught them and then we said good-bye.

These were the last words we heard as we paddled downstream, "Won't you come back?" Their words have been ringing in my ears hundreds of times since, "Won't you come back?" These Indians are without the gospel and are still crying out "Won't you come back?"

The scriptures say, "I sought for a man to fill up the gap, but found none." God grant that some will hear His call tonight and surrender to Him.

After a full year of deputation work representing the work of the Mission, the time drew near for Willie to return to Brazil. There was a foreboding atmosphere everywhere in Great Britain. The Great Depression had set in and this was accompanied by general unrest. Thousands of people were out of work with no prospect of any sort of job. Many Ulster people emigrated to United States and Canada in search of better opportunities.

In Brazil, Dr. Getúlio Vargas had been brought to power and made President in a military coup. There had also been a change in the make up of the Heart of Amazonia Mission. The mission now came under the wing of the newly formed Unevangelized Fields Mission. Notwithstanding all these developments, Willie McComb knew that there was a job for him to do in Brazil. Besides, he had a very important date to keep with Margaret McKnight in Belem.

The voyage to Brazil in 1931 on another Booth Line ship was uneventful. Willie already knew the ropes having crossed the ocean twice before. Like an old salt, he took the voyage in stride. Much to Willie's delight, he discovered on arrival in Belem that Margaret had become quite adept in her Portuguese. Although she had been busy helping at various churches in Belem, she had been counting the days for Willie to arrive and was keen to launch into the mission's work among the indigenous Indians, but realized she could not do this until after they were married.

After travelling to Manaus to pick up his few belongings, Willie McComb returned to Belem to complete final plans for the wedding to Margaret McKnight. It took place on Saturday, 7th November 1931 at the Pará Anglican Church in Belem. Leonard Harris, the field leader for Unevangelized Fields Mission, and missionary Leonard Bland were the witnesses on that special day, with many missionaries and local believers present to share in the happy occasion.

After a brief honeymoon at Mosquiero, a small town not far from Belem on the Atlantic coast, Willie and Margaret McComb were assigned to work among various Indian tribes on the tributaries of the lower Amazon. Again Willie wrote of those days:

> The missionary who is called to work among the Indians must be prepared for a rough life. It was my wife's first long trip into the interior, and it was a supreme test on health and stamina. The journey to Altamira, the station to which we were going to take over from Fred Roberts, (one of the "Three Freds" who was later martyred by the Kayapó Indians on the River Xingú,) took about fifteen days on a paddle steamer. We travelled from São Luiz, in Maranhão, to Engenho Central. Near to this town we stayed in the home of Sr. João da Costa, a fine Christian with whom Fenton Hall spent a considerable time. It was his son, Domingos, who accompanied Fenton Hall on the last journey overland. After the death of Fenton Hall, other faithful servants of the Lord continued the task in whose footsteps we were following.
>
> It was a memorable moment when we stood at Fenton Hall's grave in the company of a converted witch doctor. The site was marked by four poles and surrounded by long grass which was infested with snakes. We bowed our heads and prayed that we might be made not only like this pioneer missionary but also like the Saviour he so faithfully followed.
>
> The journey from Central was by dugout canoe which was paddled by Indians who had come to meet us. When our baggage and supplies for one month were packed into it, the canoe was barely two inches above the water level. After travelling for about six hours, we arrived at Colonia, the last contact with civilization. Here we considered it wise to leave some of our trunks in the home of the leading man of the village.

This good man, though he carried a revolver on each side of his belt and could use them when angered, suggested that we stay the night with him and hold a meeting in his home. We were pleased to do this. Our joy was complete when, at the end of the meeting, he expressed a desire to accept Christ. Subsequent visits to his home assured us that a great change had taken place in his life.

It was with more confidence that we continued our journey, having left behind three heavy trunks at this friend's house.

The River Pindaré presented a problem for transport. It was very narrow and at almost every bend there were fallen trees which had to be chopped through. Occasionally we encountered a nest of wasps - which are attracted by sound and attacked us when the first blow of the axe was made. The only consolation was that we were not the only targets of these angry wasps. Probably half a dozen others from our group were stung at the same time.

Besides the obstacles on the river, there was also a lot of discomfort. Margaret and her companion spent each day perched on top of the baggage, waving a monkey's tail around their heads to keep off the clouds of pium — a small insect that draws blood to the surface of the skin, leaving all exposed parts covered with little red spots. When darkness comes, these insects go to sleep. It is then that the mosquitoes take over. We never seemed to get used to the pests' system of earning a living!

For eleven nights we slept in the forest, sometimes under the cover of palm branches quickly erected by the Indians but often under the open canopy of heaven. It was not a pleasant experience to be awakened by the noise of thunder and the flashes of lightning at two or three o'clock in the morning. At least we had time to untie our hammocks before the tropical rain came and continue the journey.

At times it was necessary to travel in the dark before arriving at a suitable place to spend the night. One night after arranging our hammocks, lighting the fire and settling in for the night, we discovered that we were on top of an ants' nest.

Our life with the Guajajaras was uneventful. After an early breakfast we conducted a short service for the Indians. Much hard work by faithful missionaries was put into the study of the language. A small hymn book was printed, together with several portions of the Word of God. These early missionaries had already organized a school which began at eight o'clock and continued until noon. It was amazing how quickly some of the children learned to read in their own language, Tupi-Guajajara. Many of them had not seen paper before coming to the village. It was not easy for the children or the teachers, including my wife, to study and teach in the intense heat of small classrooms. The atmosphere was made worse by the windows being covered with screening to keep out the stinging pium.

Meetings, at which most of the Indians would pray, were also held nightly. The women, while praying, would always drop their long black hair in front of their faces. It was encouraging to witness the working of the Holy Spirit in their lives.

While travelling with a party of six Indians, we discovered that the river had overflowed and the forest on each side was completely flooded. From early morning until darkness fell, we saw no land. When we finally arrived at a place where we could tie our hammocks, we disembarked, weary and sore from sitting in a canoe all day. As soon as I had my hammock tied between two trees I collapsed into it and was soon drifting off to sleep. Just then I was suddenly rebuked by an Indian calling, "Guilherme," Willie's name in Portuguese, "are you not going to pray and thank God for bringing us safely on our journey?"

It was our custom to pray each night, and it gave us much joy to know that the Indian expected us to pray with thanksgiving to God. It was on this trip, while travelling with a very fast current through the inundated forest, that we ran into a decayed tree causing a huge branch to fall on my head. This brought forth a roar of laughter from the Indians. Grace enabled us to enjoy with them their perverted sense of humour.

It was with great delight that William and Margaret greeted the birth of their first daughter in Belem in August 1932. The arrival of little Irene not only brightened the McComb home and gave a lot of pleasure to her proud parents, but also it opened many doors of opportunity for her parents to foster friendships among Indians and Brazilians.

For the next three years the McComb family was based at Altamira on the River Pindaré. It was tough trying to provide a balanced diet for a baby. The locals furnished everything from monkey heads to tins of condensed milk that were so old the milk had become like brown toffee. At times the Indians found arrowroot but this was mixed with earth and grit. Before cooking the arrowroot it had to be washed and dried in the sun. After the first year, Irene's food consisted mainly of bananas which were mashed, boiled or fried, and tempered to give them various flavours.

From Altamira, Willie continued to travel on the rivers to the Indian tribes in that area. Being absent from his family brought problems that can be seen by this report Willie McComb prepared.

While on a journey for ten days with the Indians, disaster struck. It was at the end of the wet season and the river was rapidly rising. When we were still a long way from the Altamira I had a bout of dysentery and was naturally eager to return home to my wife and child. During the last leg of the journey we paddled all day in an effort to arrive before dark.

It was about 8.00 p.m. and quite dark when we approached Altamira. We soon became aware that all was not well. Everything looked different. The field in front of the houses had been transformed into a lake. There was no light anywhere and as we drew nearer we could barely make out the form of the houses. We paddled our canoe up to the door of our house. There was no one in the house. Margaret and baby Irene were gone and the house was under two feet of water. The whole village was deserted.

Because there was water everywhere, we could not even light a fire. Having travelled all day with practically no food the Indians were very hungry. There was nothing we could do but try to find where our families had gone. Another hour's paddling brought us to Central, another small village.

Most of the natives had taken refuge in a large disused sugar factory. My wife and little Irene were given the use of a six foot square room in a mud house. With all our baggage, a camp bed and the child's cot, we were left with standing room only and the peace of God in our hearts! In all such circumstances we have proved that His grace is sufficient.

Some time elapsed before the water receded and we were able to return home. It was not long before we discovered many snakes around the house. Almost daily we encountered one of these slithering reptiles. Occasionally we would be awakened at night by the presence of a snake in our bedroom, sometimes on top of our mosquito net or even over Irene's cot.

One day my wife discovered a snake poised in a corner ready to strike at Irene who was only three or four feet away. An Indian had me kill another snake which was hanging from the rafters of a corridor through which I had passed several times in the dark, totally unaware of a snake lurking just about a foot above my head. We took a photograph of a snake twisted around a crocodile which the snake had crushed to death. That snake was twenty-one feet long and the crocodile was seven feet. Upon opening the stomach of the snake we found a complete crocodile about three feet long! We treat all snakes as poisonous. Those that are not poisonous crush their victim to death and swallow it whole!

In the missionary's life, the supreme delight is "to see the heathen bow in prayer" and to witness before others his acceptance of Christ. It was an unforgettable day when sixteen of these Guajajara Indians were baptized and then later took part in the Lord's Supper. It left a deep impression on us all. This was the seed springing up; the culmination of years of hard work and tears of the early missionaries.

These river trips give some insight into the conditions the early pioneer faced to fulfill Christ's command to take the gospel to every creature. For those who serve the Lord on river evangelism, conditions have not changed too much. Furthermore, the love of Jesus Christ is the same compelling motive as that which constrained Willie and Margaret McComb over seventy years ago.

Chapter Four

FACING NEW FRONTIERS

Children are the joy and crown of every home. Besides the excitement surrounding the infant's arrival, the parents mark every milestone in their child's growth: the first tooth, the first step, the first year, the first word and the first day at school. Grandparents also love their grandchildren: love to hold them, cuddle them and please them. They generally are the proud onlookers at every stage of the baby's progress.

Missionary parents are no different. Sadly, distance and time often rob them of the pleasure of sharing their children's development with grandparents who have never looked into the cute faces of their little grandchildren.

Young Irene McComb was almost four years old when she set her tiny feet in Northern Ireland for the first time. Her grandparents were glad to see their Brazilian granddaughter for the very first time, not to mention her parents. Although she understood English, the little Irene found it strange that no one in Northern Ireland understood her Portuguese. All of that was to change soon.

Having made a great impact on Northern Ireland's Christian community during his first furlough five years earlier, Willie and

Margaret McComb were soon in great demand for meetings all over Ulster. They both spoke enthusiastically of the Lord's work in Brazil and recounted their stories of amazing conversions, God's provision and His protection. Many were spellbound and challenged by their dedication.

As the months of their furlough flew by, they inevitably had to consider dates and plans for their return to South America. There was no thought of staying at home, but both Margaret and Willie had a great burden to consider returning to the Acre Territory. Willie could not escape from the story he had heard from the colporteurs at the British and Foreign Bible Society seven years earlier. Upon inquiry, he learned that still no missionaries had ventured to that distant part of Brazil.

The Acre is an area larger than Ireland and is bounded in the South by Peru and Bolivia. Until early in the twentieth century, the Territory of Acre was part of the Republic of Bolivia. Much blood was shed in a revolution when it was annexed by Brazil and became known as the Territory of Acre. Fifty years later the Territory was approved for statehood with twenty-one town districts and Rio Branco became the State capital. Along the banks of the many tributaries that flow through the Acre, thousands of souls lived and died in spiritual darkness.

At first Willie and Margaret made their burden a definite subject for their personal prayers. The more they prayed, the more convinced they became that God wanted them to accept the challenge of this formidable task. When they were sure of their convictions, they approached the leaders of their Mission and shared with them the burden and challenge of their hearts.

The mission leaders considered the matter and while they understood the McCombs' opinions they also felt that opening up a new front in such a distant region of the Amazon would be difficult to administer. For that reason they gave a negative reply to Willie and Margaret's suggestion.

Willie McComb later spoke of that occasion:

It was while on our second furlough that the challenge of the Acre came to us afresh. Again we could hear the call from Acre, "Come over and help us."

In order to obey this call it became necessary for us to sever ourselves from the Mission, our only source of income. We were led by the Lord to send to the mission, under whose auspices we were serving at the time, all the finance we possessed. This meant starting off with a clean sheet and with the many exceedingly great and precious promises of God.

In retrospect, how thankful my wife and I are for the privilege of being asked of the Lord to do this. He was testing us and trusting us. With a wife and child, such a step demanded clear guidance. His gracious message came to us from Psalm 31:15: "My times are in Thy hands." This gave us the courage to launch out and trust God.

It was only after we took this step that the Lord gave us a group of true and trusted friends who eventually formed themselves into a Committee to support us at home. The Lord wonderfully opened doors for deputation work. We felt clearly led not to make any public appeals for funds. In nine months we received the handsome sum of £600 before sailing for Brazil.

Besides the Lord supplying our financial needs, He also gave us a coworker to assist us in this new venture. Miss Mollie Harvey had already finished her Bible and nursing training and felt God's call to join us in the mission to the Acre Territory.

Separating from the Unevangelized Fields Mission was painful but amicable. Willie's letter of resignation was acknowledged by the General Secretary of the Mission, Mr. George Byrnell:

30th September, 1936.

My dear Mr. McComb,

At the last meeting of the Council I read your letter of resignation. It was received with very great regret indeed. I was unable to give them any reason for your resigning beyond that you had felt definitely led to take that step. I was asked to express on their behalf their deep appreciation of all your self-sacrifice and labours of the past eleven years, and also for the past five years service of Mrs. McComb. The Council has especially valued your help while on deputation.

We trust that Mrs. McComb will recover her health completely and that you both may have many happy years of united service for the Master in whatever field He may appoint. I shall always be glad to hear from you.

Yours because His,

George Byrnell

Mollie Harvey had not only been converted through the influence of her friend Margaret McKnight in 1923, but she was also introduced to Northumberland Street Mission Hall on the night after her conversion. Mollie was greatly struck by the fervour of Willie McComb leading the singing at the Hall. She owed a lot also to Mr. Flack's Monday night Bible class which became her source of spiritual nourishment, and the prayer meeting on the following night became the hour of missionary challenge. As a consequence of this repeated missionary exposure, Mollie left home to study at Redcliffe Bible School in London. This was followed by nursing training at London's famous Mildmay Mission Hospital.

Mollie returned to Belfast to supplement her nursing training with a midwifery course at the Malone Place Maternity Hospital. Her arrival home corresponded with Willie and Margaret McComb's furlough and the crisis which had arisen over their step to venture to the Acre on the upper Amazon without a Mission agency.

Mollie related the steps that led to her volunteering for Brazil in 1937:

> After finishing my training at Bible College, Willie and Margaret were on furlough. As I listened to them speak, the Lord gave me a great burden for the people of

Brazil. I knew that He wanted me to serve Him there. When the reality of such an expedition sank in, I was more than a little frightened. Nevertheless, I trusted the Lord and took one step at a time. Very soon the Lord opened the way and I felt I should join Willie and Margaret as part of a team going to Brazil.

All of these steps were steps of faith and at times we dared to trust God for the impossible. As we went out we had no mission structure behind us. God raised up men who promised to stand by the home end of the work while we went forth. We thanked God for these faithful men who would form the basis of the Committee which later would become the Acre Gospel Mission. They, along with us, were prepared to trust God to supply all our needs according to the promises God had pledged to us in His Word.

Because we were going to a new pioneer area of Brazil and so far into the Amazon jungle, it was felt that I should have a medical checkup. Initially the doctors thought I had a heart murmur and would not survive more than a year in such a tropical climate. We were not foolhardy but we were clear about God's call and stepped out on His promise and command.

It may be difficult for us to imagine what such a step meant for a single lady who allegedly had a heart murmur. Faith is not a leap in the dark. It is stepping out believing that God's promises give to us a sure footing for the future. Rather than a leap in the dark, this was a great leap of faith.

Besides trusting God to supply their needs and stepping out into the unknown future in a formidable region of the Amazon, there was still another great price involved in this step of obedience to Jesus Christ. Young Irene McComb was not yet five years old. For Willie and Margaret returning to Brazil was the obvious step to take, but they agonized over the dilemma of what was best for Irene. To take her to such a hostile and remote environment as the Acre was reputed to be was considered inadvisable. The thought of leaving her at home broke their hearts. The parents painfully wrestled with this dilemma until finally they made the smarting decision that it would be best for Irene to remain in Northern Ireland while her parents went to the Acre for four or five years.

Willie wrote of the experience later:

> Never shall we forget the experience of sailing down the Belfast Lough as we set out for Brazil. We were leaving behind our only child Irene, four and a half years old. This sacrifice was the greatest we were ever called upon to make. We loved our daughter and the separation was heartbreaking. At that time we did not realize that, because of travel restrictions during the war, the separation would last for almost eight and a half years. We now realize that it was a great sacrifice for our daughter.

Perhaps Mollie Harvey was able to give a more objective account of the pain that was felt by both.

> For Willie and Margaret to return to Brazil, they would have to leave behind their only child Irene, a lovely little girl just four and a half years old. In those days they felt it unwise to take her on such a journey into the unknown. Instead of going back to the lower Amazon, the Lord had placed a burden and a vision on Willie's heart for the people who lived in the Territory of Acre, two and a half thousand miles from the mouth of the mighty Amazon.
>
> The Lord helped Willie and Margaret stand by that decision when a very kind school master and his wife, Mr. & Mrs. Evans from Ballywalter on the County Down coast, offered to keep Irene while her parents were in Brazil for what was hoped to be a four or five year term. Mr. and Mrs. Evans had a little girl the same age as Irene and she was a great playmate for her.
>
> One day Irene overheard her parents speaking to friends explaining why they felt it unwise to take her with them.

She began questioning them each night as her parents prayed with her prior to going to bed. Her question was always the same, "Daddy, Mummy, you wouldn't go away and leave me, would you?" Not wanting to lie to their little daughter, the parents had to run out of the room to shed their own tears.

Finally, the day of departure came. As a parting gift, Willie and Margaret bought Irene a lovely doll which they gave her as she was leaving Belfast to go to the Evans family in Ballywalter. With little Irene's attention wrapped up in the new dolly, suddenly the car door shut and Willie and Margaret's little daughter was away. On that day I was glad I was not married. The thud of the car door closing and the sight of the car going down the road and disappearing in the distance was relived many times. That was the last view Willie and Margaret had of Irene for eight and a half long years. Their plans for a shorter term in Brazil were to be dashed by the outbreak of the Second World War.

A special farewell meeting was arranged for the three missionaries at the Welcome Hall, Cambrai Street, Belfast, on Thursday, 20th May 1937. Two weeks later, on the morning of Friday, June 4th, 1937, a friend from Northumberland Street Mission Hall arrived at Mollie's house in Cambrai Street with his horse and cart to transport her baggage to the Liverpool boat. As they loaded the cart, the rain pelted down on the baggage, the horse and them. Mr. Harvey kept saying that everything on the cart was getting soaked, but the poor man did not have a cover for the cart or the trunks. After loading all of Mollie's earthly goods on to his cart, he left Cambrai Street and went for Willie and Margaret's baggage.

Hundreds of people from different churches and mission halls gathered at the quayside to wish the missionary trio God's speed as they embarked on their gallant mission. Among them was the Pastor Olley of Newtownards Baptist Church, who had promised to act as chairman of the group of men who had formed a committee to look after the affairs of the three missionaries.

Also included in the crowd that night was a teenage girl who accompanied the group from Pastor Olley's church. On that very night this girl made a vow that she would pray for the three missionaries every day. God answered her prayers in an amazing way. That dedicated young girl was Dorrie Cavan, who later would become Dorrie Gunning. Little did Dorrie know that twelve years later she would join Mollie in Brazil.

During the fifteen-day voyage to Brazil, the Lord graciously eased the McComb's burden of leaving their darling daughter. Mollie studied and practiced her Portuguese on the passengers from Brazil and Portugal. After their arrival at the mouth of the Amazon, they embarked on a flat bottomed, wood burning river steamer and for six weeks they travelled up the meandering Amazon River and its tributaries to the Acre. The old steamer with a paddle at the rear stopped every three days to take on a fresh supply of logs for fuel.

The steamer stopped at Manaus to take on more supplies and cargo and then continued travelling west up the main artery of the Amazon, the River Solimões. After two days it entered another great tributary, the River Purus, and headed slowly upstream in a southwesterly direction for over a thousand miles to Rio Branco, the capital of Acre.

Ever eager to win people to the Saviour, Willie McComb witnessed to everyone from the captain to the poorest passengers on the lower deck. He sold Bibles and distributed gospel literature whenever they were permitted to go ashore. He even had small bundles of tracts which he threw to people when it was not possible for them to disembark. Willie also encouraged Margaret and Mollie to help him treat various illnesses they encountered while visiting the river dwellers and even some of the crew and passengers.

Willie was made aware of how careful they had to be on their journey when he awoke one evening as they docked.

By nature I am a very heavy sleeper, and seldom would rise during the night. The steamer stopped about 3.00 a.m. and I was awakened by the noise. Normally I would have turned over and gone off to sleep again, but on this occasion I was constrained to get up and deliver tracts to those who were visiting the boat.

After giving out a few leaflets, I strolled round the deck and glanced momentarily at our baggage. I instinctively noticed that a large cedar case containing our portable organ, specially made for the tropics, was missing. I took action immediately and found that it had just been lowered into a canoe which was about to leave. Immediately I called to the first officer who soon had it restored. The culprit's excuse was that he had malaria and was not aware of what he was doing!

During the six weeks' journey, the boat stopped at dozens of towns and small villages, and they were struck by the fact that they met no missionaries after they entered the River Purus.

Arriving in Rio Branco presented the couple and Mollie with some problems. They knew no one in the town and had no place to stay. Initially, they spent a few weeks in a dingy and bug ridden hotel for which they paid inordinate rates. They learned from the proprietor of the hotel that other missionaries had arrived in Rio Branco but left again because the cost of living was too high. Mollie wondered why the cost of living was so expensive for there was no motorized transport or even a bicycle in the town. Most people got around on horse back and transported goods either by canoe or ox cart. Electricity for the town was provided by only one generator which broke down frequently. The sole supply of water other than from the muddy river was from the deep wells that many people had dug at the rear of their houses.

They also discovered that to rent a house in Rio Branco was very difficult and not cheap. However, they were offered a wooden dwelling on the outskirts of the town. This property had sufficient capacity to house the three missionaries. They had a front room and verandah where they could start some meetings so they moved in.

Willie lost no time in inviting people to their home for the meetings. Within weeks he had as many as fifty packed into the house. Margaret and Mollie visited the ladies in the immediate area and soon found they were called on to treat the sick. At home they were busy typing and binding a homemade hymn book with a good selection of hymns and choruses for use in the meetings.

In Rio Branco interest in the gospel grew steadily and many people were converted, but the work was not without its drawbacks. Unexpectedly one day the owner of the house gave them short notice to vacate the property. At first this appeared to be a disaster for the fledgling work, but in the end it proved to be a blessing. Larger premises were rented nearer to the centre of town. Within a short time this house also was too small to hold the increasing numbers who seemed to be hungry for the Word of God.

Willie was able to acquire an old house on a sizable piece of ground and started renovating the building to erect the first evangelical church in Rio Branco. Writing home in 1938, Willie informed his prayer partners:

There are times in the lives of all missionaries, I suppose, when they find themselves confronted with enough work to keep three or four people fully occupied. At present, we find ourselves passing through such a phase. For the past month I have been working, almost daily, at the church. There is much to be done. Twenty-seven of the wooden piles had to be taken out of the ground and other new ones had to be put in. The floor, which had many bad boards, had to be taken up and then the best of the old ones and the new boards were put down again. Many of the boards around the wall had to be taken out and replaced with new ones also. We are putting an entire new front on the house with two doors where the windows had been.

Some of the believers have loyally helped us by giving to the church one or two days work free of charge each week. We are also blessed in having a carpenter in our midst. He is a solid believer, whom we baptized some time ago. He has given several days work voluntarily, although he finds it very difficult to get the free time. He is employed by the Government.

Besides all this manual labour, there are also five meetings during the week for which we have to prepare, in Portuguese, with all the other duties that fall to the missionary of the Cross. While we are extremely happy in this work, we regret that it is not possible to attend to all the letters we receive as we would like. Our friends will understand and be patient.

As Willie stated, one of the encouraging things for him was that some of the new converts offered voluntary labour. Even a man who was not a Christian delivered five hundred bricks by ox cart to the site. Another man cut down trees and made benches to provide seating for the church. On the opening night, the building was too small to accommodate the crowd who came for the inaugural service.

Soon the church had a full programme of regular services, Sunday School, children's meetings and ladies' meetings. Margaret and Mollie were in increasing demand for their midwifery skills to the poorest and richest families in Rio Branco.

The church soon became a springboard for five other open-air preaching points in other parts of town. Some believers made good use of their embroidery skills and provided the church with large banners on which Bible texts were displayed. These were used at each open-air meeting.

Having spent so many years working among the Indians, Willie was eager to reach beyond Rio Branco to some of the accessible tribes in the Acre. He therefore arranged to travel down river to Boca do Acre and Sena Madureira. Willie and Margaret travelled but Mollie remained in Rio Branco. When they returned after twelve weeks, Willie wrote of the journey in a news letter he sent home in 1939:

My wife and I have just arrived from the River Purus where we have had an interesting evangelistic tour. When we left Rio Branco, it was our intention to spend about six weeks, but the opportunities were so many and the needs so great that we were fully engaged for nearly three months.

With this long spell away, we were unable to enter all the doors that were open to us. We had even hoped to spend at least a week on the River Caeté, an effluent of the Iaco where there are great possibilities for gospel work, but time did not permit us to do so.

The last time I wrote I made reference to our journey down the River Acre. We had over four days of travel before arriving at the Boca do Acre. There was some disappointment when we arrived there to find that a boat had just gone to Sena Madureira. We had to content ourselves to wait for the next one.

In this delay we saw the Lord's hand, as we had a blessed time with meetings each night. On the second day I got in touch with the local mayor to ask permission to have a public meeting in the main square. He proved to be a gentleman and gave us every help, offering the town square and also the seats from the school.

We had a splendid meeting, with about two hundred and fifty present, including all the leading men from the town. Although we felt much power in the meeting, we were conscious, too, of the presence of the enemy of souls. Boca do Acre is about as evil a place as one could find on the face of the earth.

We had a great sale of scriptures in the town. After the open-air meetings, some asked for as many as four or five New Testaments. Our great regret was that we were unable to supply all the demand.

While in Boca do Acre they met a young woman, Dona Nené Jacinto Ale, who was married to a Syrian immigrant. She was the only believer in her town and appealed for the missionaries to remain in Boca do Acre. Willie and Margaret were grieved to decline the invitation but prayed that one day the Lord would send someone to that needy town. The answer to that prayer would not come until fourteen years later. Willie's report continued:

After four days waiting at the Boca, we started off on

another little launch up the River Purus. This river is known to the Brazilians here as a Paliteiro, which is a little stand for toothpicks. It was given this name because of the large number of fallen trees and old stumps, that stand out of the water in many parts.

On the second day, we arrived at a rather bad rapid and found another launch in difficulty. With the few men aboard, they were unable to pull it through against the terrific force of the current. Fortunately, on these rivers, there is a mutual, unwritten law that each helps the other. In this case it worked splendidly, as we needed their help too. After a few hours we both got through, the other boat eventually getting ahead of us. We were surprised to meet up again in less than half-an-hour's distance from the rapid. It had run into a fallen tree which opened a hole in the side of the craft. Fortunately, they were able to make it to the river bank and make a temporary repair. In some cases there is no time to get to shore, and the launch goes down with all the cargo. Just a short distance from where this incident took place were the remains of a boat which sank last year.

After four days' travel, we arrived at Sena Madureira on a Sabbath evening. On the following day we were offered a little house. It was in a filthy condition, with a bad odour. It looked as if it hadn't been cleaned since it was built twenty years ago. With the help of a little boy, we washed and disinfected it to make it a little more habitable.

At night we were awakened continually by the weirdest and strangest sounds, which we thought to be rats. Afterwards we discovered the noise was being made by vampire bats which suck one's blood. With much difficulty, a little boy climbed on to the roof and killed thirty-eight of them. The killing of these ensured that we had more restful nights thereafter.

In Sena Madureira, there were a few believers who gave us a royal welcome. They are living in a sad condition spiritually, most of them being very much mixed up with the things of the world. However, they had a large unused government building to hold meetings each week, although sometimes only three or four were present.

Sena Madureira is a sleepy little town that once boasted to be the capital of the Acre but is now in a state of decadence. The arrival of my wife and me was the talk of the place. It was not a surprise to see the meetings packed to the utmost, often with curious people who had come to see the little organ played by my wife.

During our stay of almost five weeks at Sena, we had meetings almost nightly with often about one hundred and fifty inside the building and a good number outside. The meetings in the outlying districts sometimes took us two hours journeying into the forest, and two hours returning again. We were tired but happy to take the gospel to those that sit in darkness.

We were grateful to the authorities of Sena Madureira for their help. In no place in Brazil have we been shown more civility. They gave us the use of the public park for a lantern meeting. There were about three hundred present.

After five weeks of evangelistic work in and around the town, we decided to visit the Jamamadee Indians who live on the River Purus. We started off in a little canoe with four Brazilians. The canoe was well loaded as we took the portable organ, lantern projector, etc. with us. There was no cover so we had to travel all day in the burning sun. At 5.00 p.m. we arrived at a little Brazilian settlement called São Bento.

On the following day we set off for Campo Grande, travelling again for a full day in the burning sun. I know of nothing else so weakening. It leaves one quite limp. One of the Brazilians became ill with a temperature of over 102.5.

We spent three nights at Campo Grande where we had four meetings. These were well attended with people coming from a distance in their little canoes. The curse of these rivers are what the people call "festas" which are a mixture of dancing, drinking and immorality.

Through the kindness of the leading man at Campo Grande, we were given the use of three animals to take us to the Indian village which was another seven hours' journey from the river. The track along which we followed is used in the wet season for taking out Brazil nuts which are put into sacks and tied to the sides of the animals. The result of the constant trampling is that the track was left in a shocking condition, leaving huge holes every few feet apart. The little mules on which we travelled were very sure-footed, leaving us amazed to see how they went down the steep hills without rolling over.

At times when we travelled down a steep incline, I was trembling in my shoes expecting at any moment to have one's neck broken. The animals stopped and chewed a leaf or two from the undergrowth and then headed down the sheer drop as if to say, "If you are afraid, I certainly am not."

We thoroughly enjoyed this journey through the forest as we travelled most of the time in the shade of the tall trees, although my mule had a narrow escape from trampling on a poisonous snake.

We arrived at the Indian village before five o'clock in the afternoon. The Indians were not surprised at our coming, as news of our trip had gone before us. They had all put on their best clothing for our arrival. In ordinary life they are naked.

The village was a most interesting one and different from any other I have seen. There were only about thirty Indians present but they all lived and slept in one large hut measuring sixty by thirty feet and having the appearance of a haystack. It was closed right down to the ground and had only one little door. During the day it is quite dark inside, except for the light from the many fires that are burning. The only advantage I found is that in making the building almost airtight, it kept the insects out since they do not like smoke. After some time there, I understood their thinking for I was stung six times by wasps in one day outdoors.

A few days after our arrival, six Indian men came from another village a day's journey off. They were the most degraded set of men I have ever seen. When night came, we discovered one of the causes of their evil appearance. I was preparing the lantern in front of the Indian hut when I noticed to my right a group of about ten men, squatted on the ground, around two earthenware vessels from which they appeared to be eating. On closer examination I found that each man had his mouth full, with one side of the cheek very much enlarged. One of the vessels contained leaves from the cocoa plant from which cocaine is extracted. The other vessel held a mixture of red cinders and ashes which contained snuff. The leaves were pressed into the side of the mouth and every few minutes, with a little stick about four inches long, they rubbed in some of the ashes. This whole thing was carried on in the darkness and in almost complete silence. It seemed to make the presence of the Devil very near. These men showed very little interest in the lantern slides or the gospel message. They seemed to have sold their souls for this vice.

On two occasions while we were with them, the Indians performed their tribal dance. Only the men took part, forming a circle with their arms around each others' shoulders. They commenced by chanting the weirdest tune with no more than three notes in it. At first, to one not accustomed, the sound was that of a swarm of bees. It eventually became louder until they were chanting quite audibly. They sang to every conceivable animal and bird in the forest. These dances were performed at night and continued until daybreak.

There is always a peculiar joy in preaching the gospel message to people for the first time. In this case we had the lantern, which greatly helped in explaining the message.

There are always a few who show interest from the beginning and are willing to talk about spiritual things. It was touching to hear some of the big, strong men asking us to sing the song about Jesus. We taught them choruses in Portuguese, which a few of the men understood fairly well. We regretted very much that their language was entirely different from what we had learned from other Indians. We faithfully preached the message nightly and showed the lantern four times. We must leave the results with the Lord. As is the case in most parts of Brazil, these Indians are greatly reduced in numbers and it would not seem advisable to have a missionary permanently among them. We shall only pay occasional visits to them. They are a seven days' journey from Rio Branco.

The Indians were loathe to let us go and spent much time in asking questions. We gave them a good supply of medicines, including iodine, medicine for snakebite and toothache. It was interesting to notice that those who were steeped in witchcraft refused to take them.

I shall never forget the morning of our departure from the village. Three of the Brazilians who accompanied us deserted our group after three days with the Indians. They were afraid and could not cope with the lack of food. For the eight days we were there, our main food was a root known as macacheira. We had it morning, noon and night.

Those who deserted left us with a youth of sixteen years who on the day before we left went down with a temperature of almost 103°. To make matters worse, one of the animals that was to take us back to the river ran away. This meant that I, with the sick man, had the prospect of a seven-hour trek through the forest. Just as we were about to set off, heavy rain fell, which meant we had to wait until it passed.

Besides this, our food rations were exhausted and we could not possibly wait for another day. So on we pressed, with the sick man and me walking and Margaret on the mule. Occasionally, my wife walked while we mounted the mule. God answered prayer. The sick man did not deteriorate any more and we were able to reach our destination without much more rain.

We had another meeting that night at Campo Grande, and the following day we set off in the canoe again. I was obliged to paddle the hour trip to Regeneração, since the sick man could not help. We were fearfully tired when we arrived but were given strength to have another meeting, which was well attended.

Space forbids my telling more. Please continue to pray for us.

Besides blessings during their trip, Willie and Margaret were greatly encouraged when they returned to Rio Branco and found Mollie well, and learned that the church had maintained its bright witness in spite of their absence.

Although Willie and Margaret's lives were full of satisfying work in the Lord's service, not a day went by in which they did not shed tears in remembering their daughter Irene back in Northern Ireland. Letters assured them that she was being well cared for in Ballywalter, but Willie and Margaret knew they were missing out on the various stages of their little girl's development. How they longed to just hear her voice or to hold her in their arms. Their busyness in the work kept them occupied, but it did not make them immune from the pain and distress which they constantly felt.

Despite the success of the work in Rio Branco, the missionaries were also exposed to dangers. Mollie had one unforgettable experience on a Sunday night, 23rd January 1938:

I was put through an ordeal which nearly proved fatal. The tropical rain had poured down all day. Those who had come to the Sunday morning service had arrived with wet clothes, and by evening it was still raining. All the roads were flooded so there was no evening service.

Willie and Margaret were in their room, and I was sitting at the table in the dining room reading the scriptures. As I read Psalm 71, verse two seemed to grip my attention,

"Deliver me and cause me to escape." I then noticed verse four, "Deliver me out of the hand of the unrighteous and cruel man." I really believed that God was telling me something. Could this be a warning to me?

As I sat at the table contemplating on the reading, I was startled by someone suddenly clapping their hands loudly outside our door. I wondered who might be outside.

For some weeks I had been helping a very nice little woman, Myrtle, who was expecting her first baby. I figured I must be needed at her home. Sure enough, standing there in the pouring rain was her husband. He apologized for having to call me out on such a terrible night, but I did not mind. I soon gathered my medicine bag and followed him through the floods to his house.

I was there for several hours when the baby girl was born at 1.00 a.m. She was their first baby, and they were delighted. We all then enjoyed a cup of coffee and a rest before the new father escorted me back to my house. I noticed that he was carrying a rather heavy stick, and although I thought this a bit unusual, I did not ask any questions. I thought he must have seen a snake when he had come to call me.

The following week he told me he had brought a stick with him because he had felt someone watching us as I attended to his wife Myrtle. This was quite possible as the house was very open, only being enclosed halfway up the wall. The bedroom was the only room which was completely enclosed.

By the time I arrived home, the rain had stopped but the slippery mud made the road treacherous. I came into the house as quietly as possible, using only my flashlight so as not to waken the others. Soon after taking my muddy shoes off, I again heard someone on the verandah making a terrible noise, clapping and calling out for me. I tried to calm and hush him. I asked, "Is it Myrtle again? Whatever is wrong?"

By this time the noise had wakened Margaret and she told Willie that I had been called out to see Myrtle again. Like me, she was sure it was Myrtle's husband. But this time, we both were wrong.

I went out to the end of the verandah where I saw a tall Bolivian Indian. He had his head and face almost concealed behind a grey blanket. In the darkness of the early morning, I could not see him very clearly. He seemed quite nervous as he asked me to come quickly to his wife who was having their fifth child and having complications. Because I did not know him, I asked him why he had not contacted me earlier about his wife's pregnancy. He answered that they had come to live in Rio Branco only a short time ago.

Even after his explanation, I was still wary of him. I asked him how he knew I was a midwife and how he knew where I lived. He told me, "Dona Gertrude told me about you, and she said you would come at once."

Dona Gertrude was a believer and a member of our church. She was a widow with a large family, and she attended and assisted many ladies at the time of their delivery. For this reason we knew her as "the handy woman." Mention of her name disarmed me, for one day not long before this as I was passing her house, I stopped in for a chat and she told me about a difficult confinement she was worried about. I told her never to hesitate to call me at any hour of the night or day and I would gladly go to help her. Little did I know that this Bolivian was in her house talking to her son at that time and had heard every word that was spoken.

Unaware of any danger, I prepared to follow him to give help, as I thought, to Dona Gertrude. But Dona Gertrude knew nothing about this Indian, who had neither wife nor children.

I told the man to wait outside as I went back to get my midwifery bag. I was soon ready and we were off. The heavy rain had ceased and we began the hazardous walk to his supposed house, slipping and sliding down the muddy road to the bridge. Because of the heavy rain that had fallen throughout the previous day, the water was rushing angrily under the bridge. At times I thought that the water would wash the flimsy bridge away.

As I walked on to the bridge, the Indian caught my arm and said, "No, come this way."

I knew the place well, since I knew that the way he was pulling me led only down to the River Acre. I then realized my earlier suspicions had been well grounded, and that this man had only evil intentions; I began pulling one way and he the other. As we struggled in the darkness, he pulled my midwifery bag from me and threw it into the raging river. He then grabbed the flashlight from my hands and began smashing it into my face. Thankfully he did not have any other weapon but with this flashlight, he managed to smash out several of my teeth and badly injure my left eye.

I know without a doubt that God was my help and deliverance that night. As I desperately struggled for my life, God gave me strength. The Indian was very tall whereas my height was only five feet, but I managed to thwart his evil intentions. His hands went around my throat and he began choking me; but for some reason he changed his mind. He dragged me, fighting all the way, to the side of the bridge and threw me over into the raging torrent.

As the dark swirling water engulfed me, I thought I was dead, but this was part of God's plan. The cold water shocked me back into action, and although I was already tired from the struggle, I floated in the stream. As I was swept down river by the rushing current, I was too tired to swim and thought I would be carried all the way out into the main flow of the River Acre. Suddenly my arm brushed against the stump of a tree, and I held on with all my strength.

Immediately I heard my attacker crashing through the brush at the edge of the river, and for the first time I began to cry out, "Help! Somebody help me."

I called urgently and repeatedly as I saw the Indian coming closer. I saw that he now had something in his hand, perhaps a tree branch, with which to strike my arm and loosen my grip. By this time the new day was dawning, and my cries for help were heard. He hesitated for a moment then dropped the stick and ran off over the bridge in the opposite direction. He was frightened as he had heard someone running toward the bridge.

Farther up the hill there was a small house where two young soldiers were living. They were to be on duty at four in the morning and were getting ready to leave when they heard my cries for help. They could tell someone was in trouble because of the tone of my voice, but I was so scared I didn't realize I was calling out in English so they didn't understand what I was calling. As they drew near, I could hear one soldier say to another, "Could it be the missionary midwife in trouble? Perhaps there is a snake or a wild animal on the path."

When they reached the bridge, they looked over and saw me in the water. They jumped into the swift flowing current and reached me just as I thought I could hold on no longer. They pulled me to the riverbank and supported me as we made our way back up the hill toward the mission house. I had been in the cold water so long that my legs felt numb. When I tried to walk on my bare feet, I felt like I was walking on tiny pieces of glass.

Willie and Margaret got a rude awakening when we arrived on the verandah. I was soaking wet. By this time my left eye was swelling shut and my mouth was still bleeding where my teeth had been knocked out. Margaret, thinking I had gone back to Myrtle's, told the soldiers that Myrtle's husband had been the one that had done this to me. Of course, the poor man knew nothing about what had happened and must have been terrified when the soldiers pulled him from his house and accused him of attacking me. When I heard what was happening, I was able to tell them the true story. We asked the poor man to come to the house, and we explained the error and told him how his name had wrongly got mixed up in this incident.

That night I learned again that our Heavenly Father neither slumbers nor sleeps. I had been delivered "out of the hand of the unrighteous and cruel man," and He had caused me to escape as He had promised in Psalm 71, which I had been reading before I went out on that dreadful Sunday night.

While friends prayed at home, God delivered His child even as He had promised. Mollie took some time to recover from the frightening ordeal but she did not forsake her work. She continued to serve the people to whom the Lord had called her, fully persuaded that the same Lord was also caring for her.

Chapter Five

WHAT SHALL WE CALL THE MISSION?

Just as the apostle Paul depended on anonymous Christian friends in Damascus to hold the ropes while he escaped over the city's walls in a basket, so every Christian missionary values those who hold the vital ropes of prayer and practical support. Without his friends, Paul could not have escaped from danger by descending the Damascus' walls in a basket and without supporters, few missionaries would be able to remain at their work or know God's blessing on their labours.

While the McCombs and Mollie were busy in their missionary programme in Acre, Pastor Olley and the group of faithful friends channelled out the unsolicited financial support that came in for them. Mr. R. Evans, young Irene McComb's guardian, acted as secretary for the home based committee and kept supporters informed of the progress of the work in Brazil through a quarterly prayer letter. He was also faithful in keeping the McCombs informed of their daughter's welfare and progress as well as filling them in with general news from Ulster. Mr. Sam McIlvenna, who was treasurer of the small committee, was constantly amazed that although there was never an abundance of money, sufficient funds always arrived just in time.

After the missionary team had been in Brazil for two years, ominous events took place in Europe which indirectly had a profound effect on the development of the work in Brazil. Hitler's armies had marched into Czechoslovakia and were already threatening Poland. All over Britain, people were preparing for an inevitable war. The situation was frightening.

However, for Willie and Margaret, there was some good news to report. In mid 1939 Willie wrote a missionary prayer letter in which he included the following:

> Some of our friends already know that Mrs. McComb and Miss Harvey have gone to Manaus. My wife is expecting a happy event in August and the two doctors on whom we depended here in Rio Branco left for the South in April. It was therefore decided that it would be best for Margaret to go to Manaus where there would be better medical attention, if needed. Margaret was very reluctant in leaving me alone for such a long time, which will be more than six months. Her concern was that I had not been faring too well with my digestion and had to be very careful. I felt that I could not leave the work at this stage and must see the building through.
>
> We did everything possible to secure another missionary who might work with me during Margaret and Mollie's absence but without success. In a recent letter from my wife, she informs me that there is a young missionary in Manaus who would be able to come at the end of this month; but I regret to say that it will be necessary for me to make a trip to Manaus for medical treatment. Some of our friends at home already know that I suffered from a pain on my left side which still persists. I sleep with it, wake with it and sometimes during the day it is so severe that I can only work for a short time and then must lie down until the pain passes. This pain is the result of several attacks of dysentery I suffered over a

prolonged period six years ago. With the absence of my dear wife, and the lack of her treatment and loving care, the symptoms became aggravated. The extra work too has not helped, as I find that the best remedy is rest.

A short time ago I decided to pay a visit to a young doctor who has recently arrived from the border of Bolivia. He diagnosed my condition as colitis and advised me to have an X-ray. Rather than wait until my wife returns and then have to make the journey to Manaus, I have decided to pay a flying there visit before she returns. In Manaus I shall have the X-ray and any necessary treatment. What has been causing me a little concern is that I have been rapidly losing weight. Since my wife left over two months ago, I have lost almost four kilos. At best I haven't a great amount of flesh to lose.

Towards the end of 1939, the quarterly prayer circular reported more news from Willie in Brazil:

During the past weeks we have seen how wonderfully God has been planning for us. Up until almost the last day before leaving for Manaus, my wife was tempted to remain at Rio Branco and have the baby there. Had she done so, she may not be alive today. Her case needed the most skilled medical attention and even then we despaired of her life. I too was reluctant in leaving the work, but was obliged to do so. When I got to Manaus, I found that it would have been necessary for us all to have been here before the end of the year in order to get registered under a new Brazilian law. All other missionaries in the interior have had to come to the large towns to have it done.

On 14th August the Lord gave us another little daughter, to whom we have given the name of Eleanor Bailey. It was a Sunday afternoon and I had to spend many hours finding a doctor, who arrived at 6:30 p. m.. After an anxious time the little darling was born at 1:30 a.m. My wife was in a very weak condition afterwards. Eleanor has bright blue eyes and a pair of lungs like a pipe organ.

According to our plans, we had hoped to leave Manaus in the month of October to return to Rio Branco, but that has not been possible, as Margaret has had a series of sicknesses since the birth of the child. We took her in the ambulance to the doctor's surgery for an examination. He informed her that she was suffering from a slight touch of bronchitis and ordered an X-ray to be taken. I am glad to report there is nothing seriously wrong and that she will soon get better with treatment.

I am also glad to say that I too am feeling very much better. An X-ray revealed the parts that have been affected by the dysentery. I have had treatment, which seems to have helped. I have come to the conclusion that my best treatment is diet and rest but for a missionary in a very needy country that can be difficult. We are thankful to God for the improvement. The pain remains but is not so severe.

Friends of Miss Mary Harvey will be pleased to know that she is enjoying very good health. We are very thankful to God for all her help during this trying time. May she be long spared in the glorious work.

By the time news of baby Eleanor's arrival reached home, the Second World War had already begun. Many young men were leaving for the battle front in Europe. In many ways being in the hinterlands of Brazil was probably the safest place on earth in 1939. However, just after the war started, the missionary committee ran into a major problem in channelling the necessary funds to the three workers in far off Rio Branco. Under emergency legislation the Government froze the movement of personal assets out of Britain. This effectively meant that the McCombs' and Mollie's financial support could not be sent to Brazil because they were not a registered Mission.

A solution had to be found quickly to the predicament since the missionaries were already existing on a small allowance. Correspondence to and from Brazil was too slow to inform the missionaries of the dilemma or seek their counsel on the matter.

Early in 1940 it was agreed by the committee that several of its members should go to the bank through which Mr. McIlvenna had been sending periodic drafts to the Banco do Brasil for the missionaries and try to untangle the problem. The manager of the bank in Belfast explained that there would be no problem in sending funds to Brazil if the committee legally registered the mission as a charity. He could send their money immediately if they set about the registration of the mission agency. One of the first hurdles they had to clear was resolved in the bank manager's office when the manager asked, "What will you call the Mission?"

The members of the Committee looked at each other and then the manager asked again, "Where do Mr. & Mrs. McComb work?"

"Acre. They work in the Acre," was the reply almost spoken in unison by the committee members.

"Why not call it the Acre Gospel Mission? I will send the money to them from the Acre Gospel Mission if you will register under that name."

The name was almost obvious and struck an accord with the committee, who lost no time in registering Mollie and Willie and Margaret McComb as members of the Acre Gospel Mission. From mid-1940, all news letters from the three missionaries in Brazil were circulated under the name of the "Acre Gospel Mission." The first members of the committee became the trustees of the newly formed mission and Pastor Olley continued as its Chairman. Mr. Evans assumed the role of honorary secretary and Mr. McIlvenna as treasurer.

Finding a name for the Mission and a way to channel funds to Brazil was simple compared to the dilemma the McCombs faced in Brazil. Although they were overjoyed with the arrival of their little blond baby girl, they lived in hope of being reunited with their other daughter after four years in the Amazon. Alas, the outbreak of war on such a global scale imposed a virtual embargo on transatlantic passenger sailing and it became nearly impossible for the three missionaries and the new baby to return to Britain even though the newly formed committee sent repeated requests for them to come for a needed furlough.

If the absence of their daughter already put a strain on Willie and Margaret, the discovery that they would not be able to return until the hostilities of the Second World War ceased just about crushed them. At that time, no one knew how long the war would last. The McCombs had no idea when they would see their darling Irene again or when she would ever meet her new sister.

While they were in Manaus for Eleanor's birth, Willie received letters from various committee members asking him to consider trying to return to Northern Ireland in view of their ill health and the worsening situation of the war. In the first missionary prayer letter of 1940, under the new name of Acre Gospel Mission, Mr. Evans, honorary secretary of the missionary committee which cared for the trio in Brazil, wrote a footnote to the prayer letter:

> Mr. McComb has asked me to write a little paragraph at the end of this circular letter. It is all so interesting that I feel there is little I can say. However, we think it right that all those interested in this glorious work for God in that needy land should know that the Committee some time ago requested that Mr. and Mrs. McComb and Miss Harvey should come home for a period for furlough. They all emphatically declined to leave their post. We were really anxious about their health hence the request. Mr. McComb's old trouble is still there and those of us who know him intimately, know that he often works under great strain and difficulty. After the birth of little Eleanor, now almost a year old, Mrs. McComb was in poor health.
>
> We do indeed praise God for their determination and we also praise Him for the very valuable instrument Miss Harvey is, not only to them in their weakness, but to all the lost souls with whom she comes in contact, especially the expectant mothers. Her work is often trying and difficult and facilities are often lacking as she exercises her trained powers among the women. May the Lord

abundantly bless all their efforts in the salvation of the lost in that dark corner of the vineyard.

Irene, now almost eight years old, is such a darling child and educationally is developing remarkably well. She will be in third standard by the time this letter reaches its readers. She has also commenced to study music and is making considerable progress.

In relation to this announcement by Mr. Evans, Willie McComb sent a letter to the chairman and members of the committee:

A few weeks before we left Manaus for the Acre, we received a letter from the friends at home, urging us to return for furlough because of illness and informing us of the difficulty of sending funds because of the war. As we had already made plans for returning to Rio Branco, and at the same time were very conscious of the Lord's leading, we felt compelled to follow the plans already made. To have left the work in its present stage would have been humanly speaking, disastrous, and certainly would have meant great sorrow to us. We sincerely thank the friends who have taken such personal interest in our welfare.

It was a memorable day of mixed feelings when we left Manaus to travel back up river. The letter calling us home arrived only three weeks before embarking, so it gave little hope of an answer to our reply, except by wire, and that proved impossible.

Never shall we forget the feeling when we embarked. The three of us with little baby Eleanor, were going to a place one thousand three hundred miles farther from home. We had received the news of the difficulty of sending out funds; we had enough to keep us going for a few months. The rest was in the Lord's hands. We felt a little of what Abraham must have felt when he left his native land. We certainly were never more conscious of the presence of the God of Abraham.

The Lord brought us through to the place where, like Paul, we were willing to labour with our hands, if that need were to arise. After two and a half months, we have just received an encouraging airmail reply informing us that the difficulty of sending funds has been cleared away. We praise God for this and go into the future with confidence.

As one can gather from these letters, a lot of hurtful emotions were stirred in making these difficult decisions. More grief followed when, not long after the missionaries returned to Rio Branco, Mollie received word of her father's death. Her last memory of him was his concern for her baggage being soaked as it left the house for the boat on the grey morning of her departure from Belfast. However, in spite of her compounded sorrow, Mollie was content to continue in the work that God had called her to.

During the war years Willie, Margaret and Mollie kept themselves busy. After they returned to Rio Branco, Willie obtained a small launch to enable him to travel more on the surrounding rivers. Also, in 1940 a young Norwegian missionary, Sander Tonnesson, arrived in Rio Branco and threw his weight in with Willie McComb and the ladies while he waited for news from another Norwegian missionary coming to the Acre.

Sander accompanied Willie on several river journeys as they preached the gospel and distributed evangelistic literature. Willie also recruited two young Brazilians, Julio and Leonzio, whom he trained and supported as evangelists in the region. He travelled widely with these two evangelists along most of the tributaries accessible to them from Rio Branco. Hundreds of souls were led to faith in Jesus Christ on these trips. While in Rio Branco, Willie also continued to spearhead the development of the church and the various preaching points.

Mollie was a great asset to the church work. Her midwifery became legendary in Rio Branco and she was even invited to the Governor's Palace to care for the Governor's wife and deliver their child. Willie also put his microscope to good use, classifying various strains of malaria and intestinal parasites and then dispensing the appropriate medicines. He also became very gifted at photography and developing his own films. He was able to pass these skills on to some local boys who went on to make a handsome living from their acquired expertise.

Auntie Mollie was always a favourite with young Eleanor who, although preferring Portuguese, enjoyed conversations with Mollie in English. Margaret had great delight with Eleanor as the little girl developed through her infant years. She was a great comfort to Willie and Margaret when news came through that Margaret's mother and Willie's father had passed away.

As time went by, Margaret took on the role of mother/teacher and tried to give Eleanor a start in reading, writing and arithmetic. As well as these commitments, Margaret kept up her total involvement in the church work.

It was a dark and wet day late in 1945 when the team of Ulster missionaries had to leave Rio Branco for a long overdue furlough. Hundreds had gathered at the riverside to see them off. Mollie later wrote of them leaving Brazil and the arduous trip back to Northern Ireland after an absence of almost nine years.

> As the horn blew, it gave the signal that finally the boat was ready to move. We heard many lovely promises from the Scriptures being shouted to us from the believers. Tears were in our eyes as we watched the boat slip farther and farther away from them, but the farther this boat moved down river, the more I knew in my heart that one day I would return to Acre. This was the beginning of our long journey home.
>
> World War II was over and many missionaries who were not able to travel during the war, were now returning home. Willie and Margaret McComb were very lonely and had great longings for their elder daughter, Irene, who had been left behind at home eight and a half years earlier. Now they were taking another daughter, six-year-old Eleanor, home for the first time.

From Rio Branco to the mouth of the Amazon is a long tiresome journey in a small boat. On reaching the coast and the city of Belem, we discovered there was no hope of any boats taking passengers to England. In Belem we found suitable accommodation and Willie went to the port every day to inquire if there was any ship bound for England. We prayed and waited.

One day he came back very excited and told us to get our things packed again as we were going to New York on a Polish cargo vessel. He had spoken to the captain, who offered to take us to New York for a very small sum of money. Needless to say, we were all delighted at this answer to prayer. We boarded the vessel the next day since it was sailing that afternoon. The captain was a gentleman and treated us very kindly, as did the crew.

Although the sea was very rough all the way to America, the trip was not all that unpleasant because we knew that at last we were going home.

Near to Trinidad, in the Caribbean, we were caught in the dying throes of a hurricane. The captain ordered us to remain in our cabins where we were locked in for our own safety. The boat was tossed about on mountainous waves like an old leaf at the mercy of a turbulent flood. I must admit I was very concerned when I saw some of the heavy deck cargo being thrown overboard into the angry sea. Just when I feared the worst, the hurricane diminished and soon it was relegated to only a tropical storm and then died away completely.

After two weeks we arrived in New York. Quite a crowd was there awaiting our arrival and as the ship sailed in, the people were cheering. They seemed to be happy to see the ship safely in port even without much of the heavy cargo, which by this time must have been lying half covered in sand and silt at the bottom of the ocean. Unknown to us, news had been given on American radio about the ship being in difficulty and having to jettison its cargo at sea to save both ship and passengers.

Once on terra firma, we were advised to immediately place our names on the waiting list for a passage to England, which we did. Happily, because we had been so long in the tropics, we were told that our names would be at the top of the waiting list in the shipping office. We then took a train to Canada to stay with Mrs. McComb's sister and family near Toronto. They received us warmly and we had a very welcome rest.

After we had been in Canada for a month or so, a telegram came one night at 10.00 p.m. giving us the good news that passages had been granted to us on the *HMS Queen Elizabeth*. We were to be on board the ship the next day at noon. We praised the Lord for answering both our prayers and those of the caring Acre Committee in Belfast.

That day we rushed around packing our cases and were ready for the midnight train from Toronto to New York. The train was so full that many of us had to sit on our cases for most of the journey, but some kind folks shared their seats with us during the night. The train reached New York in good time and when we arrived in the harbour, I can remember feeling quite dizzy as I looked up at the height of that wonderful ship, the *HMS Queen Elizabeth*. It was not as posh as before the war because it had been used as a troop carrier during the years of combat.

Once on board, I was placed in a cabin with eight other ladies. There were two thousand passengers on board, which included people from all classes and walks of life. Hundreds of them had just been released from prisoner of war camps in Japan. Many of these still looked ill and emaciated but were well cared for on the journey by the male nurses and doctors who accompanied them.

Finally, we arrived and disembarked in Southampton. Again, thousands were gathered at the docks. The cheers were thunderous. The prisoners were home at last! In some aspects, the war had made prisoners of us all since we could neither come nor go from our respective lands.

"Land of Hope and Glory" was never sung with such gusto as reverberated from shore to shore at the harbour on that fine day. Many missionaries on board were welcomed by their loved ones. At the call of the King of kings, they had gone to distant lands before the war began and each could tell of precious souls they had seen delivered from darkest paganism to a new life in our wonderful Saviour, the Lord Jesus Christ.

At Southampton, we boarded a train for Euston Station in London. The weather was extremely cold, and we were informed that no train was leaving for Liverpool until next evening at 6.00 p.m.. Just as we had begun to look for accommodation, right outside the station, we found an old lady who offered us two attic rooms in an apartment house. I think we would have been thankful for a hole in the ground to get out of the bitterly cold station.

The next morning, at breakfast the old lady told us that many policemen were lined up outside her door in Euston Square. We knew that this meant some member of the Royal Family must be arriving on one of the trains and if we stood on the steps outside, we would probably manage to see them.

Soon we heard cheering from down the street. The sound became louder and louder until there was a great crescendo of cheering and clapping. Just then, Queen Elizabeth and the two princesses passed by us in a beautiful open carriage. The Queen must have noticed this little fair haired jumping bean with us and bent forward a little and waved back at her. Little did Her Majesty know how far this little child had travelled, and on this her first day on English soil, Eleanor got a wave of the hand from the Queen of England!

The following day we went by train to Liverpool where we finally boarded the Belfast Steamer for the overnight sailing home.

At Belfast we were given a lovely welcome by family and friends. Waiting at the quayside was Margaret and

Willie's daughter, Irene, who had been left in Ulster so many years before. The small girl who did not want her parents to leave nearly nine years earlier was now a tall teenager. She was a little apprehensive and unsure of how to greet her parents, who had been only a memory for so long.

The three missionaries were glad to be home after a long term in the distant Acre. Before commencing a quota of deputation work, Willie and Margaret needed time with their family. Their two daughters needed to get acquainted and Willie and Margaret needed medical attention. Very soon, invitations for the missionaries to speak began to accumulate. They were amazed to see how much interest had been generated in the work in Brazil. At that time, Willie McComb wrote a resume of his last term in Brazil:

It is almost nine years since we last sailed for Brazil. At that time, we went forth relying on the fulfillment of His exceeding great and precious promises. We also had a few faithful friends whom the Lord had given to us who eventually formed themselves into a committee. We would like to record our grateful thanks to these dear friends, for their most faithful and sacrificial service during these past years. They have done it heartily as unto the Lord.

It never was our intention to form another mission. We had hoped to labour in our needy part of the Lord's vineyard, supported by the friends whom the Lord had given to us. The war came, and we were informed by our friends at home that the Government would not permit any more money to be sent to us, except enough for our passages home. This news came as a challenge to us, and a further test of our faith in Him who hitherto had so wonderfully supplied all our needs.

At the time the letter came we were in the town of Manaus, one thousand five hundred miles from our base, and Eleanor was only a few weeks old. After much heart-searching and prayer, we decided to return to Rio Branco, our base. The Lord had made us willing for anything, and we had resolved, if necessary, to labour with our hands as we worked in the service of seeking the lost.

In the meantime, our friends at home were leaving no stone unturned in an effort to get funds out to us. Eventually the Government authorities agreed that if the work were given a name, they would recognize it as a Mission and would allow a certain amount to be sent out. It was thus that the Acre Gospel Mission came into being, and the name was coined by the committee on their own initiative. It may be necessary to alter the name later should the work develop into other parts of Brazil.

As we look back over the past years, there is one thing that saddens us. It is the fact that there were so many open doors we were unable to enter because of the lack of labourers. It is difficult to express the feeling one has when leaving an Indian village or a civilized Brazilian town, where the Gospel has been preached for the first time with a good response, and to which we may not again return. We would repeat the words of the Lord Jesus, "Pray ye the Lord of the harvest that He may send forth labourers."

On the other hand, we thank God that He has given us a part in this great programme of evangelizing the world, and we rejoice over the many thousands of souls who have heard the Gospel for the first time. Praise God also for the thousands of copies of His precious Word that have been placed in the hands of many people. In this branch of the work there is an open door like never before. We have not yet done a journey when supplies did not run out before completing the territory we had planned to visit.

We are making plans to have a sum of money sent out to the colporteur in the Acre for the purchase of Scriptures. This will be sent each quarter while we are at home.

Since drafting the above letter, we received a letter from our friend, Dynes McCullough, an American missionary of Baptist Mid-Missions, who entered into our work before we left Rio Branco. The news is most encouraging and rejoices our hearts. Dynes was able to acquire another American missionary from Manaus for a month's Mission. This proved to be a time of reaping, for forty-two souls made the great decision.

Miss Harvey, my wife and I have been kept busy with meetings. We would covet your prayers as we face the problems of the future, that in all things His perfect will may be done and His worthy name glorified. In the meantime, our task is deputation work on behalf of the millions in the vast hinterland of Brazil, who cannot speak for themselves.

Willie and Margaret began to make plans to return to Brazil. They had already purchased some items of equipment but at the back of their minds, they knew they had not made a sufficient physical recovery to face the rigors of life in Acre again. After intense treatment, the doctor faced Willie with the truth, "It would be suicidal for you to return to the tropics."

Willie was stunned by the thought of not going back to Brazil. Missions had been his life and passion. It took some time for the doctor's ultimatum to sink in, but finally it became apparent that Willie and Margaret would not be able to return to Acre because of the physical toll that repeated intestinal illnesses had taken on them.

They prayed about the future of Acre Gospel Mission and wondered what would happen to the work and to Mollie. Their speculation was expressed in the following Mission prayer circular of February 1947:

As we placed all these things before the Lord, there seemed to be only one answer — service for Him in the homeland. It is not easy for my wife and me to lay down the gospel sword which we had planned to carry to the end. But we humbly bow to what we consider to be the will of the Lord for us. In the meantime, we are seeking to know the place of His choice for us. We are assured that He will open up a door of service.

We shall never cease to take a keen interest in the work in Brazil. The Lord has given us the following plan, which we are now putting into action. We intend, through the British and Foreign Bible Society, to send scriptures to the value of £50 to Rio de Janeiro. We shall request that these be divided among three (the number to increase as the Lord guides) of His faithful servants there — Sr. Targino, Sr. Leoncio, and our faithful friend Sander, the Norwegian missionary who spent some months with us in the Acre. It is our desire that the proceeds from these scriptures be retained by the colporteurs for their personal expenses. As the Lord supplies the need, we hope to continue sending more literature and thus get the precious Word of God into regions where it is hitherto unknown.

We are pleased to inform you that Miss Mollie Harvey hopes to return to Brazil. It has not yet been decided how she will return; probably as an associate of another South American Mission. We are glad to say that we have sufficient funds in hand for her outfit and passage to Brazil.

We have planned to have a Committee meeting soon to discuss matters arising through our not returning to Brazil. All money matters will be discussed and we hope to send out another Circular soon.

Did the Acre Gospel Mission have a future? Would Miss Harvey return to Brazil? These questions weighed heavily on the hearts of supporters and were taken to God in prayer.

Chapter Six

WILL YOU NOT COME BACK AGAIN?

The year's furlough for Mollie Harvey had been an exhausting and yet an exhilarating time. Undaunted by not being able to drive a car, Mollie travelled widely and unceasingly on draughty, and at times cramped buses, all over Ireland. She spoke at churches, mission halls and to small prayer groups in homes. Frequently Mollie carried a case containing her Brazilian curios for use in the meetings and her personal belongings for an overnight stay in various homes when required. Everywhere she went she held people spellbound with her arresting and imaginative word pictures of life in Brazil. Mollie won her way into many homes and hearts and forged abiding friendships with individuals and families. Nearly everywhere this amazing lady went, people pledged to stand by her if she returned to the Amazon.

For a missionary, personal support and the assurances of prayer are very encouraging, but of themselves they are insufficient grounds to constitute a call to a mission field. Added to these tokens of support, Mollie had a burning desire to return to the Acre even though Willie and Margaret had finally accepted the doctor's advice to terminate their missionary career. She remembered that she had promised the believers in Acre that she would return sometime. Nevertheless, Mollie was still hesitant to make any plans lest she should find herself out of God's will. She always remembered Willie McComb's admonition, "It is a dangerous thing to do the Lord's work in the strength of the flesh." That was the last thing Mollie wanted to do.

One morning in the front room of their home in Belfast, Mollie mused and prayed over these matters as she read her Bible. Just then words from Isaiah chapter 45 seemed to jump from the page and sealed a deep peace in her heart, "I will go before thee, and make the crooked places straight: I will break in pieces the gates of brass, and cut in sunder the bars of iron: And I will give thee the treasures of darkness, and hidden riches of secret places, that thou mayest know that I, the Lord, which call thee by thy name, am the God of Israel." Mollie was convinced this was God's directive for her.

She shared her plans with Willie and Margaret. At first they were a little bit cautious about her returning to Brazil alone. They recommended that she speak to the committee about the matter. The committee listened sympathetically and after some discussion they agreed that Mollie could return to the Acre, but they also shared the McComb's concern for a single lady working alone in distant Rio Branco.

Within days of meeting with the mission committee, Mollie had a visit from a young couple who expressed interest in serving the Lord in Brazil. Other people had spoken to Mollie about missionary service in the Acre but there was something about this young couple that warmed Mollie's heart. James Gunning was a joiner in the building trade and Dorrie was a secretary at Doggarts, the undertakers in Newtownards.

James and Dorrie shared with Mollie how that since their conversion, they had followed with interest Mr. & Mrs. McComb's work in Brazil. Dorrie had not only been to the Belfast quayside on the evening in 1937 when Mollie and the McCombs left for Brazil, but in the intervening years she had also corresponded with the missionaries. Their pastor, Mr. Olley, had also kept them informed of how God was at work in Miss Harvey's life.

As they talked, Mollie asked James and Dorrie to share their testimony with her.

James had been led to Christ in 1932 at an evangelistic mission conducted by Mr. Tom Bailie in Newtownards. Through the instrumentality of Mrs. Ravey, her Sunday School teacher, and the influence of a school friend Dorrie trusted the Lord Jesus as her Saviour in 1930. The couple met each other at Newtownards Baptist, where they became very involved in the work of the church. In 1934 the young couple began to go out with each other and they were married in 1944. By that time, James was a deacon in the Church and superintendent of the Sunday school while Dorrie taught a Sunday school class.

Like many other newly married couples, James and Dorrie furnished their first home to their pleasure and comfort. They were united in the Lord and committed to Him and wanted to use their home to give hospitality to God's servants.

After the wedding in 1944 the happy couple went to Portstewart for their honeymoon which was planned to correspond with the annual Portstewart Convention, Northern Ireland's Keswick. Always keen for the Lord and the study of the scriptures, James and Dorrie attended most of the meetings at the tent. On the Friday morning, they were present for the traditional missionary meeting. One missionary after another gave the challenge of their work and at the end, the chairman made an earnest appeal for young people to offer themselves for the Lord's work wherever He needed them.

James or Dorrie made no public response to the appeal but the Lord had spoken to James and he knew it. In his heart he surrendered his life to Christ for missionary service. However, he would not impose such a life on Dorrie without her also feeling God was in it. James wanted Dorrie to hear God's call also so that both of them would be convinced of the Lord's leading in their lives. Although he never mentioned it to his new wife James talked to the Lord about it frequently and waited for *His* time.

True to their aspirations, James and Dorrie used their home to the glory of God. However, the Lord had other plans for them. Just over two years after the meeting in Portstewart, Dorrie attended the Baptist Women's Fellowship meeting in Newtownards where Mrs. Jump, a missionary in Africa with the Sudan United Mission, was speaking. It was most significant that Mrs. Jump had been led to the Saviour through Willie McComb's outreach on the Shankill Road. During the meeting, beyond Mrs. Jump's audible voice, Dorrie heard God speaking to her and challenging her about serving Him in Brazil.

At the close of the meeting the ladies sang "Take my life and let it be consecrated Lord to Thee." Dorrie sang every line as if her heart was bursting in devotion to Christ. She just wanted all of Him and be all He wanted her to be.

Back home over supper, James asked how the meeting went. When Dorrie said it was a very good meeting, James further pressed, "Do you think the Lord spoke to you, Dorrie? Do you think He is calling us?"

Dorrie stopped for a moment. Her eyes filled up with tears as she deliberately looked up into James' eyes and said, "James, I don't think the Lord spoke to me. I am sure of it."

James shared with his wife how God had spoken to him during their honeymoon at Portstewart. Following that memorable time of prayer, they resolved to arrange a visit to Mr. McComb and then with Mollie Harvey. James and Dorrie invited Mollie to their home where she heard the story.

As Mollie listened to the young couple, her heart was more stirred than ever. She could hardly believe what she was hearing. This was the very confirmation she had been longing and praying for. Mollie recognized this was a tremendous step for the young couple to take, but James and Dorrie were more conscious of the sacrifice their parents would make.

At a further meeting with Mr. McComb and the Acre Committee, it was recommended that the young couple go to the Bible Training Institute (B. T. I.) in Glasgow for some preparatory experience before following Mollie to Brazil at a later date.

The Mission had a Valedictory meeting in Donegall Square Methodist Church for Mollie on 15th May 1947, where James and

Dorrie gave testimony of their call to the work. Within three months, the young couple enrolled as students at the B. T. I. in Glasgow. Just before they left, Mollie experienced another emotional farewell from her family and friends at the Belfast quayside when she sailed to Brazil as the only missionary of the Acre Gospel Mission. The committee had recommended that she should not return to Rio Branco, so she was just taking one step at a time and trusting God to open the right doors for her. She later wrote of how God honoured those steps of faith:

> From the day I left Belfast in June 1947, the Lord helped me get through each day travelling as a single lady until I arrived in the city of Manaus many weeks later,. When I reached Manaus and was able to clear customs, the Lord's provision for me was a lovely surprise. Willard and Grace Stull, American missionaries whom I had just known since arriving in Brazil in 1937, were home on furlough and knowing I was coming to Manaus, they left me the key to their furnished house for my use as long as I would need it.
>
> During my time in Manaus, I was much in prayer as to where in the Acre the Lord would have me work for Him. I was attending a church in the city and had begun to be acquainted with its members. One day I had the opportunity to share with the church what was on my mind and how I was hoping to go to Acre. A nice couple came to me later and said they had lived and worked in the town of Sena Madureira for years. They said that there was a missionary there, but he was leaving soon to go back to Norway to visit his family. Sander Tonnesson was a Norwegian and had not seen his family since the beginning of World War II. Years earlier he had stayed for some time with Mr. & Mrs. McComb in Rio Branco. It was some years after that visit that Sander and another Norwegian missionary went to Sena Madureira.
>
> I listened with interest to all that the couple told me about this new town and I began to wonder if this could

be where the Lord would have me go. I believed this was God's first witness to me about a new opening. I wanted to be sure so I asked God to confirm this to me.

Willard and Grace's house, where I was staying, was just across the road from a corner on which there was a medical clinic. Each morning crowds of people gathered to see a doctor and receive treatment. Open tramcars passed up and down the road in front of the clinic and brought patients from all over Manaus. Every day I watched an old lady come out of the clinic and stand in the hot sun. She would try to cover her eyes with her hand as she stood waiting for the tramcar. One day I could stand it no longer, so I went up to her and asked her to come over to the house for a cup of coffee and a chat.

In the house, she told me she attended the clinic every day to get drops in her eyes. With tears she confessed that she feared she was going blind. Looking at her eyes, I saw she had cataracts clouding her pupils. I asked her where she lived, and to my great surprise, she told me she lived up in Acre in a town called Sena Madureira. She also told me that her daughter was a believer who knew the missionary well and that the meetings there were very good.

When I told her I was planning on going to Acre but had to wait until the water level was higher on the River Purus, she was delighted and said, "Oh, will you take me to the Acre with you after I have the operation on my eyes? Please go to Sena Madureira with me."

Of course, I could make no promises, but I felt that this was the Lord's confirmation that I had been seeking. However, I was still not sure and like Gideon, I prayed that God would not be angry with me for asking for yet another sign.

Soon after, I received a letter from Sander Tonnesson. He had heard I was in Manaus and in his letter he asked me to pray and consider working for the Lord in Sena

Madureira since he was soon leaving for Norway. He finished the letter by saying that the church members had been much in prayer and were awaiting an answer. This was the third and final confirmation. Therefore, with a joyful heart I thanked the Lord for confirming His call to me so definitely.

Back in those post war times, it was not easy for a single lady to arrange her travelling itinerary to the distant Acre. The Brazilian government had conscripted thousands of men during the war. A large number of these conscripts from North East Brazil were sent to work in the distant States of Amazonas and Acre where they were trained to extract rubber latex for the Allied cause. It was for this reason they gained the nickname "rubber soldiers." When the war was over, some of them tried to return to their homes in the North East, but the majority settled in the Amazon. These disbanded soldiers and their families swelled the population of the region which meant that great numbers of people travelled up and down the Amazon's tributaries on all sorts of craft to reach distant towns and settlements. In the Acre Gospel Mission's quarterly prayer circular, Mollie wrote of her own experience in 1947:

"I found great difficulty in getting a boat to take me up river to Sena Madureira, one thousand five hundred miles away. Things have changed for the worse since Mr. and Mrs. McComb and I did this same journey. I was promised a passage on a boat going part of the way and had all my luggage ready on the verandah of Willard's house. I even called for a man to transport the baggage, but at the last moment the owner of the boat decided not to take any passengers. That meant I had to unpack my luggage and wait for another month.

At last a boat did arrive which was willing to take me. We only travelled three days on this vessel when we were met by a small paddle steamer to which we had to transfer for the journey to Boca do Acre. I have never seen a boat so overcrowded. We were not long on the river when a boy of five years fell into the water. Thankfully he was rescued in the nick of time.

I had many opportunities to witness on board this paddle steamer. The captain was very nice, but somewhat embarrassed by the poor conditions and the inferior food. He admitted to me that it was not his fault. Twice a week I was able to have a meeting on the lower deck. I took down my little portable organ and besides singing choruses, I sometimes told the gospel story with the help of the flannel graph. Many people soon began to learn the choruses, and I spent numerous happy hours with them. During the trip, I discovered that out of more than one hundred passengers on board, only one man had ever heard the gospel before. Most of them were going to a town called Xapurí, which is farther up river from Rio Branco and where there is no gospel witness. One of the men said to me one day, "Please come up to Xapurí with us and we will soon learn more." Please pray for them and for the gospel booklets which went with them.

The paddle steamer only took me as far as the Boca do Acre, where I had to say good-bye to most of these dear souls.

Arriving at the Boca do Acre was the biggest test of the long journey. We arrived at six o'clock on a pouring wet morning. I don't know of any place more miserable than this place on a wet day. I looked at the mud on the bank of the river and wondered where I could put my baggage and myself. I also had the old lady whom I had been treating for eye trouble in Manaus, since I was bringing her back to Sena Madureira to friends. In such difficult times, the Lord is ever near to bless and show us the way.

I went to ask when I might get a boat or any craft to take us up the River Purus to Sena Madureira, which was at least another three days up the River Purus. I was told there would be a boat going in several days time. When the man saw my predicament, he told me I could leave all my baggage in his little office. I knew that in Brazil this was a very risky thing to do, but I felt this to be the Lord's provision. I got all the baggage taken off the paddle steamer and left the whole matter in the Lord's hand. He did not fail and nothing was stolen.

Next I found a room for the old lady and myself in a house where the family was supposed to be believers, but sad to say, I saw no spiritual life in any of them. Boca do Acre is a real Sodom. I remember being there several years earlier with Mr. & Mrs. McComb, and I can still feel the power of the enemy. During the four days I was there, I had three meetings which were very well attended. Dona Nené Jacinto Ale, the lady believer whom we had met almost ten years ago, is still firm in her faith and pleaded with me to send missionaries to her town. I left the Boca do Acre with a heavy heart as I thought of the spiritual need and darkness. I prayed that God would soon send a missionary to this needy town.

On the little boat to Sena Madureira, I was given the only cabin which was also used as a dressing room for the ladies. I often wondered if I would not have been better off with my hammock swung out on the deck with the rest of the women. However, I did not want to offend the owner, since he had very kindly given me the cabin as a special favour.

On the Sunday afternoon, I looked at the little children and the mothers and felt an urge to share the gospel with them. We had a nice time together. The heat was terrific, but they listened well.

We finally arrived in Sena Madureira on a beautiful sunny morning and received a very warm welcome from Sander and a nice crowd of believers who came down to meet the boat. The old lady who had been my travelling companion for more than a month was delighted to see her daughter who was also a new convert in the church.

Sander introduced Mollie to the believers in Sena Madureira over the following few weeks. She also travelled to many outlying areas in the forest to visit various groups of people in scattered clearings where a witness had been established. Mollie wrote home of those first days in Sena Madureira.

> I saw sad sights on these journeys. In one house where we rested, there was a dear little girl with her nose completely gone and her brother was almost in the same condition. They told me there was yet a third child in a similar state. Sadly, they all have leprosy. There is a small leper colony here, but there are only about twenty patients in it. They are all really bad cases. There would be hundreds in it if all the leprosy patients were certified. I was shocked during our visit to see the awful conditions. There are about six palm leaf dwellings. In one, I saw men, women and young girls all living together. No treatment seemed to be given to them. We stood outside in the pouring rain while singing the Lord's sweet message to them. One dear woman was very ill. I asked her if she was trusting only in Jesus as her Saviour. She nodded her head, meaning to say that she was. She died just a few hours after our visit. It was well worth the soaking just to give this soul another opportunity to hear the Gospel.
>
> Now that Sander has gone to Norway, I am feeling a great responsibility for this growing work. It is not only here in Sena Madureira, but also in the forest and on the rivers. What a wonderful centre this is for all the surrounding rivers. I feel that the house where I am staying will have to be enlarged if it is to be used as a future base. There are so many rivers here that are yet to be evangelized. Where are the labourers? Who is coming to help in this glorious task? Oh, how happy I am to be here

in the centre of His beautiful and perfect will. No place on earth is dearer.

I find there are many more snakes here than in Rio Branco. Two were killed right outside my door not long after I arrived. We saw many on the journey through the forest. To be truthful, I never seem to see them, but the quick Brazilian eye misses few of these deadly snakes. Some of them are the exact colour of the trees. Many times on the journeys the believers had many a laugh at me. I know I should have a healthy respect for snakes, but if I was to let them get to me too much, I would be too afraid to even put a foot to the ground or go through the forest on these journeys.

In the same circular that gave news of Mollie's arrival in Sena Madureira, there was a snippet of news about James and Dorrie at BTI in Glasgow:

Mr. and Mrs. Gunning have just finished their first year in the Bible Training Institute. They have had a most encouraging time and have been very conscious of the Lord's help in answer to your prayers. Please remember them as we seek guidance for their immediate future.

What did that future hold?

Chapter Seven

REINFORCEMENTS NOW APPEARING

James and Dorrie had been to the Belfast docks many times before to see various missionaries depart for different parts of the world. This was different. Now family and friends had gathered at the same docks on Thursday night 3rd February 1949, to say farewell to them. They had never witnessed such a crowd. Besides James and Dorrie, Hugh and Sadie Mitchell, were also being farewelled on the same boat. Hugh and Sadie were bound for Peru with the Irish Baptist Foreign Mission (now Baptist Missions). The two young couples, who were embarking on a lifetime of service for the Saviour in Latin America, separated in England. James and Dorrie boarded the *SS Hilary* with its distinctive three funnels at Tilbury docks near London for their journey to Manaus, while the Mitchells left on a separate boat for Peru.

After six weeks at sea, the new missionary couple were glad to be welcomed so warmly in Manaus by Mollie's friends, Willard and Grace Stull, Baptist missionaries from Iowa who opened their home to all Acre missionaries. James and Dorrie were in transit to join Mollie in Sena Maduriera and did not expect to be in Manaus for more than a few weeks. They knew it would be another three weeks on a river boat en route to join Mollie. However, they were soon to learn that nothing in Amazonas moves too quickly. James sent news to their friends back home:

It is with grateful hearts to our loving Heavenly Father that we write this letter to you. Dorrie and I have again proved the truth of our risen Lord's promise, "Lo I am with you always, even unto the end of the age." Together we experienced the conscious sense of His presence during our long journey up river to Sena Madureira.

After staying two months in Manaus, we believed it was the Lord's time for us to move on to Sena Madureira. The Lord very definitely led and guided with regard to a boat, the *Almir Ratala*. On Thursday, 5th May, we bade farewell to our missionary friends in Manaus and we commenced the journey to the place of the Lord's choice for us at five o'clock in the afternoon.

We were told on leaving Manaus that it would take thirty days for the boat to reach Sena Madureira, but alas, this was far from the truth. Instead, it was forty-five days before we arrived at our destination. The delay was largely due to the fact that the river level had fallen rapidly and it was not safe to travel at night.

We shall never forget the kindness of all the people on board. They did everything to make our journey as comfortable as possible even though conditions were far from ideal. Fifty passengers shared one bathroom and toilet. The captain, Sr. Daniel, even brought tea with him on the journey for his "English passengers." You can guess how delighted we were to have a cup of tea each morning and evening instead of the strong black coffee. Willard had told us to take a few tins of cream crackers with us for the journey and this proved to be a blessing. We had many chats with Sr. Daniel for he spoke English very well. We do believe he was impressed and we covet your prayers for him.

Although we could not speak much Portuguese, we were able to witness in a small way for our blessed Lord. There was a young lady also travelling to Sena Madureira. When she saw us trying to read our Portuguese Bible, she offered to read a chapter for us each day in order to help us with pronunciation. This attracted the attention of many other passengers who listened to the reading of God's Word. Do pray that the Word of God may find an abiding place in their hearts and bring forth fruit in a coming day.

We had often heard about the great need for workers in Brazil, but we never realized the need was so great. Day after day we passed groups of little houses along the river. There were such large families in almost every house and sad to say, they seem to have never heard the story of the Saviour's love. During the forty-five days of travel on the river, we stopped at many of the small towns. In every place, we were told that no missionaries had ever been along this river. Oh, what a need! Yes, the "fields are white already to harvest, but the labourers are few."

We spent two days in Labrea, a little town halfway between Manaus and Sena Madureira. Here we were thrilled to meet a believer, Sr. Luiz Marinho. He came on board to purchase some Bibles. We were glad that we had a few Bibles with us. We had sweet fellowship with him. He told us there were only three families of believers in Labrea who were longing and praying for a missionary to come and open up a work there. We have been greatly burdened about this little place ever since.

At the Boca do Acre we met another believer, Dona Nené Jacinto Ale. Miss Harvey had sent a telegram to her telling her we would be arriving. We had sweet fellowship with this dear woman. She asked us to consider coming back to start a work in Boca do Acre.

Going from the Boca do Acre to Sena Madureira was the worst part of the journey due to the river being so low. We had to change into a smaller boat on which we had very little comfort and very few conveniences. Yet, notwithstanding all this, we had perfect peace in our hearts. The Lord was very precious to us during these days and gave us many sweet promises from His own Word. We arrived in Sena Madureira looking fit and well. Praise His Name. Yes, the Lord takes care of His own.

We shall never forget Sunday, 19th June. As the launch drew near to Sena Madureira we could see dear Mollie in the distance and then hear her shouting "Hallelujah."

Yes, it was something for which to praise the Lord. We could hardly wait for the plank to be put in place for us to go ashore. We were off immediately and what a reunion we had. Words fail us at this moment to describe our meeting. Many of the believers came down to the riverside and gave us a great welcome.

Mollie then took us up to our new home, and what a lovely little home we have got. We only wish you all could see it. There was great excitement all day as the visitors were coming and going. We could not get a word in with Mollie, but as soon as the church service was over and everyone had left, we settled down for a real good "Irish chat." We talked until five o'clock the next morning. We are still talking. Our hearts are so full of gratitude to our Saviour for ever leading the three of us to this very needy land.

Mollie is doing a wonderful work here. The church is packed out every Sunday night with many souls seeking and finding the Saviour. It rejoiced our hearts to see such a lovely choir of young women, and my, they can sing. There is also the children's choir, and just to look at them is an inspiration. Yes, the Lord is surely blessing His dear child and she is loved by everyone here. Not only is the Lord using her for the healing of the body, but also in leading many to the Great Physician.

We really feel very unworthy to be Miss Harvey's coworkers. Already we have proved the Lord's blessing with us. On Sunday night, I gave the message in English and Mollie interpreted for me. At the close of the service, she had the joy of leading a young man to the Lord.

Mollie's account of James and Dorrie's arrival corresponded with Dorrie's report.

> It was a beautiful Sunday morning and as the church service was nearly finished, we heard this long and loud, blast of a horn announcing the arrival of a boat. We all hoped it was the long awaited vessel bringing James and Dorrie. Many believers joined me as we rushed to the riverside. As the launch came nearer, we could see James and Dorrie standing at the front waving to us. For them, this was the end of a long and wearisome four month journey. They told me afterwards that they heard me shout "Hallelujah" as they disembarked.
>
> They had endured forty-eight days travelling on that launch with no comfort whatsoever. During that time, they had to sit in their hammocks by day and then sleep in the hammocks at night. There were no cabins on the boat, so the hammocks were slung anywhere and everywhere as darkness fell. It is at this hour that swarms of mosquitoes appear in the thousands for their daily feast on a new source of rich Irish blood.
>
> In Sena Madureira, all the church members had waited after the service to greet the new missionaries, and what a welcome they got. After the initial greetings, we made our way to our small house.
>
> I had tried to make the house as nice as possible with a few curtains on the doors and some cushions on the wicker chairs I had bought in Manaus. The table was set for a greatly longed for cup of tea. The tea-set we used was one of Dorrie's own wedding presents she had given me just after the war, since I could not afford to buy one. After pulling off her white (or what had been white) shoes, dear Dorrie sat down and looked all around the small wooden house, now overcrowded with church members, and her first words were, "Why, this is just like home."

(Indeed, Brazil became their home for the next forty-two years.)

Because they had arrived on the Lord's Day, they were given the opportunity to give their testimonies by interpretation at the evening Gospel service to a more than packed church. Within a short while, they began to participate in many of the activities and meetings. Many of the new converts were ready for baptism, and after a few months studying the language, James had the joy of baptizing them in a creek not far from the church.

After unpacking their baggage one of the first jobs James worked at was to make a bed for Mollie and then a double bed for Dorrie and him. Soon they discovered that they had arrived just in time, for they found Mollie shivering from the effects of malaria. She needed immediate attention and someone to care for her. James and Dorrie cared for Mollie during this bad bout of illness. Mollie had also acquired the help of a local girl whose parents and sisters attended the church. Corina was a shy girl but a lovely Christian. She took an immediate liking to James and Dorrie who had no children of their own. Corina was to become as a daughter to them who not only lived in their home but also accompanied them on most of their trips.

Another letter from Sena Madureira gave news of James and Dorrie's development with the work:

On Tuesday we had our first visit to the Leper Colony. Quite a lot of the believers accompanied us on the four mile walk to the colony and then returned to town with us again. We were deeply moved as we saw these dear souls, disfigured with this awful disease. Many times we were touched when reading about them in the Bible and how the Lord Jesus cleansed them, but here we were actually seeing them with our own eyes. We had a lovely service and we believe many of these young men and women were concerned.

On Wednesday we had a baptismal service, for five recent converts. One was the daughter of the old woman that had travelled with Mollie from Manaus. She is a lovely soul. I had the joy of baptizing them. The Lord did help me with the language.

We are very happy with dear Mollie and we have settled down very well. At times we just cannot realize we are in Sena Madureira. We can of a truth raise our "Ebenezer" and say from our hearts, "Hitherto hath the Lord helped us." We would value your prayers as we continue to study the language. We are now having more liberty in speaking to the people.

James and Dorrie had good reason to speak of how well the people in Sena Madureira esteemed Mollie. Since her arrival in the town less than two years earlier, she had endeared herself to the people with her medical attention to the suffering and her midwifery skills in delivering many children. Besides this, many in town admired the courage of the "English lady" to cope with various hardships such as when the town was flooded during an exceptionally severe wet season when the river broke its banks. The muddy and foul river water streamed through the town flooding Mollie's house. Mollie only became aware of it when she stepped out of bed into dirty muddy water ankle deep. She worked with two deacons from the church and raised what furniture she had above the water level. By lunch time the water had risen above knee level inside the house.

The church next door was soon under four feet of water, and Mollie had to move out to a house on higher ground until the waters abated. Notwithstanding the floods which brought snakes and other unwelcome creatures indoors, Mollie organized the Sunday services in a house kindly loaned to her. The majority of the congregation arrived for the meetings by canoe.

God had an amazing purpose in allowing Mollie's programme of meetings to be disrupted during that week. João Marinho, a "rubber soldier" from Rio Grande do Norte in North Eastern Brazil who had settled in Sena Madureira, was an ardent Roman Catholic and was intensely opposed to the arrival of missionaries in the town. Before he left his home town of Malhada Vermelha, he had made several pilgrimages walking barefoot for eight hundred miles each time on a return trip to Joazeiro do Norte to venerate a deceased priest. He did his penance on his knees through the town until his knees and feet bled profusely. For a while he remained in the city of pilgrimage where he gained a job making figures of the various saints.

With the outbreak of war, he left this moneymaking business to be conscripted into the Brazilian army. While many Brazilian soldiers went off to fight in Italy, João was sent to the Acre with thousands of others. For João, this was three thousand miles from home.

After the war, João and Maria his wife settled in a small wooden house in the forest not far from the edge of town. Although he was only five feet tall, many believers were afraid of this fanatical Romanist. Several of them tried to speak to João about Christ but he refused to listen. João was flabbergasted when he discovered that his neighbours on both sides had become evangelicals. He was determined to give an answer to these Bible-carrying evangelicals who were growing in number at the expense of his own Mother Church.

To refute their error, he realized that he needed to be better versed in his own Catholic Bible. When João requested the Catholic Bible from Padre Agostino, the Italian priest in Sena Madureira, the priest sold it to him in instalments. The Bible cost the equivalent of a month's wages. Slowly João read through the New Testament, only to discover that one of the most recurring words in the Bible was the word "believe." Little by little, the reading of the Bible created a hunger in João's heart to read more of God's Word and to his amazement, he found that there was little in this Book that he could charge against those evangelicals.

At the peak of his search in the scriptures, João unwittingly marched past the house to where the meetings had been relocated because of the flood. At first when he heard the singing, he put his fingers into his ears to block out the sound. However, when he arrived home, he could still hear the distant singing wafting across the otherwise calm forest.

On the following Sunday morning, he approached the house during the Sunday School hour and stood at the door to see who was attending these meetings. As he lingered, he began to listen. Mollie was at the front of the assembled group with flannel graph illustrations and was explaining the story of Joseph, the son of Jacob. João reasoned to himself, *I don't believe that person is telling lies, because I have read this same story in my Catholic Bible.*

At the end of the Sunday school, some of the believers who knew João went to shake his hand and told him how glad they were to see him. He asked, "May I come back again tonight?"

The church members happily assured him that he was most welcome to return that evening and he did. Sander Tonnesson, the Norwegian missionary, had returned to the town and was the speaker at the evening service. Sander stood near the old paraffin lamp from which the black smoke ascended into the darkness. With the Bible in one hand and gesturing with the other, he gave a clear gospel presentation. At the end of the service, the mixed choir sang in Portuguese,

> *"Christ for me, Christ for me,*
> *From all the fear of what men do or say,*
> *Christ for me."*

Just as the meeting ended, Sander noticed the diminutive figure of João Marinho slinking out into the night air. Earnest prayer went up to God for João that night. Undoubtedly, that was the reason why João tossed and turned in his hammock that night and was unable to sleep. Finally he got up from his hammock and by the light of a old tin lamp, he pored over the pages of his Catholic Bible.

On the following night, João arrived at Sander's house and explained that he wanted to trust Jesus Christ as Saviour. Sander opened his Bible and showed João the simple way of salvation through faith in Jesus Christ alone. This man, who in previous years had walked barefooted over stony ground until his feet bled in an attempt to atone for his sins, now found peace with God through Jesus Christ and was rejoicing in the freedom from his sins.

From the day of his conversion, João Marinho had a great desire to tell his old companions and relatives about the good news of the gospel of Jesus Christ. Within a short time João became a very effective colporteur and evangelist, at times trekking through swamp and deep jungle where there were no paths while suffering bleeding feet, loneliness and hunger. For the next fifty years, he gladly endured many hardships for his new Master's sake.

With the benefit of hindsight, it is possible to trace how the Lord was providently shaping lives for future days and ministry. James and Dorrie, who arrived in Sena Madureira not long after João's conversion, found in him a firm colleague. The progress of language study corresponded with João's development in ministry.

Soon after James and Dorrie settled into Sena Madureira, the dry season was at its peak. They and Mollie made plans to trek to Itapira, a rubber plantation far off into the jungle where José Soares had his home. José was not a Christian at this time, but the neighbours knew the missionaries were coming and they sent word to their family and friends in the forest to gather at José's house for some meetings.

The unspoiled beauty of God's creation displayed in the forest caused them to marvel at the greatness and goodness of God. But it proved to be a long walk in the hot sun. The missionaries left Sena Madureira at 7 a.m. One of the church members knew the forest trail very well and he led the way while a few other believers accompanied the missionaries. They set a fast pace in order to reach the house before the darkness invaded the forest at 5.30 p.m.. At midday the energetic leader allowed a half an hour interval in an empty house, where James gathered sticks and lit a fire to boil water for a cup of tea.

Soon they were on their way again and the pace-setter purposely ignored telling the new missionaries of the bridges they would have to cross on the way to the plantation. These bridges were nothing more than long narrow logs which had been stripped and crudely thrown across a creek. There were no hand rails or even a rope to help the ladies balance as they edged their way across the narrow logs. At times the logs were very wet and, as if the effort to cross these improvised bridges were not bad enough, the men had to balance heavy loads on their backs while they cagily made their way over the slippery tree trunk.

In many places the creeks were so full of raging and cascading streams that the water sometimes splashed over the makeshift bridge. In other places the water level was so low that the missionaries dared not look down, in case a misplaced step could result in a disastrous fall.

When they arrived at José's forest clearing, James and Dorrie could not help but see that José's simple house was chiefly made from trees that he had felled and covered with palms to provide a secure roof. José's wife led the three missionaries away from the house to a hole into which a trickle of muddy water was slowly running. A few pigs wallowed in the surrounding mud at this first hole so the lady directed the missionaries to another site which had even less water. Mollie and Dorrie turned a blind eye to the nearby pigs and discreetly washed their hands and faces before returning to José's house.

Some time after dark José and other people began to arrive at the forest house from all parts of the jungle. Several families lived nearby while other friends walked for hours, some with babies in their arms. Each person brought a hammock and a change of clothing for an overnight stay and an enamel plate and mug. José killed a pig, a few chickens and some other animals he had hunted in the forest. Everyone tucked into the various barbecued meats that they ate with rice and roasted manioc

After everyone finished eating, it was very late. The cacophony of nocturnal life echoed from the forest as the people gathered for the meeting in a dimly lit hut. Soon the forest noises were drowned out by the singing of the choruses which Mollie taught. After the singing finished, the voices of the missionaries echoed in the night air as they taught the Bible verses and spoke of God's simple way of salvation through Jesus Christ. Most of those who gathered had never seen a Bible or heard the gospel before. Mollie read the story of the Prodigal Son and from this well-known parable she preached the gospel.

It was well into the wee hours of the morning by the time the meeting finished, but in spite of the late hour, José, his wife, his brother and another man accepted the Lord Jesus as their Saviour.

After the meeting finished, the simple jungle house took the strain of many hammocks as more than forty people settled down to sleep in José's humble house that night. Some did not sleep but preferred to chat all night. Their mumbled prattle mingled with the coughing and crying from little babies which pervaded the small dwelling.

Early the next morning, Dorrie helped Mollie attend to the huge crowd of sick and suffering people who had waited to speak to the "English nurse." While Mollie attended to her patients, nearly everyone else crowded into José's house for breakfast before leaving for their trek back through the forest to their isolated dwellings.

This was the first of many meetings conducted in Itapira in which many people trusted the Lord as their Saviour. This work in the forest grew so much that soon José and his friends built a simple little church near his house where both missionaries and José conducted regular meetings for the forest people.

James and Dorrie not only progressed with Portuguese, but Dorrie learned a lot of midwifery skills from Mollie as they attended numerous maternity confinements all over town and sometimes in the jungle. Mollie invested time in teaching Dorrie about ante-natal and postnatal care of their patients so that within a short time, Dorrie became very proficient in delivering children in Sena Madureira.

About a year after James and Dorrie arrived in Sena Madureira, Sander returned from furlough in Norway. He soon got to know the new couple from Ireland who had joined Mollie. Sander and James worked very well together as they planned a strategy for work. Initially, James took responsibility for the work in Sena Madureira while Sander concentrated a lot of his time travelling on the rivers. During Sander's absence in Norway, João Marinho had greatly developed as a personal worker. He became a close colleague of the Norwegian missionary and travelled with him on various pioneer journeys. Together they navigated many tributaries in the region around Sena Madureira and often their trips would last for months as they travelled right up to the borders of Peru.

While the Gunnings and Mollie made great efforts for the work in Sena Madureira, there was an increasing prayer involvement for their work among friends back in Northern Ireland. The volume of prayer ascending to God and the deepening interest in the work of Acre Gospel Mission sent out its own challenge to young people who were anxious to serve the Lord. A note in the Mission Circular

in 1950 gave news of a young man who was soon to increase the
ranks of the Mission in Brazil.

> We would covet your earnest prayers that we may be
> guided regarding the future policy of the Mission. Another
> application from a young man, who has completed three
> years' study at the All Nations' Bible College, London,
> and is about to commence a year's study of medicine, has
> just been received. Others in training have their eyes on
> the Acre. The question that faces us now, as a Mission, is
> "Shall we go forward?" We would like each interested
> prayer-helper to seek the Lord's answer to this question
> and pray that we may be willing to accept it, cost what it
> may.

There was no turning back for this work. Jack Finlay, from
Dundonald near Belfast, had heard Mollie Harvey speak during her
furlough and was deeply touched by the challenge she presented of
the needs in the Amazon. Not long after Mollie returned to Brazil,
Jack proceeded to the Bible College and afterwards applied to the
Acre Gospel Mission.

Jack was a dedicated young man with a will to work. He was
accepted by the Mission Committee and his presence in Brazil not
only increased the numbers, but his wit and good humour was greatly
enjoyed by the Ulster missionaries.

As Jack got down to language study in Sena Madureira, Mollie
began to prepare for her return to Northern Ireland for another
furlough. She left Sena Madureira with a touch of sadness as she
would miss her friends and close colleagues, but she also looked
forward to seeing her family and friends back in Belfast.

Chapter Eight

GREAT DOORS SWING ON SMALL HINGES

Among missionaries, it is generally recognized that great doors swing on small hinges. It should be equally acknowledged that those small hinges are almost always associated with prayer. The prayers of friends, missionaries and nationals lubricated the hinges that gently eased new doors open for the Acre missionaries, who had been enjoying God's blessing in the work in Sena Madureira.

On Sunday mornings, many people packed into the small church in Sena Madureira as increasing numbers professed faith in Jesus Christ. This growth was not confined to the church in Sena Madureira. Many rubber cutters and their families from the outlying areas of the forest were also converted. Unable to trek to the church in town every week, some forest dwellers established small congregations where they lived. On most weekends some of the missionaries travelled on foot to these remote congregations, which met in rustic palm leaf covered huts in the forest. These congregations also grew rapidly.

For Jack Finlay, there was plenty of work to get his teeth into and improve his language skills. James gave Jack plenty of opportunities as they visited people throughout the region. In Mollie's absence,

Dorrie became quite deft in her maternity and midwifery skills thanks to her involvement with Mollie. This continued to create wider opportunities for the gospel. Corina's help in the house was greatly appreciated while Dorrie attended to her duties with expectant mothers in the town. The Brazilian girl also learned a lot of new recipes from James and Dorrie who had formed a real close bond with this lovely girl.

With Sander back in town and João Marinho's increasing progress as an evangelist, the Acre missionaries felt that they should be thinking of expanding the work into other needy regions.

Mollie returned to Northern Ireland in December 1951, eager to report of the great things God had done in the four years since she left Belfast as the only missionary of Acre Gospel Mission. She also carried a burden and an appeal for the people to pray about the future of the work. However, on the way home Mollie fell victim to another bout of malaria and had to be hospitalized as soon as she arrived in Belfast. It was only after a long recuperation that she was able to resume her deputation programme and make the appeals for prayer and workers in Brazil. Mollie also met with some changes at the home end of the Mission.

Pastor Olley, the founding chairman of the Acre Gospel Mission, had accepted a call to pastor a church in Canada and Mr. Rennie Thompson had stepped into his place. On the 6th September 1951, Mr. McComb was inducted as the pastor of Castlereagh Evangelical Church and for the next nine years, he combined the dual responsibility of the pastorate and Mission secretary.

Changes were soon to develop in Brazil also. Since their forty-five day journey to Sena Madureira several years earlier, James and Dorrie could not forget what they saw in Boca do Acre and the lady who pleaded with them to return. In conversation with Mollie, she recalled her visits to Boca do Acre with the McCombs many years earlier and her own encounter with Dona Nené Jacinto Ale. Although engrossed in what God was doing in Sena Madureira, they had not forgotten to pray that God would soon send a missionary to that needy town.

Unknown to the missionary team in Sena Madureira, people in Boca do Acre were also praying that God would send a messenger of the gospel to their area. Many years prior to the Acre missionaries making their short visits to Boca do Acre, a lone colporteur had arrived in the town by canoe carrying a supply of Bibles, New Testaments and gospel booklets. Although his visit to the Boca do Acre was received with a lot of apprehension and fear, he was able to distribute his literature and sell some Bibles. Even as he left the town, the forest dwellers hailed his canoe to call in to where they were and bought copies of the precious Word of God.

As soon as the colporteur pointed his canoe down river and returned to Manaus, the town's resident Italian priest, who had been greatly angered by the visit of the evangelist, announced to his flock that all the "Protestant literature" was of the devil and must be brought to the church. When the priest recovered as much of the literature as he could, he torched the Bibles and booklets in a public bonfire at the town square in front of his church.

However, not all the Bibles were turned into ashes in the priest's bonfire. Some of them found their way into homes scattered throughout the region, and they ignited a different flame which would burn in the hearts of people for years to come. Several of these Bibles had a great influence on the opening of a door for the Acre missionaries.

Sr. Pedro and his family lived deep in the forest and several days' journey from Boca do Acre. Like most of the people who lived in these isolated places, Pedro made his meagre living from extracting latex from the "syringa" trees and gathering Brazil nuts in their season. To provide for his family, he supplemented his scant income by hunting in the jungle and fishing in the lakes and rivers.

One day while he was hunting, he came upon a deserted and derelict hut in the thick of the forest. A keen eye for anything the former residents might have left behind, Pedro searched through the dust and debris of the abandoned house. The only thing he found was an old Bible. Not only was it covered in dust, but the busy termites had feasted on the torn cover and had burrowed their way through some of its pages. Pedro picked up the old Bible which had probably been introduced to the region by the unknown colporteur or even when Willie McComb had visited the region in 1938.

Pedro blew the dust off the cover and slowly began to read the words, "Biblia Sagrada." He did not read very well but knew that this was a holy book. He placed it into his latex covered bag which held his hunting rations and continued his pursuit of wild animals to provide food for his family.

When the hunt had finished, Pedro returned to his simple and rustic dwelling which had no walls, but was little more than a bamboo floor and a palm leaf roof. At the hour of the evening novena, Pedro gathered his wife and children around to read to them from the holy book. Slowly and hesitantly, he began to read the gospel to them for the first time. These stammering readings continued every evening at the same hour and after reading, Pedro prayed for his family. They had never met a Christian nor seen a missionary but the Bible made a profound impact on their lives. One evening Pedro told his wife, "I don't know what we have to do but I believe Jesus Christ died to forgive and save us. Let us ask God for His forgiveness."

Pedro experienced a new peace in his heart. Often in a free hour he read the Bible alone and wondered who could explain more of this holy book to them. Their children needed better opportunities in life, so they moved to live on the outskirts of Boca do Acre at the Praia do Gado. Pedro and his wife began to pray that God would send them someone who could explain more about God and His Word.

Pedro's prayers were an important hinge on which a door would swing to open the way for James and Dorrie to go to Boca do Acre. Like Pedro, Dona Nené Jacinto was also praying that God would send someone to start an evangelical work in her town. She remembered meeting the McCombs many years earlier with Mollie and then the Gunnings on their way to Sena Madureira, but she felt frustrated that these missionaries were always in transit to somewhere else.

Although she was a believer, for many years she did not possess a Bible. However, Dona Nené had one page from a hymn book which she greatly treasured. When any friends in town died, she went to the house and read to the family from that page. For years she longed and prayed for the day when God would send a missionary to Boca do Acre. Gradually, another hinge was beginning to help swing open a door for the Acre Gospel Mission to enter Boca do Acre.

Meanwhile, James shared with Jack Finlay and Sander that he sensed God was speaking to him that it was time for them to branch out to another needy area. However, this decision was not taken easily. They waited for God's time and His direction.

Periodically, river traders and government officials from Boca do Acre passed through Sena Madureira and occasionally some of them would drift into the meetings at the church, which was one of the biggest public gatherings in the town. One of these government officials was Sr. Emetério. He showed great interest in the gospel and told James that Dona Socorro, his wife back in Boca do Acre, was a believer. James encouraged Emetério to come to the Saviour and assured him of their prayers that soon he also would become a Christian.

As the missionaries prayed about their future and where they should go next, James was constrained to write to Emetério and inquire of the possibility of accommodation in Boca do Acre. He sent the letter with some people who were making the three day trip down to Boca do Acre. Several weeks later James received a reply from his friend telling him that not only had Emetério received the Saviour, but for the missionaries to come as soon as possible. Emetério assured them that he had a place for them to stay. James was convinced that the Lord was leading the Mission into Boca do Acre.

Within a few weeks, the Gunnings and Jack Finlay packed up all their belongings and at the beginning of May 1952, made the journey down river to Boca do Acre. Besides being aware that people at home were praying for them in this venture, they were also assured of the prayerful support of the believers in Sena Madureira. Corina had become like a daughter to James and Dorrie and with the encouragement of her parents, accompanied the missionaries on this new venture.

Boca do Acre is located on the southern bank at the confluence of the rivers Purus and Acre. The low lying land is surrounded by swamps which contribute to the town's frequent floods in the rainy season. Because of the frequent inundations of the overflowing river, most dwellings were elevated four or five feet above the ground on wooden stilts. Boca do Acre was an important trading post where, during the rainy season when the rivers were full, large vessels from the coast navigated the winding rivers for more than a month to reach Boca do Acre. They traded rubber latex and Brazil nuts at this distant town. These large vessels met up with smaller river craft which came down river from the distant borders of Bolivia on the River Acre or the frontier of Peru on the River Purus.

The river trade which converged on Boca do Acre brought men from all walks of life to this small Amazonian town. With the merchants and crews came all the vices associated with loose living. As a result, Boca do Acre became a byword for gambling, drunkenness, violence and immorality.

When the missionary trio arrived in town, Emetério and Socorro were delighted to welcome them as God's servants. Even before they arrived, there had been some opposition to their plans to live in the Boca do Acre. Emetério and Socorro had arranged a place where the missionaries could stay and conduct their meetings but these plans were thwarted. However, a lady who heard of the difficulties volunteered to partition her house and provide one half of the large wooden structure as accommodation for the new arrivals

Soon bags and boxes were unpacked, beds were put in place and the missionaries were installed in their new makeshift residence. This was the first foothold in Boca do Acre.

Dona Socorro was a teacher at the local primary school and she said that she had arranged for them to conduct their first evangelical meetings in one of the classrooms. However, that very week the priest had heard about the venture and put pressure on the school authorities to deny the missionaries the use of school premises. Dona Socorro had prayed too hard for missionaries to come to Boca do Acre to let them be disappointed by such a setback, so she determined to turn her wooden home into a meeting place.

At first, on the day of the meeting, the couple moved all of their furniture out of the house and made room for the invited guests. Besides Socorro, Emetério and the missionaries, six people turned up at the first meeting on Sunday. Dona Nené Jacinto was one of those present and she was so pleased that at last someone cared enough to come to Boca do Acre.

On the next Sunday, the congregation had more than doubled so Dona Socorro moved her bed and belongings out on to the street to make room for the people. Night after night, James explained the gospel in a simple way to the assembled group while Dorrie taught some choruses. Jack gave his testimony of how he came to faith in Jesus Christ and then they mixed freely with the people after the meeting.

Many showed interest in the meetings. Dona Nené was overjoyed at the response in the town. It was like a dream for her, especially when José Rodriques became the first person to accept the Saviour after the missionaries arrived. Several of Dona Nené's children also trusted Jesus Christ as Saviour.

Soon Sr. Pedro, the hunter who had found the Bible in the forest, heard about the evangelical missionaries in town and the meetings at Emetério's house. He walked with his family from the Praia do Gado one Sunday and after the morning meeting, he related to James the amazing account of his conversion to Jesus Christ through finding a copy of the scriptures in the forest.

Little by little, a nucleus of converts came together and the missionaries became quite well known in the town. Sr. Eduardo Rocha took a particular interest in the newly arrived missionaries and felt that they needed better living accommodation than sharing a house with another family. He therefore arranged for them to rent a large wooden house from Dona Cecília Leite. Although the missionaries moved to a larger residence, it also became evident that Sr. Emetério's house was becoming too small to accommodate the growing congregation. Besides, they felt that it was not fair to Emetério's family for the congregation to continue to use their home. James and Jack were aware that before long they would have to build a proper church building.

Besides the meetings in town, James and Jack travelled up the River Acre and then into some of the tributaries which branch off the main river. New convert José Rodriques showed a lot of zeal and accompanied the missionaries on their trip. For six weeks they paddled the canoe by day and preached the gospel to the river dwellers in the evenings. Most of the people were hearing the gospel for the first time and many of those responded to its message.

Once back in Boca do Acre, James and Jack decided they needed to get started to provide a structure to house the growing congregation. During James and Jack's absence, Dorrie continued to conduct the meetings in the town as others had received Jesus Christ as Saviour. The missionaries were able to acquire a strategic site facing Emetério's house, right in the commercial centre of the town and near to where most of the river traffic docked.

The living allowance from the Mission was pitifully small and did not allow for any extra expense and certainly not to build a church. Their tithes and offerings had been used up in the purchase of the site and what little money remained would not be put to the best use by employing workers or purchasing the raw material. This dilemma helped James and Jack decide to go into the forest and cut down the trees to provide the wood.

James and Jack took José Rodrigues with them and headed down river in a large dugout canoe. They then walked through the forest selecting the best trees from which to saw long planks for the church's walls and floor.

After finding a particular tree and chopping it down, they tied thick ropes around their waists, attached the ropes to the tree trunk and then pulled it to a previously erected platform on which they suspended the log. A hole was dug under the platform and the log put in place. James stood below the log and Jack above it. Then they began to move the large double-handed woodcutter's saw up and down, always following the straight carbon line they had drawn with the aid of a tight string soaked in ash. The rhythm of the up and down movement of the saw went on for hours each day. Although it was not only exhausting work and very dangerous, the Lord protected His servants.

After several boards were sawed, José trailed them to the river's edge and then down the steep bank to be loaded into the canoe. After the canoe was filled, the three men paddled back up stream against the current to Boca do Acre where Dorrie had a good meal ready for them. The boards were placed in an upright position to dry. The drying process generally took a few months, after which the planks had to be trimmed and planed by hand.

For months James and Jack worked at the wood every day. Meanwhile, the meetings continued to be well attended in Emetério's house. Dorrie was fully engaged in children's meetings and also in afternoon gatherings for ladies. Emetério and Socorro gladly rearranged all their furniture to make room for the Sunday services. Nearly every week people from the forest came to the meetings and many trusted the Saviour.

As she had done in Sena Madureira Dorrie was again able to put to good use the midwifery skills she learned from Mollie. It was demanding work since she was called at all times of the day and night. Her ante natal care, the attention she gave in delivering the baby, and subsequent visits to the mother and child unlocked many doors for the gospel and forged lasting friendships with local families.

Little by little, the church was being erected. When the main structure was finally completed James and Jack worked at making a very fine pulpit, communion table and enough pews to fill the church. It was a great day when the church and the furnishings were all finished. It was the talk of the town. People were amazed that the two foreigners had been able to erect the building right from the raw materials from the forest.

Mollie arrived in Brazil just before Christmas 1953 and made her way back to Boca do Acre instead of Sena Madureira. With Mollie, two new missionaries from Calvary Baptist Church in Liverpool arrived. Jack and Joan Mawdsley had been challenged about the work after hearing Willie McComb speak at special meetings in Liverpool organized by Nurse Causer from Whiston. Not only were Jack and Joan accepted by the Mission but Nurse Causer became the English representative of the Mission, which was creating increasing prayer interest and support beyond Northern Ireland.

Mollie was astounded at the developments in the work since she left almost two years earlier. The town that she had previously called "the Devil's den," was now home for the Acre Gospel Mission workers. The meetings in Emetério's house were packed with new converts and the new church building was nearing completion.

When heaven rejoices, hell rages. Significantly, near the date of the new church's inauguration, all of the missionaries of Acre Gospel Mission were almost wiped out in a tragic accident. The large house which had become home to the missionaries at Boca do Acre had three front windows that offered a good view of the activities on the River Acre. During the rainy season when the river was in flood, the large boats going up river to Rio Branco passed within yards of the front of the Mission house.

Early one morning, two large boats arrived from down stream and docked on the other side of the River Acre. Always looking for fresh provisions and the possibility of buying a few biscuits or onions which were luxury items in the interior, the ladies persuaded James to take them across the river to the boats.

While Corina remained at home, James and Dorrie, Mollie, Jack Finlay and the new missionaries, Jack and Joan Mawdsley, all embarked into the large canoe which was kept tied up outside the front door of the Mission house during the flood. At James' insistence, they took an ample supply of gospel tracts in Portuguese to give to the crew on the boats.

James started up the outboard motor as he moved the canoe out from the river bank and into the middle of the river. Even though he was just going across the river, he had to head upstream to compensate for the strong current which would sweep them down river. Even as he did so, he could feel that the strong flow was so forceful it was pushing against the canoe. James increased the throttle accordingly, but even this was not enough to resist the force of the strong current which threatened to sweep them down river past the large boats. James carefully tried to balance the play of throttle on the outboard motor against the force of current as he eased the canoe closer to the stationary boats. The other missionaries were absorbed watching James' manoeuvre from where they sat together under the shade of the canoe's aluminum canopy.

Another large canoe was tied securely to the side of the *Victoria*, one of the boats the missionaries planned to visit. This large canoe blocked the approach of the missionaries' craft and the fierce current drove the two canoes dangerously close to each other in the swirling waters. James fought to swing the front of his canoe back toward the middle of the river to avoid a collision. His efforts were in vain. There was an ugly thud as the two canoes collided. The two river craft were locked against each other and the strong current threatened to push the heavily loaded missionary canoe under the other canoe and down into turbulent flow.

Suddenly, the muddy brown river water began to rush into the missionary canoe. Their craft was quickly being forced under the stationary craft by the unrelenting flow. There was panic and confusion. The missionaries scrambled from under the canoe's canopy. The Mawdsleys and Jack Finlay were in the middle of the boat when they were picked out of the canoe by the *Victoria's* crew members, who had been looking on in helpless horror.

James straddled between the larger boat and the canoe trying to help Dorrie escaped the doomed craft. Several men tried to grab Dorrie as she cried for help but then suddenly let her go and she almost went under. Just before the canoe plunged under the angry torrent, several other men on the *Victoria* grabbed Dorrie's outstretched arms and dragged her out of the angry river. After they hauled her on board she collapsed immediately. Her legs and body were badly bruised.

All the missionaries were soaked and in a state of shock. They looked around in stunned disbelief. All had been accounted for but Mollie. "Where is Mollie?" Jack shouted in Portuguese.

"Did she get out of the canoe?" another bellowed.

"She's gone down with the canoe," came the answer from people in a boat close by. The frenzied atmosphere of the moment was compounded by deep sobbing. There were shouts in English and Portuguese, as well as screams of panic and grief from missionaries and Brazilians. People, alerted by the screams, quickly gathered on the river bank to watch what was happening. They knew this was a dangerous stretch of water and that quite a few local people, including a Roman Catholic priest, had lost their lives in the waters at the nearby confluence of the Rivers Acre and Purus.

Several moments seemed like an eternity as everybody scanned the river for any sign of the missing missionary. Dorrie knew that Mollie could not swim, therefore, it seemed impossible that she could ever survive this tragedy. James was already frantically turning over in his mind how he was going to break the news of Mollie's death to her family back home.

A long time went by as the worst fears began to sink in. Suddenly, there was a loud shout from bystanders pointing their fingers, "There she is. There she is." Just then the prow of the canoe emerged out of the water more than a hundred yards downstream. As the forward part of the boat slowly emerged out of the muddy water, it exposed Mollie doggedly clutching the wheel with her two hands, her handbag was still secured by its straps to her arm.

James and another friend dashed in a canoe to where Mollie was hanging on for her life. She was paralyzed with fear and could not move. Furthermore, it was too dangerous to try to remove Mollie from the canoe which had only its prow partially protruding above the water. The two men moved in carefully and courageously as they put a rope around the prow of the canoe. Slowly they towed the illfated craft to the water's edge on the town side of the river. Once in the shallow water, Mollie was helped from the stricken canoe and rushed to the Mission house.

Miraculously, Mollie had been rescued from certain death. There were shouts of "Hallelujah" and "Praise the Lord." Mollie's colleagues welcomed her back from what had seemed like a watery grave. They were all soaked and still in a state of shock, but at the same time, exhilarated to have survived the ordeal. Later Mollie, who fell victim to pneumonia as a result of her frightening episode, wrote of what happened when she went down on the canoe.

> I had been sitting at the front of the craft and at the moment of impact, I was thrown forward. I faintly remember catching hold of the wheel, my handbag still on my arm. As the cold, strong fingers of the current gripped me, I prayed to God for deliverance. Witnesses said that our boat disappeared below the two other boats. The people said they were sure I was lost. My missionary colleagues were stunned. Although they had been delivered from a watery grave, they were distressed for they thought that I had drowned in the submerged canoe.

Down river, at the confluence of the Rivers Purus and Acre, is a dangerous spot where, because of the raging currents, many lives have been lost. Everybody was sure that I was another victim of this treacherous river. After what seemed an eternity, in the mercy of the Lord, the prow of our canoe came into view above the water on the far side of the two boats.

Although dazed and feeling I had been to the grave and back, I was still holding on to the wheel with my handbag still on my arm. At the same time, an old man travelling in his canoe spotted me. He hurried over near to our emerging canoe, shouting at me to come to him, but I did not know how I was able to go to him. It was then that James and a friend drew near and were able to secure a rope on to the canoe and slowly tow it to the side of the river. I felt as though a miracle had taken place and immediately thanked God for His deliverance.

As I came ashore, I must have been a terrible sight. I had lost my shoes, my long hair was hanging around my face, I was shivering with shock, but my handbag was still safely tucked under my arm. I was told that if I had let go of the wheel, I would have certainly drowned. However, I was sure that it was not my holding onto the wheel that had saved me, but rather it was our wonderful Lord holding onto me.

Crowds from the town had gathered on the river bank to see the outcome of the frightening experience. Many said they had been praying for us in those awful moments. God hears the prayers of His children. Since we had not been in Boca do Acre very long, we felt that this accident was an evil attack on the new work in the "Devil's Den."

The official opening of the new church on a Saturday afternoon early in 1954 was a great milestone. The building was packed full for the occasion. Several officials of the town's administration attended the service. Everyone spoke highly of the new building, modest by the standards of the outside world but quite impressive in

an interior jungle town. The missionaries were more impressed to
see so many new converts at the meeting. This was the fruit of
eighteen months of hard work, for they represented the building of
the spiritual and mystical church of Jesus Christ.

The arrival of Mollie with the new missionaries also coincided
with an announcement from Jack Finlay. He was hoping to go to
Manaus to make plans to marry Betty Berry, an American missionary
with Baptist Mid Missions. When Jack first arrived in Manaus in
1950, he spent several weeks with Mollie's friends, Willard and Grace
Stull, while his baggage was being released from customs and a
suitable boat was found to take him to Sena Madureira. It was during
this delay that he met Betty who was also a new missionary with
Willard's Mission. Friendship blossomed into romance, which was
subsequently carried on by correspondence and rapidly developed
to the point of Jack proposing marriage. The wedding was to take
place in the United States.

James and Dorrie were due for furlough after five years in the
interior forests. With Mollie's return, plus the arrival of the new
missionary couple, it was an opportune time to go to Northern Ireland.
Furthermore, Jack's decision to marry Betty Berry resulted in him
reluctantly resigning from the Acre Gospel Mission to seek
admittance into Baptist Mid Missions. His colleagues, although they
were sorry to see Jack sever his links with the Acre Gospel Mission,
also knew that Jack and Betty would still continue to work with the
Irish missionaries and that their home would always be open to their
colleagues. This arrangement was to prove a great blessing in years
to come.

A large crowd of friends lined the side of the river as Jack Finlay
and the Gunnings embarked on a Catalina flying boat that would
take them to Manaus. This was the first airplane flight for all three
and they were the only passengers. As they soared into the air above
the jungle, they felt this was the end of a great chapter of missionary
service. Their hearts were filled with thanksgiving to God for the
privilege of seeing the door open for them to go to Boca do Acre.
Their joy was tinged with a measure of sadness as they were leaving
so many believers and friends at the Boca do Acre.

James and Dorrie were especially sorry to be leaving Corina, who returned to her parents in Sena Madureira to await her adopted missionary parents' return a year later.

The flight to Manaus took six hours, a journey which would have taken almost four weeks on a river steamer.

Chapter Nine

LET ME BURN OUT

Willard and Grace Stull were glad to welcome James and Dorrie to Manaus and especially glad to see Jack Finlay. During their five years in the interior, Dorrie maintained a regular correspondence with the American couple and felt at home in their company. It was only on arrival in Manaus that they learned that the Booth liner, the *Hilary*, would not reach Manaus for another month. James, never one for sitting around, volunteered to use his time to help Willard put a new floor in their home at Rua Urucurá, which was near to one of the churches Willard had founded.

James and Dorrie waited eagerly each day for the arrival of the ship from Liverpool. Not only were they going home on the liner, but a new missionary couple from Belfast was due to arrive. Fred and Ina Orr were the latest recruits of the Acre Gospel Mission and were arriving to enter into the work God had called them to. James and Dorrie had never met Fred and Ina before, but Mollie had told them much about this couple from Belfast who had applied to the Mission.

Fred and Ina Orr came from the Castlereagh district of Belfast and were members of Castlereagh Evangelical Church where Mr.

McComb was the pastor. Both had been converted as children and as teenagers they lived a stone's throw from each other. Although Fred's chief pursuit as a youth was football, which he was very successful at, it was only when he started to date Ina McMurray that he became more involved in the Castlereagh church.

They were married in the Castlereagh Evangelical Church and went to live at Knocknadonagh outside Lisburn. In spite of moving out of Belfast, they still remained totally absorbed in the work of their home church. Ina taught Sunday school and Fred led a large Bible class and the Young People's Fellowship.

Fred was first challenged about missionary work as a result of a special missionary offering collected by the young people to be donated to the Worldwide Evangelization Crusade (WEC). Until then, although successful in business with his father, he showed great promise of possibly entering into pastoral work in Northern Ireland. At that time, missionary Emma Munn was home from Guinea and was invited by the Castlereagh young people to speak of her work. At the end of the meeting, Fred handed over the designated gift on behalf of the young people's fellowship with a sense of honour almost bordering on pride. Miss Munn, although grateful for the gift, bluntly asked Fred, "Why aren't you thinking of going to the mission field?"

Fred was stunned. First, he was taken aback by Miss Munn's bluntness. However, the question rocked Fred and that was the beginning of a process that eventually resulted in Fred and Ina going to the Worldwide Evangelization Crusade Missionary Training College in Glasgow in 1950. Initially Fred and Ina, challenged by Len Moules' book, "Three Miles High," felt that the Lord was leading them to India. They were willing to go to India, but through a series of circumstances and largely through the influence of Mollie Harvey, who was on furlough in 1952, the Lord definitely called them to Brazil.

Both Fred and Ina were exceptionally gifted people. Ina's musical talents greatly complemented Fred's preaching ability and they both engaged in evangelistic activities before embarking for Brazil. They also were gifted in children's work and while they were still at the Bible College in Glasgow, a representative of Child Evangelism Fellowship (CEF) approached the couple about possibly working with their agency. Fred declined the offer but introduced the representative to Sam Doherty, a school teacher in Lurgan who a few years earlier had trusted the Saviour during a visit to Fred and Ina's home near Lisburn. Sam and Sadie Doherty received the man into their home and as a result, they accepted the challenge of pioneering the work of CEF in Ireland and then beyond to many other parts of Europe.

On Sunday, 14th March, 1954, there was a special farewell service for Fred and Ina at Castlereagh Evangelical Church. Willie McComb was the pastor and led the service. Fred gave a moving and challenging testimony of how God had unmistakably called them to Brazil. It was a memorable night and those present never forgot how Ina sang with great feeling what were almost prophetical words:

> O Lord this world is lost in sin,
> And few there are who care,
> Many of whom profess your name,
> No burden will help to bear.
> We need a passion Lord for souls
> To bring the lost back to Thee,
> Our hearts must be stirred
> Until all have heard,
> At least once of Calvary
>
> Let me burn out for Thee, dear Lord,
> Burn and wear out for Thee.
> Don't let me rust, or my life be,
> A failure, my God, to Thee.
> Take me and all I have, dear Lord,
> And get me so close to Thee,
> 'Til I feel the throb
> Of the great heart of God,
> And my life burns out for Thee.

Crowds were at the Belfast harbour on the following night to say farewell to a young couple who had so much to entice them to stay at home. However, God had called them and they painfully said good-bye to friends and family before sailing down Belfast Lough to the echo of hymn singing from the large company of well-wishers.

After visits to the exotic ports of Portugal, Madeira, Barbados and Trinidad, the *SS Hilary* finally entered the mouth of Brazil's mighty Amazon River. Fred and Ina's hearts were filled with joy for they felt that after five years of marriage and training, this was the land to which the Lord had brought them.

When they arrived in Manaus six weeks after leaving Britain, they received a warm welcome from James and Dorrie and their American missionary friends. The new couple from Belfast were also welcomed to the Stulls' house, which was always open to the Acre missionaries. James and Dorrie had ten days to acquaint themselves with Fred and Ina before they left on the same ship that had brought the new missionaries from Britain.

After the Gunnings left, Willard and Grace Stull took Fred and Ina on a tour of the various churches in Manaus. During the day, he attended to releasing their baggage from customs and trying to secure a place for Fred and Ina on the Catalina flight to Boca do Acre. At each meeting, Willard gave Fred an opportunity to speak while he interpreted for the congregation. He also tried coaxing Ina to sing, but she was reluctant to do so since she felt there was little point in singing English when no one could understand her.

Fred and Ina did not want to be delayed in Manaus unnecessarily, for they knew that Mollie was preparing for their arrival in Boca do Acre. Because no places were available on the plane, Willard arranged for the new missionary couple to travel by river on a wood-burning paddle steamer that had a flat bottom and large rotating wheel at the stern. It would take several weeks to reach Labrea and then Fred and Ina would have to transfer to a smaller boat that would take another ten days to reach Boca do Acre where Mollie and the Mawdsleys awaited them.

On the night before they left Manaus, Ina finally conceded to sing at a meeting. She took the time to learn the Portuguese words of the hymn,

The Name of Jesus sweet,
I love its music to repeat

It makes my joy full and complete,
The precious Name of Jesus.

"Jesus," O how sweet the Name
"Jesus," every day the same;
"Jesus," let all saints proclaim
Its worthy praise for ever.

Ina's voice penetrated into the night air like the voice of an angel and arrested the attention of many passersby who stopped to listen. They came to the door of the church to gain a better view of this unknown singer. Even a passing bus transporting people to town, stopped outside the church and let the passengers listen to the young missionary singing. They were not aware that this would be the last time Ina would ever sing for the Saviour on earth. Appropriately, she expressed her purpose of being in Brazil as she sang the last stanza of the hymn,

No word of man can ever tell
How sweet the Name I love so well
Oh, let its praises ever swell
Oh, praise the Name of Jesus.

Fred and Ina had never seen anything like it. Even as Ina sang and before Fred spoke, people came to the front of the church to accept the Lord Jesus as Saviour. During those days in Manaus the couple had not only won souls for Jesus Christ but also gained many friends in Manaus. They were really taken aback the next evening when they arrived at the boat that was to transport them up river. Many of the believers came to the floating harbour where the boat was moored to say farewell to the missionary couple. The believers sang to them and presented Fred and Ina a heart-shaped cake that was beautifully decorated as an expression of their love for the young couple they had gotten to know so quickly.

Fred and Ina were glad to leave Manaus even though they had thoroughly enjoyed the time spent with Willard and Grace. They felt that their place was farther into the interior where many had not yet heard the gospel of the Lord Jesus.

The boat was small but the captain had given Fred and Ina a cabin on the steamer's upper deck. He also insisted that they eat their meals with him. Although they could not understand what he was saying, they appreciated his kindness and sat with the captain at each meal. They smiled at his complimentary comments although they understood very little of what he said.

The meals consisted mostly of meat, rice, beans and manioc followed by a dessert of bananas and thick jam made from guavas. Fred and Ina ate most of what was set before them without too much inquiry about what they were eating. However, Fred did avoid drinking river water for fear of falling victim to typhoid or dysentery which was so prevalent in the area. He brought plenty of bottles of soft drinks to drink and Ina even cleaned her teeth with bottled lemonade.

Every six hours the steamer stopped at a clearing in the jungle to replenish its supply of firewood that the river dwellers chopped down from the forest. These people made a modest living selling firewood to the passing steam boats for a pittance. Fred and Ina enjoyed meeting the simple people and their children in their basic bamboo houses, which were clustered together in occasional clearings atop the steep clay river banks.

After six days of travel, Fred and Ina were sitting at the table having another meal with the steamer's kind captain. It was Saturday about 6.00 p.m. They completed their meal and returned to their tiny cabin. Once inside, Ina expressed her concern to Fred that she had eaten a piece of rotten meat at the table rather than offend the captain. Fred was annoyed that Ina had eaten the foul meat rather than decline, but he also knew how sensitive she was to the feelings of others.

Little more was said about the incident and they slept through the night in their tiny cabin. During the night, the steamer continued to make its slow progress upstream. The next morning they had their customary breakfast with the captain. Around noon on Sunday, even though it was hot and humid, Ina said to Fred, "I feel freezing. I'm shivering."

Fred wrapped his wife in what few blankets were available while Ina lay on the lower bunk. Soon the shivering stopped and Ina started to burn with fever. Both suspected the fever was the result of the bad meat Ina had swallowed on the previous day. Fred put a thermometer below Ina's tongue. The mercury mark read 104°. As he held on to the thermometer, Fred had a strange premonition that this fever was more than just a passing chill. *Is God taking Ina?* he asked in the quietness of his heart. *Don't even think that way*, he chided himself. He prayed but had no real assurance that God was going to heal Ina.

On the boat, there were very few medicines but Fred gave Ina some aspirin to try to help sweat the fever out of her system. Ina had little or no appetite but took small sips of the bottled lemonade they had brought on board with them.

The high temperature persisted even though she had no pain. Fred felt helpless to alleviate Ina's plight. The steamer was taking them farther up river every day and it seemed that they were getting farther and farther away from any help. Fred held Ina's hand and prayed that the Lord would touch her. Still, the fever raged. Together they quoted the promises God had given them and reaffirmed their commitment to God's call on their lives and their love for each other.

As the boat steadily made its way up river, Fred and Ina talked of their lives and Ina shared with Fred that she always knew God would take him to the mission field. She also said that she prayed he would not go until she was ready. "Now," said Ina, "I am so happy, happy to be here with you, happy to be in the will of God. I am the happiest girl in the world."

One night, near midnight Ina said to Fred, "I would give anything for a drink of soda water, something that wasn't sweet like these drinks we've brought."

Fred wondered to himself, *Where would I ever find soda water out here?*

They sat talking until after 1.00 a.m. Just then they heard the steamer pull into a small town which they afterwards would learn was Canutama. Fred heard a hullabaloo outside his cabin where he had been keeping vigil with Ina and went out to see what was happening. Just then a man came aboard the steamer and the captain introduced him to Fred. Fred, still not able to converse in Portuguese, got his little English/Portuguese dictionary out and began to look up the words that would translate to "soda water." In spite of the lingual difficulties, Fred was able to communicate to the stranger what he was looking for.

The man disappeared into the night and soon returned with six bottles of soda water. *Where did he get these from*? thought Fred. The bottles were so old that the tin tops on them were rusted. Evidently, they had lain unwanted in a store for years.

Fred returned to the cabin and said to Ina, "Here's your soda."

"Where did you get that?" Ina asked with evident surprise.

"If the Lord is able to furnish a table in the wilderness, He can provide soda water in the jungle," Fred replied. The soda water was a welcome change to the sweet drinks Ina had tried to imbibe.

Fred and Ina were deeply touched by the Lord's provision. Fred later learned from Sr. Osmar, the man who gave him the bottles, that the soda had been left in the town years earlier by an American team of engineers who passed through that region. Perhaps the unknown American team used the soda water as a dilution for their whisky. Whatever their use of it might have been, they had no more need for the remaining bottles and left them with Oscar in his store. Soda water was unheard of in the town and no one liked it. It was the Lord's provision for Ina just at this precise time.

As they pulled out of Canutama, the captain of the steamer and all his crew were very anxious for the well being of their young passenger, but they were confined to expressing their feelings by making gestures with their hands to encourage Fred. It was frustrating not being able to communicate orally. The captain tried to tell Fred that there might be help in Labrea, a town four days up river from Canutama.

Fred seldom left Ina's side. He continued to pray for Ina and with her, but all the time he had no satisfaction that God was going to answer his prayers by healing his wife. Home and help seemed so far away. Each day they travelled farther into what was commonly known as the "Green Hell," and Fred could not help think of why all this should be happening to them.

That same week back in Britain, Roger Bannister had just been acclaimed as the first athlete to run the four minute mile, and tennis star Maureen Connolly had just been crowned queen of Wimbledon for the third successive year. While these remarkable athletes enjoyed the plaudits of the world, this young couple, in obedience to the call of God, had forsaken their lovely home and a promising career and were slowly winding their way up river through the green hell.

Even though Ina was very ill and the fever continued to rage, she had no sense of alarm or fear. At times she chided Fred for showing anxiety and doubt. There was little sleep for either of them. Their waking hours were spent conversing, reminiscing, reading the scriptures and praying.

On the following Friday just after dawn, the slow moving steamer finally arrived in Labrea, which was located on a sharp bend of the river and on the opposite side from Canutama. This was the end of the journey on the steamer, the half way point between Manaus and Boca do Acre. Fred had to think of arranging their baggage and transferring it to another boat for the next stage of the journey that would take him and Ina to Boca do Acre. In the back of his mind, he was thinking how was he going to change from one boat to another with his wife so ill?

To everyone's surprise and relief, they discovered there was a doctor in Labrea just as the captain had said there might be. Hopes were raised when the doctor was brought to the steamer to see what he could do for the lady missionary. Alas, it was already too late. Ina grew weaker during the afternoon. Fred never left her side. At one stage she called Fred, who was trying to mask his real feelings of doubt and fear. Try as he would, he could not hide these real feelings from Ina. Again, she questioned why he was doubting and pointed out that to doubt was a sin. Before long, at Ina's insistence, Fred was on his knees beside Ina's bunk, confessing to God his doubts and asking for forgiveness.

After he prayed, Fred looked straight up into Ina's eyes. She noticed there was a smile on his face and Ina said, "Now that's the Fred I know. You go and get on with your work and I am going to have a little sleep."

The work Ina was referring to was arranging the baggage, but those were Ina's last and very significant words. Ina fell asleep in Christ at eight o'clock that evening, Friday, 4th June, 1954. She was only twenty-nine years of age and had been in Brazil for just over six weeks.

Fred was bewildered. He did not know what to do or where to go. The captain would not leave Fred's side. If he had to be away for an hour, he detailed someone else to be with Fred. Curious people from Labrea came aboard to see the young foreigner who had just lost his wife, but Fred stayed in his cabin. The captain arranged for a carpenter in town to make a coffin and for a grave to be opened the next morning for burial at the town's cemetery.

A thousand thoughts filled Fred's mind, as he sat in his cabin in the early hours of Saturday morning. He thought of Mrs. McMurray, Ina's mother back in Belfast who just a short time earlier had lost her husband. *She is not only going to hear that Ina's ill. She will be shocked to hear that her only daughter is dead. How will she take the news?* He thought of his parents and their anxious thoughts about him. Besides the family, there were also their friends at the Castlereagh Church and a myriad of other friends at home. *How will I get word to Mollie and Mr. McComb?*

While these thoughts crowded in on his mind, Fred felt constrained to read his Bible even though he was in a spin of confusion. In the back of his mind was the haunting question, "Why did God allow her to die if He has called us out here?"

At times it seemed as if the Devil whispered to him, "You should never have come out here."

Fred was not in the habit of opening his Bible at random and looking for a verse. However, he still cannot recollect how he got his Bible open to John 13. Immediately, Fred's eyes fell on the page of his Bible and it seemed that verse seven stood out in large bold letters right across the page, "**Jesus answered and said unto him, What I do thou knowest not now; but thou shalt know hereafter**."

The words shook Fred. He looked back and could not see the verse again in such bold letters. He had to search to find that the quotation was in John 13:7. This word was the voice of God to His child and gave Fred the great assurance and peace that he needed in the midst of his frustration and heartbreak.

Not long after the sun came up on Saturday morning, Fred and three other men carried the simple coffin up the steps of the port in

Labrea. In the early sunlight, Fred got his first inhospitable view of a town that would soon become his home. The small entourage made a diagonal crossing of the town square and then half a mile down a mud road to the town's cemetery.

Over the open grave, Fred read Psalm 23 in English and prayed with thanksgiving for his darling wife Ina and her mother and family at home in Belfast. It was a heartbreaking moment but Fred stood around until the gravediggers had filled in the grave. Two of the men who help Fred carry the coffin, Sr. José Carirí, one of the town's drunks, and Sr. Rosena, later became Christians under Fred's ministry in the town. The latter still serves as a deacon in the church where Fred is pastor.

As he left the cemetery, he felt enshrouded in a sensation of loneliness. Again it seemed as if Satan whispered, "Now you are all alone."

Almost immediately God gave an assuring reply. Although it was a sunny Saturday morning, Fred lifted his eyes to the horizon over the forest where a beautiful and clearly defined rainbow arched over the sky. It was as if God was answering Satan's innuendo and assured Fred that God is faithful to His promise for He has said, "I will never leave you nor forsake you."

The captain had bonded a close friendship with Fred through the ordeal and refused to leave his side until Fred travelled to Boca do Acre on a Catalina flight on Sunday. Fred could not get out of Labrea quick enough and vowed he would never return to this awful place that held so many dark memories for him.

While Fred and his company were at the cemetery on Saturday morning, the local telegraph operator communicated the tragic news of Ina's death by Morse code to Boca do Acre. Mollie gave an account of how she received the news:

> The believers at the Boca do Acre were planning a welcome service for the new couple arriving from Northern Ireland. The Sunday School children were to sing as a choir. The elders and deacons had planned to say a few words of welcome and I was to translate into English for Fred and Ina.

Sr. David Salgado, a Jew who lived in Boca do Acre, had a shop in town. He came one day to tell me he was going down river on a small boat to meet up with the larger steamer that was returning to Manaus. He knew about the new missionary couple arriving in Manaus and their plans to come to the Boca do Acre. He said he would be meeting the new missionary couple on their way through.

I had already received letters from Belfast addressed to Fred and Ina. David said he would be glad to take them down river and give the correspondence to the couple in Labrea. I also wrote a letter to Fred and Ina and told them all was ready for their arrival.

On the Saturday morning, an old man came to the door of the Mission house. He said he had come from the telegraph radio station high up on the hill on the other side of the river. He handed me a piece of paper and when I unfolded it, these are the words I read, "The missionary Ina Orr died on board this boat last night at Labrea. Please contact husband to arrange about burial."

The radio operator sent word to say that this was the message he had received from Labrea. He suggested that I accompany the old man to the station since he wanted to speak with me.

To this day I do not remember crossing the river and climbing that steep hill. Arriving at the telegraph station, I was dumbstruck. I could only write out the message to Fred, word by word in English. The operator transmitted the message as I had written it, "Lay Ina to rest in Labrea and come to Boca do Acre."

Within a short time I received a reply which said, "Coming on plane tomorrow, Sunday."

My Jewish friend, David Salgado, was in Labrea when these sad events occurred and was such a help and comfort to Fred. He had carried Fred's Bible to the cemetery while Fred shouldered the coffin. He said that just when Fred finished reading from the Bible at the grave side, a beautiful rainbow appeared. Fred pointed to the rainbow, then to the Bible, and then directed his pointing finger to the grave. David was very touched along with the many Brazilians around the grave.

When he arrived at the Boca do Acre, Fred was utterly exhausted. Only the Lord knew how deep the waters of sorrow were through which he was passing. We sat and talked at length, and I tried to be a good listener for him. Neither of us slept for nights.

Some days after his arrival in Boca do Acre, his baggage arrived on a river boat. Fred was not interested in unpacking what he and Ina had packed in Northern Ireland before they left for Brazil. I had to go through all their belongings and keep out what belonged to Fred. The opening of each case was a painful exercise.

Back in Belfast, Willie McComb was visiting with friends when he got an urgent call to return home immediately as a telegram had arrived from Brazil. It coldly conveyed the sad news, "Ina took fever on journey; went to be with Jesus; advise families; letter follows. Willard Stull."

Willie McComb was stunned and found it hard to believe the news. He knew how inhospitable life was in the interior forests of Brazil. Besides feeling deep sympathy for Fred, he had the unenviable task of going to Mrs. McMurray's home and breaking the sad news to her and to Ina's brother Jackie.

It was an unreal situation in Belfast, with no funeral to attend or body to see. Perhaps it was God's way of comforting the family when some days later, Mrs. McMurray received a letter which Ina had written before she and Fred left Manaus. At the top of the letter, Ina had written the words of the Lord Jesus recorded in John 17:4; "I have glorified thee on the earth: I have finished the work which thou gavest me to do." The verse was so appropriate for the situation that Mrs. McMurray said afterwards it seemed like a message straight from heaven.

The tragic news of Ina's death hit the Christian community like a bombshell, for Fred and Ina had been held in such high esteem. On receiving the news the Acre Committee immediately contacted Fred and offered the passage money to bring him home to Belfast. He declined this offer and felt he should continue in the work he and Ina had gone to Brazil to do.

Fred wrote to Willie McComb not long after Ina's death and in his letter, he disclosed a measure of the grace God gave to him under the extremely trying circumstances.

Loving greetings in the precious name of Jesus! Just a few lines to let you know that I am keeping well and finding His grace sufficient for each day. I am sure it was a terrible shock to you to receive the news of Ina's home-call. It all seems like a wild dream, and I feel I shall awake from it. At such a time as this one is inclined to ask, "Why?"; but we must trust in Him, who never makes a mistake, and seek to glorify His name in it.

I am sure you realize something of the burden upon my heart, and I ask that you would pray and influence others to pray also at this time. How many things seem to add up in these days and throw light upon mysteries of the past! I do not just say this as Ina's husband, but truly, God used her mightily, right from Belfast.

On board the ship she won the hearts of all, and I have seen big men stand at the rail and cry as she testified for Jesus and then sang His praises. The places we called at and the witness she bore there, especially in Brazil, the Lord knows. The greatest of all her witness was in Manaus, and then on the boat to Acre. The believers just loved her, and I have seen the church as well as the road outside packed, as she sang for Jesus. Many people told me that she sang beautifully in Portuguese. Grace Stull suggested that she should record some hymns, since there are very few hymns recorded in Portuguese.

I had letters from Grace and Willard Stull in Manaus today. They say that when Ina's name is mentioned in the church, there is hardly a dry eye. The other evening, the evangelist in Willard's church asked the people to rise and observe a moment's silence in honour of Ina.

Afterwards they sang "Whiter than the snow," which was one of the last pieces Ina sang there.

On the boat she again won many hearts, including that of the captain, who was a real father to us both. We spent hours on the bridge with him, and we lacked for nothing.

Never once did Ina complain. She was actually running over with joy. She would say to me, "Freddie, why are you afraid? Don't you trust the Lord?" She was an inspiration to me and even made me kneel at her bed to confess my sin of doubting, and ask for faith to trust in Him. This was early in the morning of the very day she went home.

Right from the start she had no pain, and as far as I know, she had none right until the end. She became delirious on Friday afternoon, and then went unconscious about 6.00 p.m. and passed away two hours later.

God alone knows what a week I spent, as Ina slept very little and I sat with her right until the end. The Lord seemed to be preparing me for what lay ahead, for I could not get the thought out of my mind right from the start. Ina's condition did not do this of itself, for as I have already said, she never seemed to be seriously ill. Her temperature was very high, although one day it was almost normal again. She actually sat on deck for a few hours on two occasions, though the second time she had to go back to bed because she felt a little queer.

The doctor took a blood slide and said that there was no sign of malaria. She went so quickly that it is hard to believe, especially since she was in the best of health previously. Even the doctor said that she was very strong, yet in six days, she was gone.

Thank God, He is still my trust. To Him be all the glory. The way before looks dark, but I feel that He who called us to serve Him has all the answers. Ina never doubted her call and was emphatic that she was where He would have her, even during her sickness.

This was a sacrifice of monumental proportions. In almost all of Fred's correspondence to this day, he heads the letter with 2 Corinthians 9:8; "God is able to make all grace abound toward you; that ye, always having all sufficiency in all things, may abound to every good work." He most certainly would be justified in endorsing this verse with the words, "tried and proved to be true."

Some time later, recollecting on the events of Ina's final days and how God spoke to and sustained him, Fred wrote these appropriate words:

I cannot always understand
The way God works His mighty plan,
But this I know, His love to me
Is greater, deeper than the deepest sea.
Some day soon His face I'll see,
And then His promise unto me
Will be made real, I'll understand
And praise Him for His guiding hand.

He drew me out of nature's night,
And o'er my pathway shed His light.
I've walked with Him the narrow road
That leads my spirit up to God.
Some day soon His face I'll see,
And then His promise unto me
Will be made real, I'll understand
And praise Him for His guiding hand.

So by His grace I'll follow on
To know the Lord, God's blessed Son.
My glory shall be in His cross,
For which I count all else but loss.
Some day soon His face I'll see,
And then His promise unto me
Will be made real, I'll understand
And praise Him for His guiding hand.

Chapter Ten

FAITH TAKES A STEP BACK

While William Carey is generally recognized as the "Father of the Modern Missionary Movement," it is to Hudson Taylor that the principle of the "faith mission" is generally attributed. During the Boxer Rebellion in China, when some of the Lord's choicest servants were murdered, Hudson Taylor wrote to a friend, "I cannot think, I cannot even pray, but I can trust." That was largely the experience of Fred in the months that followed after Ina's death. Mollie Harvey's kindness and care sustained him through those difficult days and sleepless nights when he was trying to cope with sorrow and adjust to a new culture, a testing climate and language study.

Fred applied himself to master the Portuguese language, which was not only good therapy for him, but also his efforts and focus paid worthwhile dividends. Very soon, he was speaking Portuguese exceptionally well. As he progressed with the language, he began to take part in the various meetings. The people at the Boca do Acre loved him and being aware of his circumstances, they sought to express their sympathy and support.

Jack and Joan Mawdsley became more involved in river evangelism before going to work in Sena Madureira. Fred felt he wanted to go down river to Labrea and erect something at Ina's grave, even though he had vowed never to return to that town which held such dark memories. This decision only came about after a period of resisting the thought of ever returning to Labrea. Finally, Fred surrendered to God's leading and four months after Ina's death, he embarked on a boat to travel to the town which was a journey of eight days down river.

On arrival in Labrea, Fred did not know where to go. There were no hotels in the town which was dominated by a Spanish bishop, his Spanish priests and nuns. However, as Fred walked up the bank an old lady recognized him and said, "You are that Englishman that lost his wife here a few months ago?"

By this time Fred could understand Portuguese and he nodded his head in agreement with the lady. She continued, "Would you like to go to the cemetery?"

Together they started off in the direction of the graveyard, across the same town square he had traversed a few months earlier carrying his wife's casket. On the way, she stopped and invited Fred into her home where she soon prepared a pot of strong, black, but very sweet coffee. While Fred downed the coffee, she went out to her quinteira, an elevated platform of plants and flowers at the back of the house, and cut a little posy of colourful blossoms.

Soon they were on their way to the graveyard again and on arrival, the lady looked down at what she thought was Ina's plot and began to cry. Fred lifted her chin and pointing up he said, "She is not down there. She is up there." That was the first person to whom Fred witnessed on his return to the town, which involuntarily became a special part of his life.

Still not sure where he was going to stay, he returned to the boat which was not leaving until the next day and slept overnight on board. Early the next morning, he ventured up to the town again and met a tall gaunt man with a short beard. His name was Alfredo David, a Syrian trader who had made his home in Labrea and ran a shop just at the corner of the town square.

Obviously recognizing who Fred was, he inquired of his well being. During the course of their conversation Fred told him he would love to find a place to stay in the town. The Syrian said that

Labrea was no place for a man like Fred and that he should go elsewhere. "This place has too many sad memories for you," and pointing across the town square to the Bishop's large residence, he said, "and what is more they will put you out."

Fred insisted that he would like to stay but was not sure where he could find a place. The old man disappeared into the back of his shop and called on his son, Alfredinho, to open a store a few doors up from the shop and make room for Fred to stay. The young boy duly complied and swung a hammock across the room for the stranger in town. This was Fred's first experience of sleeping in a hammock and he fell out of it more frequently than he was able to sleep in it.

The store was completely overrun with rats, which sometimes fell into the hammock. There were no toilet facilities whatsoever. When it got dark, he had the use of a little tin lamp which gave a dull amber light but filled the room with smoke. However, the smoke was not strong enough to deter the mosquitoes which came in their droves to feed on fresh Irish blood. Because it was a store, it was full of nuts, manioc, and other materials. This allowed Fred one room in which to live, sleep and receive visitors. However, it was the first foothold in Labrea and proved to be the Lord's provision.

When the mayor of the town saw the conditions in which Fred was staying, he was greatly embarrassed and offered Fred a piece of land on which to erect a house. At the town hall, he gave Fred the deeds of the land as a gift from the town in which his wife died. However, the Bishop was so powerful in Labrea that he not only overturned the legal document Fred had acquired for the land, he also had the mayor sacked from office and deported out of Labrea.

Fred stayed long enough to erect a headstone at Ina's grave and then returned to Boca do Acre. Mollie was doing a valiant work and besides the services in the church and attending to the sick and ladies in ante and post natal care, she also opened a small clinic in the needy town. There were no doctors in the town other than an occasional visit from a doctor flown in for a few hours as an electioneering stunt to boast a particular candidate or party. People travelled for many hours, sometimes by canoe and others trekked through the forest, to visit Mollie's clinic where she used both homeopathy and conventional medicines to treat all sorts of diseases.

When a lawyer friend in Boca do Acre learned that the Bishop in Labrea had taken land that had been given to Fred, he offered to pursue the matter further. Fred graciously declined the offer, preferring to let the Lord work it all out.

Within a few months Fred ventured on another visit to Labrea, constrained that the Lord had a work for him to do there. On arrival, he found that there was a lot of local sympathy for how he had been treated by the Bishop on his previous visit. In the outpouring of this emotion, Sr. Alfredo David offered to sell Fred a piece of land. Fred was grateful for the man's kind offer, knowing how much this old Syrian cared for him. However, Fred did not have the wherewithal to buy any land.

Without betraying his complete lack of funds, Fred said he would look at the various sites the man offered. Fred did not have enough money to buy even the worst site but he felt had nothing to lose in asking how much the best site would cost. Alfredo David told Fred to go ahead and fix a house on the site and then they would talk about money later. Rather than be caught out on a shortage of funds later, Fred insisted on knowing the price right away. The man urged Fred to secure the land, as he was in no hurry for money. The matter was left in abeyance as Fred was waiting for James and Dorrie to arrive back in Brazil before they would start building a house.

When news of the Syrian's offer to Fred leaked out, the Bishop saw red. He contacted the judge in town and through him, sent word to Alfredo David urging the Syrian to go ahead and sell the land to the foreign missionary. The Bishop would then use his influence to dispossess Fred and give the land back to its original owner. When Alfredo David heard this, he was angry at the connivance of the Bishop and refused to cooperate. The Bishop continued to press the matter further and told the town councillors to impound all the property the Syrian owned in an attempt to frustrate any missionary incursion in Labrea.

The saga continued to and fro for several months while Fred returned to Boca do Acre to wait for James and Dorrie just before Christmas 1955. In the meantime, the judge fell in love with the Syrian's daughter and somehow was persuaded to see things from her father's point of view. Consequently, he refused to follow the

Bishop's edict. The Syrian eventually became the judge's father-in-law. The judge then advised Sr. Alfredo David to let Fred use of the land but retain his own name on the documentation. In so doing, it would secure the land for all parties concerned.

It was a great day in Boca do Acre when James and Dorrie returned after an eighteen months absence. So much had happened since they left. Their beloved Corina had fallen in love with a young man in Sena Madureira and before James and Dorrie returned they had been married. Although they were sorry to lose her they were glad that her husband, Francisco Franco, was a fine believer from the Assembly of God. He was one of the most genial persons in Sena Madureira and in years to come he would be an immense help to all the missionaries.

James wrote about their return to Boca do Acre in the *Acre Missionary News* of early 1956.

> The journey from Belem to the Boca do Acre took longer than expected — forty-seven days in all, but this was due to the fact that the river was abnormally low for that time of the year. We had the joy of witnessing for the Lord aboard the river steamer and also at the different homes at which we called during the journey up river. We would ask prayer for the contacts made, and the Scriptures distributed.
>
> Wednesday, 21st December, was a wonderful day for us, for that was the day we arrived in the Boca do Acre. Here we were met by our dear colleagues, Mollie, Fred, Jack and Joan. The only thing which caused sadness at our arrival was meeting our dear brother Fred without dear Ina, but the Lord gave grace and is giving it daily to Fred. Do continue to pray for him.
>
> Quite a number of the believers were also down to meet us, some known to us, but there were many others we did not know for they had been gloriously saved during our time on furlough. We had a lovely time of fellowship and reunion around a nice refreshment served by Mollie and Joan. When our friends left, we then sat down and

had a "wee Irish yarn." In fact, I will tell you a secret, we did not go to bed but talked right through to the morning!

Friday night was our welcome meeting in the church. We shall not soon forget that welcome. How our hearts were gladdened to see the little church once again and above all, to see how the labour of His servants had been blessed. Praise God, for the joy of seeing souls seeking and finding the Saviour at the close of this service.

On Thursday, 1st March, Fred and I travelled down to Labrea to make plans for the future of the work there. We found in this town a real thirst for the Word of Life. Every day we met people who asked, "When are you coming to commence a work here?" The authorities of the town are very favourable to us, although we may expect opposition from other quarters, yet, praise the Lord, we need not fear when "God is for us, who can be against us?"

A foothold has been gained in Labrea at a very great cost: the seed which has fallen into the ground and died is bearing fruit. We rejoice to tell you that during our visit we had the joy of pointing two souls to the Lord. We feel that these are only a foretaste of what is to come, because we believe that the Lord has many souls in this town.

The first essential we need in Labrea is a house, and as there are none to let, we will have to build one which will be suitable both as a residence and also as a room to accommodate the meetings until a church building can be erected to the glory of God.

The site which was given to Fred is very central and will be ideal for the meetings. Dear friends, please pray very definitely for the future of the work in Labrea.

So that James and Fred could be free to work at the construction of the house in Labrea, Dorrie remained in Boca do Acre to carry on the work there. Little by little the Lord supplied the need to purchase all the materials for the building of a house in Labrea. It not only provided accommodation for the missionaries, but also a large verandah with seating for over one hundred people.

Periodically Fred was invited to preach at conferences in Manaus and Rio Branco. In his absence Dorrie joined James in Labrea. During one of these visits to Manaus, Fred became extremely ill. After consultation with a doctor, he was told that he was suffering from severe colitis and if he did not return to Britain, it would kill him. Fred resisted the thought of going home and not returning to Brazil. He refused to go home and took a stand on the promises God had given him. The Lord honoured this step and Fred was able to travel back to Labrea.

While James was busy with his joinery tools, Dorrie started meetings for the children in the same rooms Sr. Alfredo had first rented to Fred. These first meetings brought a great response and revealed an obvious hunger for the gospel in the hearts of many in Labrea.

Among those who threw their weight into the work was Sr. Luiz Marinho and his family who, eight years earlier, had met James and Dorrie on the boat that first transported them to Sena Madureira. He became James' right hand man in the construction of the house and in later years, his family would play a major part in the development of the Lord's work in that town.

Dorrie returned to Boca do Acre to stand in for Mollie, who was due on furlough late in 1956. James remained in Labrea to work at the building. This arrangement meant that James and Dorrie shuttled between the two towns until Mollie returned from furlough at the end of 1958 and brought with her a new missionary, Allen Loney from Richhill in County Armagh. Allen was a graduate from the Belfast Bible College and the Missionary School of Medicine in London.

As they settled into life in Labrea, the missionaries found that there was a very high incidence of leprosy in the town. One area near the cemetery was allocated for those who suffered from the dreaded disease. Few people ventured near them. Sadly, there was little treatment available for them. The compassion of the Saviour constrained the missionaries to visit these poor victims who unwillingly had become outcasts in their own society.

Another door opened for the work of Acre Gospel Mission in 1957 when Jack and Joan Mawdsley were preparing to go to England for their first furlough. They had completed their time in Sena Madureira when Sander Tonneson arrived back from Norway. On the Catalina flight to Manaus, they met the mayor of Canutama who implored them to go to his town. Canutama needed not only the gospel but also someone to attend to the many sick in the town. Very few of these interior towns had any medical assistance.

Although unable to attend to the invitation immediately, Jack and Joan felt that this was the Lord opening a door for them when they returned to Brazil. Meanwhile, the Lord already had a servant there. Sr. Milton Rosa, a river trader who owned a lot of land in the Canutama region and was a fine and forthright Christian, conducted open-air meetings on the street of the town. These were vehemently opposed by the town's Spanish priest who was under the authority of the Bishop in Labrea. At first, the priest instigated the crowd to stone the zealous preacher. In spite of the persecution, this courageous servant of God persisted in his witness during his frequent visits to the Canutama. He was overjoyed when he heard that an English couple were planning to move into the town.

Canutama was not only the smallest town, but also probably the poorest of all the towns into which the Acre Gospel Mission had moved to. Supplies were scarce and the incidence of leprosy was almost on a par with the situation in Labrea. Possibly, there was even less care for these victims here and no treatment for these poor souls.

Some months after Jack and Joan went to United Kingdom, Fred was also due for furlough. In his absence, James and Dorrie were separated from each other for nine months at a time as James looked after the developing work in Labrea, while Dorrie still continued in Boca do Acre.

Allen Loney's arrival was a blessing to all. Besides being very talented with several musical instruments, he also was adept at construction work and was able to help James finish the work at the Labrea house. Just about the time of the completion of the house, Dorrie joined James and Allen in Labrea and soon they started the first meetings on the new verandah. Initially the numbers were small, but one by one people trusted the Lord Jesus and the work began to show great promise.

The challenge of what the Lord was doing in Brazil was stirring many young people at home and over the next few years, new recruits helped swell the number of missionaries in the Amazon. Not only did Mollie arrive back with Allen, but Jack and Joan Mawdsley returned and accepted the Mayor's invitation to start a work in Canutama, in spite of intense opposition from the Roman church.

When Jack and Joan arrived in Canutama, they had money on hand after furlough to purchase a small house half way up the main street. The house sat at one side of almost an acre of land and had very good potential. The first meetings in the house were small but soon several people trusted the Lord. These first converts were discriminated against by the priest whose immoral lifestyle was well known in the town. Sr. Milton Rosa was quick to stand by the side of the missionaries and gave support to the new converts. He bought a prime property in town, less than one hundred yards from the church, and offered it to Jack and Joan as their residence. In later years, that house became the Mission base for Canutama. After missionaries left Canutama the house became the pastor's residence.

After a very full furlough, Fred also returned to Labrea to join Allen, James and Dorrie in the fledgling work. He was thrilled to meet with his colleagues and a keen group of new believers. Fred's return allowed James and Dorrie to visit Boca do Acre before making plans to travel back to Northern Ireland for a needed furlough.

Fred gave himself wholeheartedly to the work in Labrea, even though he had many invitations to speak at conferences elsewhere. Allen was not only able to use his practical skills to finish some jobs at the new house, he also taught some local believers the rudiments of photography, developing films and also trained a local believer how to extract teeth. This man became one of the leading dentists in town and went on to make himself a comfortable living from his acquired skills.

Each time the missionaries returned from Britain, they brought lots of medicines and clothes to help the sick and the poor. This benevolence and the midwifery work helped break down many prejudices and suspicions and also gave opportunities for the gospel witness.

Labrea at that time became the centre of an epidemic which was colloquially known as the Black Fever. This mysterious illness plagued the people of the River Purus, leaving much heartbreak and grief in its wake. The victims were mostly young people, who died within five or six days of the first manifestations of the disease. In some areas whole families were wiped out.

Black Fever became a byword that struck fear in the hearts of everyone. Many superstitions arose, attributing the disease to a curse of witchcraft on the region. The fact is that it was an unclassified condition which attracted the attention of the World Health Organization. Pathologists from around the world converged on the region to help trace the source of the disease.

Although Fred was not trained in medicine, he used common sense and the medicines brought from home to alleviate much of the suffering. With the outbreak of this disease, he was asked by the Evandro Chagas Tropical Institute in Belem to take biopsies of the liver from each victim who died of Black Fever. It was a fearful situation and a gruesome task. Fred had to perform this procedure at the cemetery almost every week, but the missionaries' contribution during this epidemic helped win the hearts of many people who were formerly opposed to the gospel.

In 1959, Anne McWhinnie, a bonny lassie from Dumbarton in Scotland, who had trained at the WEC Missionary Training College in Glasgow, joined Mollie in Boca do Acre. She had a sweet voice and soon won her way into the hearts of the Brazilians as she played her guitar at the meetings and put her mind into mastering Portuguese. The arrival of Mollie and Anne allowed James and Dorrie to travel to Northern Ireland for a much needed rest and deputation programme.

Bill Woods arrived in Brazil in August, 1960. After an initial spell with Fred in Labrea, he joined Jack and Joan to help in the construction of a new church in Canutama. Bill also trained at the WEC Missionary Training College, after which he spent some time in North Antrim with the Faith Mission at the request of the Acre Gospel Mission committee.

Bill applied himself well to language study and was soon taking a full share in the growing work at Canutama where the Lord was blessing. Besides the work in the town, Bill travelled with Jack extensively on the surrounding rivers reaching thousands of isolated people with the gospel for the first time. Scores of people trusted Christ at the first hearing of the Word of God during these pioneer journeys. Bill also became involved with Arne and Joyce Abrahamson of the Wycliffe Bible Translators in their endeavours to reach the fierce Juma Indians, whose dwellings were two days' journey from Canutama on the River Içuã.

There were many remarkable and dramatic conversions in Canutama. One lady, Dona Adelha, had followed the priest's directives and vocally expressed her opposition to the missionaries. She vowed that she would never let one of their converts over her door. Tragedy struck the home when two of her daughters fell victim to Black Fever and died within a short time of each other. Dona Adelha, heartbroken and full of despair, ran off into the forest. She could not bear to even look at her home. The poor lady thought she was going crazy with pain and despair. An indelible image of her daughters would not leave her mind and she was frightened for the rest of her children.

In the forest, Dona Adelha called on all the saints she could think of and even surrendered herself to evil spirits. The darkness and despair seemed to deepen and finally she cried out, "I will even call on the missionaries' God to see if He would give me peace."

It was only then that her heart calmed and she returned to peace of mind. On returning to Canutama, Dona Adelha went to the missionaries' house where Bill Woods was able to lead her to personal faith in Jesus Christ. After her conversion she prayed for her family and most of them came to the Lord within a short time.

It was also at Canutama, while Jack and Joan were absent from town, that Bill was called down river late one night to help a young man who was dying. Bill felt totally inadequate and was deeply moved as he prayed for the youth. Even as Bill prayed, the teenager writhed in pain and called out, "I don't want you to pray I want you to do something."

As Bill left the house and pulled his canoe out from the river bank, he could still hear the cries of the poor man echoing across the quietly flowing river and into the forest. "Help me! Help me! I want you to do something!"

The condition of that young man and the plight of the leprosy sufferers in and around the town compounded Bill's sense of frustration and helplessness. He had arrived in Brazil to be a preacher but sensed he needed to do more than preach. It was at that early stage in his missionary career that Bill felt he had to do something which would eventually constrain him to take leave of absence from the Mission to study medicine. The amazing story of Bill Woods' life and ministry, which brought relief to thousands of leprosy sufferers, is told in the book, *Angel of the Amazon.*

At Bill's invitation, a young seminary student from Manaus, Moacir Alencar, joined Bill in the work in Canutama during Jack and Joan's absence while on furlough. Besides gaining experience for future pastoral ministry, Moacir fell in love with Dona Adelha's daughter, Maria do Carmo, and married her a year later. Moacir eventually became the first national to pastor the Canutama church and went on to found nine other Baptist churches in Manaus. Twenty-five years later their son, Eliezer, returned to Canutama as pastor and erected a new brick building to accommodate the large congregation.

When James and Dorrie returned to Brazil in 1961, Hazel Miskimmin from Belfast travelled with them and was soon initiated into the work in Boca do Acre. Hazel was a qualified nurse and midwife and had trained at the Bible College of Wales in Swansea. After James and Dorrie travelled to Labrea to pick up their baggage, they proceeded on up river to Boca do Acre.

The influx of these new missionaries gave a fresh impetus to the work and freed the more experienced missionaries to travel on the needy rivers. Jack and Joan had brought a Kelvin motor from Liverpool and were able to have a boat constructed locally that enabled them to travel the many tributaries in the Canutama region. Allen moved to Boca do Acre and also travelled on the River Purus, using his dentistry skills to open doors for evangelizing the river dwellers.

Like other interior towns, Boca do Acre continued to grow because many forest dwellers left their remote forest dwellings to seek a better life for their children in the town. Over a period of time, what had been small settlements near the town soon developed into small villages. James acquired property on the other side of the river at São Paulo and commenced a work there. God moved in a marvellous way in that location and many people were converted, including an old man, Sr. Artu. He remembered the time when the unknown colporteur visited Boca do Acre and after he left, the Word of God was torched on the town square. Before long, seventy people formed a new congregation at São Paulo.

Also, downstream from Boca do Acre and on the other side of the river, James and Dorrie opened a work in Terra Firme where one of Willie McComb's former evangelists, Sr. Leoncio, lived. From there they established a further outreach at Monte Verde, which was still another half-hour down river and where there was a settlement of Apuriná Indians. Again there was a real move of the Spirit of God in these neighbourhoods and whole families and several Indians turned in repentance to Jesus Christ.

To reach Terra Firme, James and Dorrie had to cross a very treacherous stretch of the fast flowing water where the Purus and the Acre converge. Once they reached the other side of the river, they climbed up the muddy and slippery bank until they came to a steep ascent with seventy-eight wooden rungs. In the tropical sunshine, this was an exhausting journey.

All of these steps of faith and extensions of the work were fiercely opposed by the local priests who were mostly Spanish or Italians. In Canutama, the children of new converts were denied access to the only school in town. In Labrea, free food and clothing donated by the Lutheran Church of the United States for the poor people of Brazil's interior was distributed by the priests who either sold it or refused to give it to anyone who attended the meetings in the evangelical church.

The increased numbers of missionaries in Brazil also brought added responsibility at home. Consequently Mr. McComb, after nine years as pastor, resigned from the Castlereagh Evangelical Church to devote himself full-time to the work of encouraging more prayer support for the missionaries and to care for the administration of the growing work of Acre Gospel Mission.

Chapter Eleven

UP AGAINST IT

It may sound paradoxical but it is true to say that there is seldom progress in the Lord's work without the workers suffering reversals or facing adversity. Paul reminded the Corinthians that although we have the treasure of the gospel, it is carried in earthen vessels. "But we have this treasure in earthen vessels, that the excellency of the power may be of God, and not of us. We are troubled on every side, yet not distressed; we are perplexed, but not in despair; Persecuted, but not forsaken; cast down, but not destroyed; Always bearing about in the body the dying of the Lord Jesus, that the life also of Jesus might be made manifest in our body." Satan cannot touch or tamper with the treasure, but oftentimes the vessels are buffeted. Such has been the experiences of the Acre missionaries.

Travelling by canoe on the narrow or broad tributaries of the Amazon basin can give rise to many hazards and even by drowning is a common occurrence. Often the missionaries have had close calls in this respect, such as the day four missionaries and a friend from the church in Boca do Acre were returning from a visit to the Indians at Monte Verde.

In the middle of the afternoon, Mollie, James, Dorrie, Fred and a believer from the church in Boca do Acre were returning after another worthwhile time spent with the Apurinás. Little by little they were gaining the confidence of these superstitious people and on this day, they had experienced an Apuriná meal and conducted a short meeting.

It was a fine afternoon as they walked back through the forest on the path leading to their canoe. Although the air was heavy with humidity as usual, the sun was still shining brightly as it coursed its highway across the brilliant blue sky. Suddenly Mollie felt a strange sensation and remarked to her colleagues that there was a marked and eerie stillness in the air. Even the birds had stopped singing.

As they neared the canoe, the missionaries noticed that towering dark clouds had suddenly gathered on the horizon and were drawing closer and closer with unusual rapidity. Soon these sombre clouds rolled overhead and hid the bright sun. It was time to get back to Boca do Acre before they all got caught in another tropical downpour.

Mollie and Dorrie dropped wearily onto the hard benches that bestraddled the dugout canoe, thankful for a place to sit after being on their feet all day. Fred started the outboard motor and, with an eye on the turbulent sky, headed the boat up river. James remarked that the dark clouds seemed to be following them, which was not the usual direction from which storms came. After travelling for a short time, they noticed that theirs was the only boat left travelling on the river. All the other boats, large and small were tied up in their moorings on the far river bank.

Fred decided it was time to head for the opposite side of the river. Just then, the large swirling dark clouds seemed to drop from the sky and wrap themselves around the canoe, the river, and almost anything in their path. Suddenly, like a little leaf in convulsive and agitated waters, the canoe was violently thrown from side to side until everyone feared for their lives. Mollie had escaped death several times in the Amazon but thought this time her hour had come. She wrote about it later.

> Just as the cruel wind blew up into a tempest, the straining motor abruptly hesitated, coughed and then died. We were now completely helpless since we had no power

to direct the canoe. It seemed like we were at the mercy of the wind and waves. We felt the canoe being spun round and round as the current and the wind battled for supreme control. Because of the wind-driven rain, we could not see where we were headed or if anything was coming toward us.

As we held on to each other and to anything within our reach, I thought that this must be similar to what the disciples experienced on the Sea of Galilee long ago when Jesus calmed the sea with a simple command. But my mind soon returned to the situation at hand, as the canoe was quickly filling with water from both the rain and the angry waves that were washing over the sides. Large hail stones began to pelt down on us. With our light clothes it felt as if the driving wind was shooting constant showers of tiny sharp needles or darts into our skin. Death stared us in the face. Like the terrified disciples on Galilee, we cried to the same Lord for help and He answered our prayers.

Soon the wind began to abate and the rain to slacken. As the clouds, borne on by the wind, rushed away up river, we were able to see around us and knew that God had calmed the waters once again. Somehow we were able to manoeuvre the canoe into the side of the river bank. James and Fred tried to start the outboard motor again, but without success.

By this time it was getting late, and we felt very isolated in the impending darkness. Dorrie and I decided to walk through the forest while the men continued working on the motor. Eventually, we heard the putt-putt of the motor bringing the canoe around the bend of the river. Before long James and Fred caught up with us and once again, we lowered our weary bodies onto the hard benches for the final stretch of our journey to Boca do Acre.

When we arrived in Boca do Acre, we saw the severe damage that this tropical whirlwind had inflicted on the wooden structures in the town. Roofs had been ripped off and in some instances, entire houses had been torn apart. We were thankful that God had preserved our lives on the river. The badly shaken believers were glad to see us back home safely. Some of them told us that they had been praying for us.

Arriving at our house, we took the time to clean up and change into fresh clothes before gathering around the table to thank our heavenly Father for His great deliverance. We read Psalm 126:2-3; "Then was our mouth filled with laughter, and our tongue with singing; then said they among the heathen, the Lord hath done great things for them. The Lord hath done great things for us whereof we are glad." We rejoiced as we considered how the evil one had been defeated once again.

Some months after this experience, we received a letter from two prayer partners in Belfast. They told us that one afternoon, while they were sitting at their fireside knitting, they felt constrained to pray for us. They were greatly burdened and knelt by their chairs and committed us to the Lord. Our dear heavenly Father heard and answered their prayers.

Before cyberspace arrived, missionaries in the Amazon enjoyed a good relationship with the local post office, for they depended so much on correspondence from family and friends. Of course, in order to receive letters it is important to be a good correspondent. It was important that a steady stream of news flowed from the missionaries to prayer groups and individual supporters who pledged themselves to uphold the Lord's servants in prayer. It was David Livingstone who wrote home assuring his followers, "I can do without your money; I can live without your letters; but I must have your prayers."

The Acre Gospel Mission was founded upon the faith principle that no public appeals should be made for money. Members of the Mission are committed to look to the Lord to supply all their needs and each new missionary accepted into the Mission is another step of faith. There have been times when God has tested this step of faith, sometimes supplying the need at the last minute and often in the most unexpected ways. In almost seventy-five years of existence, God has supplied all that was needed, month after month, not only for the missionaries' allowances, but also for all the accompanying needs of the Mission and its workers.

Correspondence for Allen in Brazil involved more than prayer support. During his first term he had been writing to Ada Smith, a Faith Mission Pilgrim who came from near Allen's home in County Armagh. They had known each other for a number of years. While Allen was in Brazil, Ada completed her training at the Faith Mission College in Edinburgh and had been a very effective pilgrim worker in Scotland and England. It was a big day for them in April 1963, when Allen and Ada were married in Portadown during Allen's first furlough. Several months after tying the knot, they sailed for the Amazon.

Several months later, Mollie Harvey, who had come home on furlough around the same time as Allen, returned to Brazil taking Susan Scott with her. Susan had been accepted by the Mission more than a year earlier and had planned to go to Brazil, but she was involved in a serious road accident in which her brother-in-law was killed and other members of her family badly injured. Susan escaped, unscathed physically, but deeply shocked.

Like Hazel, Susan was also a nurse from Belfast who did her Bible training at the WEC Missionary Training College in Glasgow at the same time as Bill Woods and Anne McWhinnie. She was keen to put her considerable nursing experience to good use in Brazil. When Mollie and Susan arrived in Brazil, Susan remained in Manaus for language study while Mollie proceeded to the Boca do Acre where Hazel, James and Dorrie awaited her arrival.

During Mollie's absence, Hazel and Dorrie had done a lot of the medical work at the clinic and midwifery work in the homes. An insight into the blessings and frustrations of attending the sick and needy was given by Hazel when she wrote home from Boca do Acre in 1962.

The medical work continues to be an open door for the presentation of the Gospel. During these past weeks, our hearts have been saddened by the number of souls who have gone into eternity. We feel that a few of these people could have been helped with a little medical attention.

On the night of Anne's farewell meeting prior to going to Labrea, we were asked to go to a confinement. The old midwives requested us to come to a home because the case was proving to be too difficult for them. At first we were disappointed to miss the meeting for we were looking forward to giving Anne a warm sendoff. However, we sensed there was some difficulty so we went along to see the case.

On our arrival, we soon discovered that they had every reason to be concerned. The poor woman had been suffering for two days and her condition was dangerous. Four hours later she delivered a stillborn baby which we believed had been dead for some time. We do praise God for His help in all this work. If this dear woman had been left much longer, she too would have died.

In one of the little houses across the river, another woman delivered one of her twins. There was some difficulty in the second child being born. Her husband was on his way to call us when someone told him that we were already out at another case. When he got back home, he was devastated to find that his wife had already died before giving birth to the second baby.

The next day, as I was about to commence language study, there was another call. A woman who lived some distance up river was hemorrhaging. Her sister called us and said that a man would take us to her in his boat, but alas, even before we boarded the canoe, word came to say that the woman had died. The grief of this family was terrible to see. Can you understand something of our burden as we wondered just how much of the gospel that woman had ever heard? Did she, or did she not hear the way of salvation?

Just a few nights ago, we were surprised when one of the men got up in the meeting and said how the midwifery work has been a testimony for the Lord in Boca do Acre. He was referring to the first case that I mentioned in this report. The people here cannot understand how we manage to work under the difficult conditions and still remain calm. Many friends of that family have expressed their desire to attend the meetings including the young woman who was safely delivered.

As I listened to this testimony about the medical work, the words of the hymn came to me: "Love never faileth...see, they are looking learning of you, silently watching all that you do."

In Canutama, Jack Mawdsley and Bill Woods also came up against difficult physical conditions when they travelled on the rivers. Bill wrote about it in 1963.

> During the entire month of August, our launch, "Messenger of Peace," chugged for hundreds of miles up and down various rivers. It was taking Jack and me, with the message of the gospel, to the many darkened and hungry hearts who live along the banks of the rivers Tapauá, Cunhuá and Ipiranha. Day after day we travelled, going ever deeper into the interior and ever meeting those who were eager to hear the good news of Jesus Christ.
>
> In the very first home at which we stopped, we found hearts that had been prepared to receive the Saviour. The father had been reading to his family for some time from an old tattered Bible and a few days before our arrival, their hearts had been softened by the death of their son. It is thought that a huge snake overturned his canoe and pulled him down into the water. Although his canoe was only a few feet from the river bank, he was never seen again.
>
> Poverty and sickness abounded on every hand. I shall never forget going into one wee hut and climbing on my hands and knees to get under a thick mosquito net. When I got in there, I had to wait until the woman of the house

brought an oil lamp. In the dim light, I found her husband lying in an old hammock. His leg was such a rotten mess that I cannot even begin to describe it. A snake had bitten him a few days beforehand and now it was in a gangrenous mess. We gave the poor man all the medicines that we had, but that was only enough to start the treatment he needed. Today, almost three months later, I am still looking for someone going to that distant place to take more medicines to that very sick man.

We finally turned the launch into a smaller river and left it there while we travelled up the narrow waterway by canoe. Even then, it was with much difficulty that the canoe made it upstream. Often we had to get out into the water and lift the canoe over fallen trees or cut our way through the foliage that blocked our path. We rowed for eight days visiting many homes on the way upstream and preaching the gospel to those we met. It was our joy at the headwaters of this river to visit a small tribe of Indians who live in the depths of the forest. We praise the Lord for His protection, but most of all for the four precious souls, that we know of, who trusted the Lord as their Saviour.

Mollie arrived with James and Dorrie just in time for Christmas. There was a lot of news to catch up on, and the oil lamps burned well after midnight as they conversed to each other. Mollie gave all the news from home and was thrilled to hear of the developments of the work in Boca do Acre and the growth of the smaller churches in Terra Firme and São Paulo, where James had acquired two properties that were transformed into church buildings. God was continuing to bless these outreaches and people were constantly coming to the Saviour. The new church at Terra Firme was to be inaugurated on Christmas day.

James related to Mollie how the purchase of the house at Terra Firme had greatly angered the local Italian priest who vowed that he would make sure that the doors of the new evangelical church would never open. His opposition was so great that he bought the house next door to the church to start evening novenas for the people. Even as they talked about the matter, something happened that dramatically changed the priest's plans for Terra Firme. Mollie tells the story:

I had just arrived in the Boca do Acre on Christmas Eve and chatted with Dorrie, James and Hazel all through that night. Early the next morning, we opened the shutters to find the sunlight already streaming through the trees and trying to find its way into the house. We looked up the street and realized that something was wrong. People running past our house were crying; others were being carried and it was apparent that they had been injured. We thought it strange that no one had asked the missionaries for help since we were usually the first people called in any medical emergency.

We later learned that during the Midnight Mass on Christmas Eve, there had been a terrible accident at the Catholic Church. In order to accommodate the expected crowds at the Mass, the priest had built a balcony in the large Roman Catholic Church. It was erected in a hurry and was obviously not secure. When the crowds of people packed the gallery, the whole structure collapsed under the weight. The priest had been leading the proceedings on the ground floor, just under where the balcony crashed down. He and others were seriously injured and he had to be flown out to São Paulo in the south of Brazil for special treatment. We were speechless when we heard the news, for he was the very man who threatened us and vowed that our little church at Terra Firme would never open.

When we officially opened the small church at Terra Firme later that Christmas day, the believers gathered and brought many interested friends. James commenced the proceedings by praying for the salvation of those who had been injured, and especially for the priest who had already left town on the long journey to seek treatment. It was a memorable service, and we gave thanks to God for this new place that was opened to the glory of God to preach and teach the gospel of Jesus Christ.

Besides Fred's work in Labrea, he was travelling to various places for conference ministry. Willard and Grace Stull had moved away from Manaus to work in a seminary in North East Brazil. He encouraged the staff to invite Fred to visit the Baptist Seminary in the picturesque city of Natal. As Fred reported in a letter to Mr. McComb, the time there was greatly blessed by God and opened many doors for conference and evangelistic ministry for many years to come.

Many problems had arisen in the Bible School and the staff asked me to attend their special meetings to help solve them. At one such meeting I suggested we cancel all studies and classes on Friday and set the day apart for prayer. Well, they agreed, and made me responsible for the day's programme to do as I felt led.

We started to pray at 7 a.m. I had spent the previous night with the Lord and He had dealt with me and really met me in power. About 8 a.m, I spoke from Psalm 51 and then we went to prayer again. At first it was, "Lord forgive *us...we*," etc.. Suddenly the "fire" fell and the student who had been causing the worst problems got up and confessed his sins. The praying and confessing then changed from "we" and "us" to "I" and "me." The tears began to fall and one student after another confessed their sin until even the staff, one after another, confessed their sin and sought forgiveness from the Lord.

It was just then that the joy started to come. Some could hardly contain themselves as they praised God through their tears for His dealing with them. It really was wonderful! Hours and hours passed like seconds. I left with the staff about 4 p.m. for a conference meeting and when we returned at 5 p.m., the students were still praying. All the problems rolled away like a mist lifts with the rising of the sun and we were on victory ground.

What a joy it was to listen to the testimonies, even today, of how God worked in the lives of His children. Souls were saved everywhere on Sunday as the students ministered in the various churches. I had the joy of seeing three souls in my meeting come to Christ Jesus as Saviour.

My programme is so full that I never leave the seminary grounds except to preach in some church in the evening. The Lord is giving grace and strength. I'm in an evangelistic campaign in Parna-Mirim until next Sunday and six souls have already come to the Lord. The other conference I had that finished last week was also owned of the Lord as the believers were quickened and built up. We also heard four souls call upon the name of the Lord at those meetings.

Perhaps it is not surprising that times of blessing are either accompanied or followed by tragedy or difficulty. Just around that time, Fred was passing through Manaus where he spent a few days before catching a boat up river again to Labrea. He took a bus to go to the city centre. Buses in Manaus were largely improvised coaches which were built on top of a chassis of a truck. They were badly balanced and as a result, they veered greatly to one side when rounding a corner and sometimes overturned.

The bus on which Fred travelled was quite full. Fred was standing when the driver took the bus around a corner with little or no reduction in his speed. Fred lost his balance and in an attempt to avoid toppling over on the seated passengers, he stretched out his left hand toward the window to stop his fall. At the moment of impact, his arm smashed right through the window pane. The jagged glass ripped through his arm, severing a main nerve and an artery. At the sight of blood, people began screaming for the driver to stop. Fred remained conscious even with the severe loss of blood. Cradling his left elbow in his right hand, he got someone to wrap a tourniquet around his arm to arrest the blood flow. He also had the presence of mind to call a taxi, which rushed him to a nearby hospital.

At the emergency department of the hospital, a doctor stitched up the laceration and told him he was fortunate not to have bled to death with such a severe gash. He also told Fred that the main motor nerve to his left hand had been severed and it was unlikely he would regain the full use of his hand. Fred had several subsequent operations on that arm but he never regained the full use of that hand.

He made a good recovery and after returning to Labrea, he was pleased to see that the work there continued to grow. However, Fred soon prepared to go on his second furlough. For medical reasons, Jack and Joan had to withdraw from Canutama. Anne McWhinnie also had to return home.

During the time Willard and Grace Stull lived in Manaus, they willingly looked after any Acre business that needed to be transacted in the city. In the interior there were no banks, so Willard was the contact person who received the missionaries allowance every three months from the local branch of the Bank of London and forwarded the money by trusted friends to the missionaries in the interior.

When Willard and Grace left Manaus to work with their mission in north east Brazil, Francisco Franco and Corina kindly filled the vacancy to look after the Acre business in the city. After they left Sena Madureira years earlier Francisco opened an office in their apartment in the centre of Manaus. Not long after he assumed the responsibility to attend to the Mission business, there was an increase in the number of new Acre missionaries arriving in the Amazon. Francisco was also able to secure another small apartment above his own which the mission rented for the use of the missionaries passing through Manaus.

Besides the increase in the number of foreign missionaries, the churches in the interior produced gifted young men and women for the Christian work. One of these was Francisco Poderoso, a poor boy, from Boca do Acre, who trusted the Lord at the end of a children's meeting. Even as a small boy, he showed good promise. As he emerged into his teenage years, Allen Loney took time to teach Francisco how to play the accordion and an opportunity was given to young Francisco to lead the young people's work.

When he was eighteen years old, Francisco went to the Baptist Seminary of Amazonas where he became one of their outstanding students. Today, Dr. Francisco Poderoso is a pastor, Bible teacher, soloist a musician and is one of the leading pastors in the Amazon.

He also speaks excellent English and has travelled abroad several times to sing and preach.

Pedro Moraes was also converted as a lad in the children's meetings in Boca do Acre. Like Francisco, he also trained at the Baptist Seminary of Amazonas, after which he returned to his home town where for more than twenty-five years he remained as pastor of the Boca do Acre church. These two lads were only the first fruits of the dozens of other young men and women who would be commissioned from these interior churches to serve the Lord all over Brazil and abroad.

Chapter Twelve

NEW THRESHOLDS

"It's big, it's bustling, it's Brazil," is a comment that was made back in the latter part of the twentieth century about the largest of Latin American countries. Brazil is still spoken about with superlatives. It is the fifth largest country in the world and with its vast natural resources and incalculable mineral wealth, it had the potential of equalling the United States for Gross National Product. In the middle of the last century it planned and built the most modern capital in the world, Brasilia. It also has one of the world's largest cities, São Paulo, and undoubtedly Rio de Janeiro is one of the world's most beautiful cities.

Since its discovery in 1500, this vast and potentially rich nation, the largest Roman Catholic country in all the world, was enslaved by superstition and held down by false religion for almost five hundred years. By the last quarter of the twentieth century, there was a dramatic turn around and Brazil had the fastest growing evangelical movement in the world.

Running parallel to this phenomenal growth was a military revolution in the early sixties that saved Brazil from sliding into Cuban style Marxism. Among other reforms, this new government made a nationwide drive to eradicate illiteracy. Education became the number one priority throughout the country.

The missionaries of the Acre Gospel Mission were not lacking in playing their part for education in the interior towns. They were not only motivated by the government's campaign, but also because of persecution and discrimination against believer's children. Such was the case in Canutama.

Victor and Audrey Maxwell travelled to Brazil with Fred Orr early in 1965, just two months after they were married. They had long followed with interest the work and missionaries of Acre, both by attending the Mission's prayer meetings and corresponding with the missionaries in Brazil. Victor, like some of the other workers, was a student at the WEC Missionary Training College and the Missionary School of Medicine in London, while Audrey did her Bible Training in Swansea in the Bible College of Wales.

After a short period of language study in Labrea where they first learned the ropes of missionary life, they went to work with Bill Woods in Canutama. God was blessing greatly in the town. Neighbours, whole families and some notorious characters were converted. So many converts were leaving the established Roman Catholic Church that the priest solicited help from the Bishop in Labrea. This did not stop the flow of conversions so the Spanish priest forbade the children of believers to attend the parochial school which was the only one in town.

Although Bill Woods continued to be involved with his visits to the Juma Indians, he started a school in an old house at the side of the church with only a few pupils. At first this class was organized to help some children at the upper end of their primary education. As demand grew from concerned parents to allow their children to attend this new class, it became necessary to build a school at the rear of the church. Although funds were low, the missionaries sacrificed what they had to erect a suitable building. For months Bill and Victor, neither of whom were carpenters, planed wood and worked hard to erect this simple structure at the rear of the church. When the two-classroom building was completed the church employed three teachers who taught from seven o'clock in the morning through late afternoon with two separate groups of forty children each.

The growing church in Boca do Acre also called for an educational programme at São Paulo, a small village on the other side of the river where a church was already well established. So many children there wanted to study, but it was difficult to travel to Boca do Acre every day. James bought an old house next door to the church in São Paulo and soon made sufficient benches and desks for the children. About fifty boys and girls were enrolled for the school and Raimunda, Pastor Pedro Moraes' sister, became the first teacher.

A similar situation prevailed in Labrea where the town council gave the church a piece of land nearby on which to build a school. This school also had several dedicated teachers with almost two hundred pupils. Although the Canutama school closed after five years because of improvements in the local educational situation, the Labrea school continued to function for several more years. Several of the first teachers went on to secure teaching posts in the University of Amazonas in Manaus while some pupils achieved high academic positions.

Just after the school started in Labrea, Robin McCready, from Richhill in County Armagh, joined Fred in Labrea as the latest recruit to the Acre Gospel Mission. Robin also completed the course at the Missionary School of Medicine after spending some years with the Faith Mission. Robin was blessed with a superb mellow voice which he used to sing the gospel even before learning to speak Portuguese. His arrival in Labrea also coincided with the first steps of putting up a new church building in the town, as the congregation had far outgrown the capacity of the verandah at the Mission house.

During this time, there were many marvellous conversions in the town. Some of these converts trusted the Lord in the meetings, while others were awakened to their need of Christ without even meeting a missionary. Perhaps no conversion was more dramatic than that of Raimundo Lobato. As a young man of eighteen years, Raimundo lived in a distant remote part of the forest. He and those who lived in that region made their meagre living from gathering Brazil nuts and extracting latex from the syringa trees. For daily provisions they hunted and fished.

One day he and a friend went on a hunting expedition to look for wild boar or deer. When they hunted down an animal, they would salt the meat and bring it back to the settlement to share with their families and friends. After the two friends had been hunting for three days, the younger man became ill with a roaring fever. Raimundo helped his companion into a hammock which he had swung between two trees. The lad was too ill to trek back to their settlement. Raimundo fell into great despair when the young man sank into unconsciousness. In spite of all that Raimundo tried to do for him, the friend died a short time later. There was no way of carrying his body back to the settlement which was two days trek away. He was obliged to wrap his friend's body in a hammock and bury him in a shallow grave.

When Raimundo arrived back without his friend, the people were stunned to hear the news of his death. However, no one was more dazed than Raimundo Lobato. The sudden death of his companion prompted him to ask probing questions about death, eternity, heaven and hell. When he spoke to his uncle about the matter, he said that he had an old Bible that he had picked up at one time. He gave the tattered volume to his nephew who began to slowly read the scriptures. Someone told Raimundo to tune his radio to the short-wave and listen to Trans World Radio. Without ever having met a missionary or another Christian, Raimundo trusted the Saviour and called upon God for mercy in the heart of the Brazilian forest.

After his conversion Raimundo read the scriptures each night to others on the settlement at the customary hour of the Catholic Novena. Within a few months almost forty people at that jungle clearing were converted without contact from outside missionary influences.

The more Raimundo read the scriptures, the more he wanted to know about Christ and to follow Him. Eager to be baptized, he decided to go to Labrea or Canutama, the nearest towns. If he was to travel by boat to either of these towns it would have taken almost three weeks but trekking overland he could make it in ten days. He walked to Labrea and on arrival at the Mission house, he requested to be baptized. It was a memorable day in his life when Raimundo shared his testimony with the church and was baptized in the River Purus by Pastor Jose Salsa.

Having tasted of the fellowship at the Labrea Church, Raimundo decided he would go back to the forest to gather his belongings and return to live in town. Providentially, Hazel Miskimmin was working with the Labrea church at this time and she took the new convert under her wing to encourage him in his Christian life. It soon became evident that this young man had good potential and soon the church gave him opportunity to develop his preaching ability.

Raimundo Lobato was not satisfied to remain in Labrea. Within a year, he left the interior to enroll at a Baptist Bible School in Manaus. He was advised and greatly supported by Hazel in this step. While at Bible College, Raimundo met and married Cila, who came from another distant part of Amazonas. After graduation, the young newly weds went to Labrea where Raimundo became the pastor of his home church. Later he received a call to the Canutama church and after a short spell there, he and his family returned to Manaus where he has pastored several Independent Baptist Churches.

When James and Dorrie left for furlough in 1965, Allen and Ada Loney led the work in Boca do Acre and tried to cope with the growing pains of the church. The young people's work was very encouraging, yet they suffered some reverses.

Black Fever, which had already ravaged the lower Purus, had reached the Boca do Acre region. The story of one family reflects on some of the heartache that this deadly fever left in its wake. Allen and Ada wrote about Raimundo.

Just four weeks ago, we witnessed the death of one of our choice young boys, Raimundo. He was just fourteen years old. His life was precious to the Lord and to all those who knew him. Until he was six years old, Raimundo lived in the heart of the forest with his parents and five little brothers and sisters. It was then that his grandmother brought him to live in Boca do Acre, but the rest of his family remained at the forest home.

One day Black Fever arrived in that remote area. Although the mother pleaded with the Virgin Mary and all the saints that she had ever heard of to spare her children, within three months all her children fell victim to this fatal scourge. In one day, two little homemade coffins were carried out of their forest dwelling and three died in one week.

Raimundo's mum and dad left their jungle home and came to visit grandmother in Boca do Acre. They had decided to take Raimundo with them to another location in the forest farther from town. He was their only remaining child, but he also became the first ray of gospel light to shine into that home. While living with his grandma in Boca do Acre, Raimundo trusted the Lord Jesus at Dorrie's children's meeting.

Not long after arriving in the new location in the forest, Raimundo became ill. The mother was in complete despair. Again she called on the saints but nothing happened. It was then, she heard her own son pray to the Father in heaven in the name of the Lord Jesus Christ. She decided to pray to Jesus for her only son whom she thought was dying. Through that experience, the young boy led his mother to personal faith in the Saviour. She had promised the Lord that if Raimundo was spared she would dedicate him to the Lord for life.

The Lord did spare the young boy and soon the whole family left the forest to live at Terra Firme, across the river from Boca do Acre. At the church here in town, his father also trusted the Lord under James' preaching.

Raimundo was the life and soul of the youth in the church and lived for the day when he would soon be old enough to go to Bible College to train for the Lord's work. Besides studying at the local school, Raimundo got a job carrying fresh water from a well to people in town. With the money he earned, he bought material for his mother to make him a shirt and trousers for James and Dorrie's arrival.

Sadly, he never got wearing those clothes. He arrived home from town one day and was somewhat listless. Rather than eat lunch, he preferred to lie in his hammock. On the third day he went into a coma. His parents then recognized the telltale and all too familiar signs of the dreaded Black Fever. Despite a lot of attention given by Susan Scott, Raimundo passed away after only five days of sickness. He was buried across the river in Terra Firme.

Little Raimundo had been preparing the young people at Boca do Acre for the arrival of James and Dorrie, who had been on furlough the previous year. The missionary couple whom he loved greatly regretted that he did not survive long enough to meet them again. However, when they did arrive, they did not come alone. Four new missionaries were accepted for the work in Brazil and arrived in Manaus for Christmas 1966.

Dr. Tom and Ethel Geddis from Lurgan were converted as children and as teenage sweethearts, they became familiar with the work of the Mission. God had challenged Tom through Ina Orr's death while he was still a student. Besides Ethel being a nurse and midwife, Tom qualified in medicine at Queens University, Belfast and afterwards gained a lot of experience in preparation for going to Brazil. He acquired valuable surgical skills as he worked alongside surgeons in various hospitals in Northern Ireland and then, after two years as medical officer on Ascension Island, he pursued courses of Tropical Medicine at the Ross Institute in London. Following these Tom and Ethel did their Bible Training at the well-known Bible Training Institute in Glasgow before leaving for Brazil.

The arrival of Tom and Ethel in Brazil was a big step forward for the work in the Amazon, in view of the great medical needs and challenge in the interior. Until then, the missionaries had done a sterling job in difficult and isolated regions with little or no medical help, even though some were not even trained in the rudiments of medicine. To have a doctor and his wife join the team was a great boost to all the workers in Brazil and would soon give a new direction for the work.

Just a few weeks after Tom and Ethel's departure from Belfast with James and Dorrie, Hazel Miskimmin also sailed for Brazil with another two new missionaries, Thelma Peters and Lenore Graham. Thelma, a nurse and midwife from the South of England, did her Bible training at Emmanuel Bible College in Birkenhead, near

Liverpool. It was while at Bible College that Thelma heard Mollie present the needs of Brazil and through that word, God challenged her.

Lenore had known about the Mission and the missionaries since she was a child. Her parents started a prayer meeting for Mollie Harvey and the McCombs when they sailed for the Acre in 1937. Always with a view to the mission field, Lenore trained as a teacher in Belfast. After a few years of teaching in the city, she was constrained to apply for the work in Brazil after her Bible training at the Bible Training Institute in Glasgow.

These new missionaries were introduced to the work in Brazil after joining all the other workers for a memorable Field Conference in Boca do Acre just weeks after they arrived.

At that conference, several major changes took place in the work and placement of personnel. James and Dorrie had received an invitation to return to Sena Madureira as Sander Tonneson and his wife were leaving Brazil permanently to return to Norway. It was also at that conference when Bill Woods indicated his desire to study medicine at the University of Amazonas, with a view of devoting himself to a leprosy programme. Tom and Ethel were assigned to study Portuguese Rio Branco while Lenore was invited to teach at São Paulo, near Boca do Acre, after she and Thelma completed their language study in Manaus. The Lord had other plans for Thelma.

During that conference, there was a special week of meetings at the Boca do Acre church. On Saturday night, the missionaries mingled with a crowd who listened to different believers testify at an open air meeting in the town square. One man who listened attentively shared with Victor and Fred his desire to accept the Lord the following day at church. The two missionaries invited the friend to trust the Lord that very night, but he declined because he had already arranged a festa (a party and dance) at a hall he had hired. He assured them that he would be at church the following morning.

Later that night at the festa, there was a fracas. The same man who told the missionaries he would trust the Lord the following day got involved in a fight with a young man. He was arrested but the young man escaped. Early the next morning, the police took the man from the cell in order to identify the young man who lived across the river from the Mission house. As the two policemen and prisoner crossed the river, someone warned the sixteen-year-old boy that the police were coming to arrest him. Instead of fleeing into the forest, the young man grabbed his rifle and cocked it into position at the window of his mother's home. He took careful aim and then one solitary bullet whistled through the air. It caught the prisoner in the temple, and he fell from the canoe into the River Acre. His body was never found.

There was a solemn air in the meetings that Sunday when news broke out that the man who had intended to trust the Lord that day had already passed into eternity, the victim of cold blooded murder.

Following the conference, the missionaries dispersed to their designated assignments in scattered towns. Bill Woods settled into the work in Boca do Acre. Besides attending to all the work of the church and travelling extensively throughout the forest to evangelize the unreached, Bill also set up his first programme to treat the many leprosy patients he had encountered in the town and surrounding district. He acquired the help of Francisco Poderoso, who was back in his home town to serve the Lord for a year as part of his seminary course. This partnership was the forerunner of greater things to come.

Lenore completed her studies of Portuguese and returned to the Boca do Acre to work alongside Raimunda at the São Paulo School. She was most patient and dedicated in teaching the children in a rural and interior school after her former experience at home. Travelling to and from school each day was trying, as it involved negotiating a journey by canoe on a treacherous stretch of the Rivers Purus and Acre. But her work was greatly appreciated by the children, many of whom walked quite a distance from Terra Firme and the surrounding forest to learn their reading, writing and arithmetic each day.

Outside school hours, Lenore also became fully involved in the work of the church and its various outreaches in the region.

In Sena Madureira, James and Dorrie were greatly thrilled to see the development of the church. Not only were so many congregations established up river, down river and along the forest trails, but several young people were sent to study at the Baptist Seminary of Amazonas in Manaus.

In town, the church leadership also recognized their need for the education of the numerous children who attended the church but were pressurized into attending parochial schools during the week. The church was able to provide a fine body of qualified Christian teachers. Providently they were joined by Jean Starritt, a teacher from Ramelton in County Donegal, who besides her teacher training qualifications had also spent some years at the Faith Mission Bible School in Edinburgh.

When Jean joined these teachers, they made a great impact in the town and soon they had over two hundred children studying each day. In 1969 Jean sent this report for the Acre Missionary News.

> The month of March marked a new chapter in Sena Madureira when the new school was opened. About three hundred people met for a short dedication ceremony.
>
> We have four good classrooms that were constructed by James and his helpers who worked more than twelve hours some days to have it completed in time.
>
> The Lord has wonderfully provided seven Christian women and girls to teach, two of whom are being paid by the government. The others receive a small gratuity from the church. There are over two hundred pupils enrolled. The junior classes are from 7a.m. - 11a.m., and seniors are from 1p.m. - 5p.m. Each class has a period of Religious Instruction daily. Do pray that as the 'Good Seed' is sown we will see many of these young people come to know Jesus Christ as their Saviour.
>
> The school is called "Ebenezer." This is certainly a testimony to God's help and faithfulness to the believers in Sena Madureira and as we launch forth on this vital ministry we are assured of His help in the future.

Sadly, Jean had to leave Sena after only two years because of ill health. She was a big loss to the Ebenezer School but made a lasting impact on the teaching staff.

While looking for accommodation in Rio Branco, Tom and Ethel met a man who as a youth had been taught the basics of photography by Mr. William McComb and now had a thriving photographic business. He was able to secure an apartment for them to rent at a new maternity hospital in town. Now they were able to get down to language study.

While in the Acre capital, they also made contacts and built friendships with local doctors at the hospital. These contacts proved to be providential for when Bill Woods arrived from Boca do Acre with an acutely inflamed appendix, Tom was able to use the facilities at the maternity unit to operate on Bill. The fact that a bachelor underwent an operation in the maternity hospital gave rise to plenty of amusement.

On the very day Tom and Ethel transferred to Sena to complete their language study, Tom was called to an emergency. A man had arrived from the interior with a strangulated hernia. There was no other doctor in town and little possibility of the man being flown to Rio Branco for surgery. Tom had to open the barrels that he brought from home to find some of his surgical equipment. After sterilizing instruments and gowns on the gas stove and oven, he operated on the man with James in attendance.

A few days later, the man seemed to have made a good recovery from his emergency operation. The patient, an extremely poor man from the forest, was ever so grateful for what Tom was able to do but sheepishly asked James how much the operation might cost. James knew it would not cost the man anything but he courteously translated the question to Tom. With a bit of typical humour, Tom joked and said that it would not cost any more than five thousand dollars.

What was humour to the missionaries was taken rather seriously by the poor man. Fearing he might have to pay such a hefty bill, the poor man absconded from the small hospital in the middle of the night and was never seen again.

After a period of language study, Tom and Ethel were praying about where they might serve the Lord. It was not their original intention to necessarily engage in medical work. They had arrived in Brazil primarily as missionaries with a burden to plant churches and take the gospel to the unreached. However, Tom could not close his eyes to the great need everywhere he went. He worked at a small clinic in the town and treated the sick with a lot of medicines he had brought from home.

News of Tom's medical work soon got to the ears of the governor of Acre. Just when Tom and Ethel were praying about their future and discussing it with James as Field Leader, the Governor of Acre summoned Tom to the State Palace in Rio Branco.

When Tom arrived in the capital, the governor received him enthusiastically and explained that the State government was in great need for qualified doctors to work in the interior towns and asked Tom if he and Ethel would be prepared to go to Tarauacá. The *Acre Missionary News* carried a report of this move in March 1968.

> Since the last writing, much has happened about our next move. The government has asked us to go to a place called Tarauacá since there is no doctor there. After much thought, we have provisionally accepted this invitation. The authorities of the town are providing a house (just newly built!) and there is also a small hospital with about fifteen beds. We repeatedly made it clear to the authorities that we were primarily interested in missionary work. We have learned that there are no missionaries in the town but that there is a small Assembly of God Church there.
>
> The governor and the town authorities said that there would be no hindrance put in our way at all. Indeed, they would try to assist with transportation if we wanted to journey on the river to hold clinics and meetings in the different centres. We made a quick trip over to see the situation. Tarauacá is a town of about four thousand people that serves a very wide area. The potential "practice" would be near twenty thousand people scattered over an area larger than Northern Ireland. We are very happy about the move but at the same time scared stiff. If we did not believe that God is able, we would not dare to venture.
>
> We have finally arrived here. About ten days ago, the Brazilian Air Force very kindly made a special flight to bring us here, including our baggage. Praise the Lord the transport of all our baggage was free. The local authorities

have been giving us V. I. P. treatment all the way. We have been provided with a nice new brick bungalow along with the necessary furniture. Tom has been very busy. He goes to the clinic each weekday from 7:30 a.m. through to 11 a.m. He also looks after the hospital and any house calls.

At that time Tarauacá was one of the most westerly and remote towns in all Brazil, almost three thousand miles from the mouth of the Amazon River. The invitation given to Tom and Ethel was only a foot in a new door that would soon swing wide open. Tom's medical and surgical skills quickly made a big impression on the people in Tarauacá, but for the first few months, he and Ethel did not venture into starting meetings. They judged it better to work and overcome any suspicions of why a British doctor and his wife should set up home and come to work in one of the most remote regions of Brazil. This proved to be a wise strategy that later paid dividends when the first meetings were initiated.

The Mission's work was progressing on all other fronts and other happy developments took place just at that time. Robin McCready and Thelma Peters were married in the Faith Regular Baptist Church in Manaus on 10th January, 1968. After Robin's spell with Fred in Labrea following their wedding, he and Thelma went to work in Canutama to replace Victor and Audrey who had gone to take Bill's place in Boca do Acre.

Just over a year later in Manaus, on 1st February, 1969, Fred Orr and Zení Pinheiro were married at Cachoeirinha Regular Baptist Church, which was founded by their friend Willard Stull. Fred had remained a widower for fifteen years and many people had been praying that he would find a suitable partner and helpmeet in his work. Zení's family originated from near Canutama where her uncle was a deacon in the Canutama church. After her own conversion, she studied for four years at the Amazonas Baptist Seminary. Following their wedding, they returned to Labrea to continue in the work that Fred was greatly committed to.

In between these two weddings, Mollie Harvey returned to Northern Ireland for the final time after serving more than thirty years in the Amazon. She was a great woman and many will greet her in the Tabernacles of Glory because of the sacrifices she made and the long life she devoted to her Lord. More than thirty years in the Amazon in those early years was some accomplishment for a woman who was initially told that she would not live more than a year in the Green Hell. When she got back to Ulster, all the doctors who warned her had already died and Mollie lived on to be more than ninety-two years old.

Perhaps it was most appropriate that when Mollie retired from Brazil, another member of her home church, Shankill Baptist Church, should arrive in Brazil that same year. Paul and Reta Mayner arrived in Manaus late in 1969. Paul was from a Brethren Assembly in Birmingham, and Reta, a nurse and midwife, was a member of Shankill Baptist Church in Belfast. They met and fell in love while both were students at the Bible College of Wales in Swansea.

After their arrival in Brazil and subsequent language study, they replaced Robin and Thelma in Canutama. Like Thelma before her, Reta gave great medical attention to the sick and suffering of the town. Among those who trusted the Saviour in Canutama at that time was a young boy called Plinho. Later he went to a Baptist Bible School in Manaus and entered into the work of the Acre Gospel Mission in Brazil.

Another thing that marked Paul and Reta's tenure in Canutama was that they were the last foreign missionaries to work in that town. They had to leave Canutama after several years because of illness to their oldest son, David. After they left Canutama, Miquel Nogueira, an evangelist from Sena Madureira, went to pastor the Canutama church. Under his ministry, the work prospered as it never had before.

Miquel was a charismatic character who never had any formal Bible school training, but he was the person who first welcomed Mollie, James and Dorrie to his home at Itapira, an eight hours' walk into the forest. Since his conversion, he always had a passion for souls and invited hundreds of forest dwellers to his home in the jungle to hear the gospel. Now he had given himself full time to the ministry of the gospel.

It was also in 1969 that Bill moved to Manaus and started his medical studies at the University of Amazonas.

The missionaries had arranged to meet for their annual conference in Manaus in January 1969. That meant that some of them travelled eight or ten days by boat to be present in Manaus, while others required two flights and travelled almost two thousand miles to be there.

James and Dorrie, who required two flights to get to Manaus, were finding difficulties in trying to secure a flight out of Sena Madureira due to the heavy rains that had closed the town's airstrip, which was little more than a level field. However, on 13th January, an Air Force plane came to town to pick up a group of medical students who had been sent to Sena Madureira to set up different clinics for the benefit of the local people. The DC 3 Air Force plane was due to take off no later than 4:30 p.m. to make the half-hour flight to Rio Branco. The lack of landing lights in Rio Branco prohibited night flights so no aircraft was allowed to be in the air in that region later than 5 p.m. since night fall came around 6 p.m.

At the last minute, James and Dorrie were able to obtain places on the flight. They hurriedly gathered their belongings and got to the airport within a few hours. The short flight allowed them to catch a commercial flight to Manaus on the following day.

The students and Air Force crew left rather late to embark on the plane. Finally, the old plane taxied down the runway and climbed into the air at exactly 4.30 p.m., the latest permissible time for take off. On board, the passengers sat facing each other on parallel benches that ran down either side of the aircraft. James was seated farther up the plane from Dorrie. As the DC 3 levelled off above the clouds and forest, there was a lot of merriment and fun. Students undid their seat belts and began to dance the Brazilian Samba up and down the narrow aisle.

After twenty minutes, James, who was familiar with the usual route of this flight, noticed that the sun was not located in the usual direction in relation to the aircraft. Furthermore, the forest below had not begun to thin out as was usually the case when approaching Rio Branco. He said nothing but inwardly prayed that the Lord would look after them.

By the time they were three quarters of an hour into the flight, the singing and dancing ceased and an eerie atmosphere descended on the plane. After half past five o'clock, the plane was still at the same altitude and the gloom of the evening was quickly enveloping the ground down below. It would be totally dark by six o'clock. Dorrie kept looking anxiously up the aisle of the plane towards James. People around her were crying and some had their rosary beads in their hands. By the look on their faces, they might as well have been worry beads rather than prayers.

The captain emerged from the cockpit door and appealed for everyone to be calm. He admitted that they were lost over the jungle and that their navigational aids were down. He wished everyone well and said that they were doing everything possible to bring them safely to ground.

James edged down the aisle to where Dorrie was sitting and knelt at her knee. Tears coursed down Dorrie's cheeks as she said, "James what will the missionaries think when they see the state of the house we left when we ran out in a hurry? James, we'll not see our wee dog Spot again."

James consoled Dorrie as he held her hand and spoke assumingly, "Dorrie, the Lord will preserve us for when I was ill some time ago, He gave me a promise from Isaiah 46:4, 'And even to your old age I am He; and even to hoar hairs will I carry you.' James was serious as he continued, "Dorrie, my hair may be going white but I am not old yet for I am only fifty-eight."

By this time, the plane was totally shrouded in the darkness of the night as the monotonous sound of the engines droned on. Dorrie asked James to take the Daily Light out of her bag. This was Samuel Bagster's well proven daily readings from the scriptures that James and Dorrie read every morning and evening. Turning to the portion for the evening of 13th January, she read the first line, "Let not the sun go down upon thy wrath."

Dorrie was disappointed with this ironic word, seeing the sun had already gone down over the forest and they were lost. Dorrie whispered, "The evening and the morning are the same to you, Lord. Let us see what the morning says." As she read the morning portion, tears swelled again into her eyes.

January 13th   Morning

Thou wilt keep him in perfect peace, whose mind is stayed on thee.

Cast thy burden upon the LORD, and he shall sustain thee; he shall never suffer the righteous to be moved. - I will trust, and not be afraid: for the LORD JEHOVAH is my strength and my song; he also is become my salvation.

Why are ye fearful, O ye of little faith? - Be careful for nothing; but in every thing by prayer and supplication with thanksgiving let your requests be made known unto God. And the peace of God, which passeth all understanding, shall keep your hearts and minds through Christ Jesus. - In quietness and in confidence shall be your strength.

The effect of righteousness [shall be] quietness and assurance for ever. - Peace I leave with you, my peace I give unto you: not as the world giveth, give I unto you. Let not your heart be troubled, neither let it be afraid.

-Peace, from him which is, and which was, and which is to come.

Even though the tears flowed down her cheeks, yet the peace of God that she had been reading of, flooded Dorrie's heart. In that moment, she gained the assurance that all would be well even though they seemed to be trapped in a doomed aircraft.

At almost seven o'clock, the Air Force captain emerged again from the door that led to the cockpit. Everyone listened attentively as he cleared his throat and told his passengers that he had some good news. Another plane had found them and was flying above them to guide them back to Rio Branco. This other Air Force plane, also a DC3, had been dispatched from Rio Branco to search for the missing aircraft. It flew in ever widening circles from the capital until it found the lost flight on the borders of Bolivia and more than one hundred miles from Rio Branco. Everyone prayed that there would be enough fuel left to get them back to the Acre capital.

In Rio Branco, the airport authorities summoned a number of car and truck drivers to form an avenue of headlights on either side of the concrete runway to help guide the planes to land. The fire brigade and ambulance crews had never faced an emergency like this before but prepared themselves for disaster even though they were praying for a safe return of both aircraft.

When everything was in place, the first DC3 with the anxious passengers on board descended from the darkness and cautiously touched down before speeding up the lighted airstrip between the assembled cars. A cheer went up from the crowd of families and friends who had gathered in the nearby airport terminal. As this plane cleared the runway, the second DC3 with the search party on board also touched down. Again, the crowd roared their approval with shouts of relief that both planes had made it and all was well.

When the doors of the aircraft opened, the passengers poured out with obvious displays of relief to be safely on the ground. Several retched unceremoniously and suffered nausea after they descended from the plane. With the relief from tension, some adults cried openly like children. The mayor of Rio Branco and many city authorities gathered at the airport to greet the passengers and crews. Families and friends could not be restrained as they ran out from the terminal to meet their loved ones with tight embraces amid floods of tears.

A member of the crew told James afterwards that they had made it back to Rio Branco with barely twenty minutes of fuel left in the tank. James and Dorrie remembered it was Monday night. Surely people at home had been praying for them at the Acre prayer meeting. James knew that God's angels do their work well and that God's promise to carry him to hoar hairs and old age still stood firm.

It says a lot for God's grace, which enabled James and Dorrie to board another DC3 early the next morning and proceed on a six-hour bumpy flight to Manaus to meet their colleagues at the Mission conference.

Chapter Thirteen

WHAT NEXT?

One of the first obstacles the missionary must overcome is a new language. Culture shock and adjusting to a new climate are chicken feed compared to trying to learn new phonetic sounds, memorizing the conjugation of regular and irregular verbs and trying to sort out the gender of nouns. They all have made their embarrassing mistakes, and happy is the missionary who can laugh at those slips and errors and then learn by them.

Victor never forgot arriving in Brazil after six weeks at sea and feeling that he needed a hair cut. That was back in the days when all men had a short "back and sides" haircut every two weeks. On the second day after disembarking in Manaus, he ventured into what was obviously a barber's shop which had a large propeller-like fan rotating above the customer's head.

When his turn came, Victor sat on the chair and motioned to the barber to cut his hair. It was the only way he knew how to convey what might have seemed to be the obvious, but Victor needed to do that for other men were there to have their finger nails manicured and that definitely was not for him. The fast-moving barber was soon making short work of Victor's hair and within minutes his head was almost bald. Seeing the damage being done to his wavey hair, Victor was alarmed and wanted to tell the barber he had cut off enough hair but he was at a loss to know how to communicate this to him. Just then the new missionary remembered the few traffic lights in the city centre where the red signal carried the word "pare," which he took for granted to mean stop.

In vain hope, Victor repeated that same word to the barber, "Pare, pare."

The man stopped cutting instantly and looked quizzically at his client. Again Victor repeated the same two words, "Pare, pare."

It was only then that the hairdresser really went to town and completely cropped the missionary's head, leaving just a short tuft of hair at the front. The rest of his hair was virtually shaved off. Victor had unwittingly been treated to a new style of haircut that was locally known as a "militar." This style obviously gained its name from recruits having their hair cropped as they entered the army. The raw missionary realised he had said the wrong thing to the barber. Fred told him later that the barber must have thought he had said, "apare," which means to trim or to shorten. Victor made sure to learn how to speak to the barber before he made another visit to a hairdressing salon.

Children have no such problems with language study. When growing up in a foreign country, they generally learn to speak the language much better than their parents. Sometimes they are even able to teach mum and dad a few words that the missionary might never have heard before, wholesome words and otherwise.

With so many young couples joining the ranks of the Acre Gospel Mission, there soon was the pitter-patter of tiny feet in the missionaries' homes. Missionary kids, MKs, as they are often referred to, have little choice about where they live or what deprivations they might suffer. They are reared in the culture their parents have chosen to live in. Sometimes there are hardships which perhaps are felt more keenly by the parents than the children. Living in a different culture also has benefits for the missionary parents and their children. Furthermore, missionary kids enjoy the blessing of being born into a Christian home. Often for the missionary parents, their children unlock doors and break down barriers of suspicion locally.

When Victor and Audrey went to visit Tarauacá in August 1968, just a few months after Tom and Ethel had arrived in the town, their daughter Sharon was just seven months old. Although the Maxwells' stay was planned for only two weeks, events soon changed those plans. While Tom worked three days a week at the clinic and another two days undertaking surgical operations at the small São São Gomes Hospital, Audrey and Ethel put Sharon in a baby buggy and wheeled her all around town. The more they visited people, the more they sensed a hunger and opportunity for the gospel from the local people. A week into the visit with times of prayer each evening, both couples felt it was time to make a venture and start five days of children's open-air meetings down by the riverside.

On the first afternoon, a large entourage of children followed the foreigners and the baby down a rickety boardwalk that led to a wide open field near the river. The four missionaries soon got started by singing some choruses with actions. Although the meetings were ostensibly arranged for children, the missionaries were also aiming at the many adults who either peered from the vantage of their open windows at what was going on or gathered in the circle with the children .

Day after day, the numbers grew until well over a hundred children and adults were present to listen to the gospel message. By the end of the week, it became apparent that now that these meetings had started with such momentum, it would be wrong to stop at that. After some thought and prayer, it was decided that Victor should return to Boca do Acre while Audrey remained with Tom and Ethel to help them develop what they had already started.

Tom was able to purchase a house near the centre of town. It was an old wooden structure elevated on stilts five feet above ground level to avoid the periodic flooding. Some modifications were made to the old house and soon it was converted into a meeting place. Ethel and Audrey put Tom's prestige to good use and began to visit many of the town's prominent families. After several weeks, they returned to these same homes and invited the ladies to a special gathering for women at the meeting house.

The first time the ladies got together, it seemed more of a social encounter except for the fact that Ethel and Audrey sang to the ladies and gave a simple Bible study on Mary, the mother of Jesus. The women seemed to be very impressed but a little perplexed that Ethel and Audrey should speak so well of the Virgin Mary, since the priest had warned them to have nothing to do with these Protestant foreigners.

A few subsequent meetings for both children and the ladies gave good opportunity of sowing the Word of God. At those first children's meetings, two little sisters, nine and ten years old, went home to their mother and told her that they loved the meetings and wanted to become Christians. The mother was somewhat frightened lest the daughters should provoke the wrath of their ill tempered father who was not only furiously opposed to evangelicals, but was also a notorious drunkard.

One Sunday night, the two girls secretly attended the church service and afterwards they spoke to Ethel, who, having pointed them to the Lord, encouraged the girls to tell their parents of their conversion when they arrived home. Their mother was quite happy but their father was furious.

"It is a disgrace on my family," he said, and administered a severe beating on his two daughters. He forbade them to go near any more meetings. The older girl never returned to the church but the younger daughter kept attending the meetings. Her mother was aware of this but it was without her father's knowledge or consent.

Her mother, Dona Francisca, was so impressed with what her young daughter said she was learning at the meetings that soon she began listening to the gospel programmes from Trans World Radio and The Voice of the Andes. After almost six months, she got the courage to attend the church services even though she knew this would incur her husband's disapproval. Her daughter's changed life and the simplicity of the gospel message constrained Dona Francisca to accept the Saviour. She did not expect life to be easy when her husband found out about her conversion, but she remained faithful both to the Lord and her husband in spite of his occasional violent attacks.

Dona Francisca never ceased to pray for her husband and family. Although he disowned his converted daughter because she had become a Christian, she continued to show him respect and love with small presents and cards at Christmas time and on Father's day. Only many years later did they have the joy of pointing the father to the Saviour as he neared the end of his life. Interestingly, all those cards, although not acknowledged at the time, were discovered neatly tied in a bundle among his personal papers after he died.

The name of that daughter was Lucimar de Souza. Tom and Ethel, who had no children of their own, took a particular interest in this sweet little girl and invited her to live and work in their home. Most families in the town employed young people to work as a means of supporting them. This was the beginning of a friendship in which Lucimar became a permanent part of Tom and Ethel's family, unofficially their adopted daughter.

Two months after these children's and ladies' meetings began, Victor returned to Tarauacá late in November 1968 to take Audrey and Sharon back to Boca do Acre before going on furlough. Upon learning how things were progressing, he and Tom planned a week of special evangelistic meetings. Tom and Victor spent a week working in the hot sun, making benches to provide seating for those who might venture to attend the first Sunday meetings in the old renovated house.

Personal invitations were given by word of mouth around the town. On the same Sunday afternoon that the special evangelistic event was to begin, Tom and Victor walked down the broad Tarauacá main street and were startled to hear their names and the planned meetings being denounced from the Catholic Church's public address system. By his verbal attack on the missionaries, the priest had actually done them a big favour because many people in town did not know about the meetings until they heard the priest's tirade on the public address system.

The hearts of the missionaries were lifted up to the Lord in prayer throughout that day. The meeting was scheduled to start at 7:30 and by 7:15 the meeting house was still empty. Just then the bells from the church began to ring, marking the end of the evening Novena.

Crowds poured out of the Catholic church and many of them made their way to the first evangelistic meetings in that old house.

Within a short time, more than a hundred people packed into the makeshift church. Every seat was taken. Some people sat on the floor while others stood on the verandah. That meeting was the first time for most of these people to hear the gospel. Throughout that week, they came back night after night. By the end of the first week, sixteen people professed faith in Jesus Christ.

That was the beginning of a work that grew and progressed in leaps and bounds week after week. Frequently, ten or twenty people were converted each week. Neighbours who vowed never to attend a meeting listened to the gospel from the verandah of their nearby homes and were converted. People from all walks of life trusted the Saviour, some who were clean living religious folk and others who had lived exceedingly immoral lives.

The old house was extended five times to accommodate the growing numbers coming to the church, before it was finally knocked down three years later and a larger wooden church was built on the same site. At times, that building was packed to capacity with over two hundred and fifty people in attendance.

After eleven years, the wooden building was replaced with a beautiful brick structure that was well finished within and without and had a capacity exceeding three hundred people. Beyond the central church in town, church workers and missionaries established nine other congregations on the river, eight congregations out through the forest and another two congregations in town.

There was a real move of the Holy Spirit in the region, as the missionaries moved out to evangelize on the surrounding rivers. These journeys which generally lasted for a month were not easy, but they were most rewarding as scores of people accepted the Saviour on first hearing the gospel. Sometimes the missionaries and Brazilian workers were sternly opposed by the local priest but in almost every place they stopped, they were warmly welcomed by the people.

There is no doubt that medical and surgical prowess greatly benefited the preaching of the gospel in that area and helped to give the missionaries an influence and favour that they did not necessarily enjoy elsewhere. Dr. Tom's name was not only greatly respected in the town, but people even arrived in Tarauacá from the capital to consult Dr. Tom or request to have an operation with Tom in Tarauacá.

There was also an element in the town in the early days which tried to undermine Tom's presence in Tarauacá and even have him arrested. As a result of this illegal move there was almost an uprising in the town in support of Tom. It was led by the highest authority in Tarauacá, Dr. Quirino, the local judge. He uncovered a plot that was hatched by a local policeman who for many years as administrator of the hospital made a livelihood by exploiting the people. Tom's work and integrity put an end to this man's exploitation who saw that the only way to restore his lucrative activity was to use his police authority to remove Dr. Tom from the town. Because of this scary incident, in an amazing turn of events, the instigator of the treacherous move was expelled from Tarauacá and forbidden to return.

Travel to Tarauacá was not easy. The trip from Manaus to Tarauacá by airplane required two flights over a period of two days and at times this could cost as much as a transatlantic flight. To travel by boat took a minimum of a month in the rainy season or two months in the dry season. Flights between Tarauacá and Rio Branco were rare except for individuals who flew private single engine aircraft taxis back and forth each day. Tragically, many of these planes lost their way over the jungle. Some ran out of fuel or were caught in fierce rainstorms while others crashed because of the pilot's incompetence. In these all too frequent crashes, many friends of the missionaries were needlessly killed.

One day, Tom and Ethel were returning to Tarauacá from Rio Branco in a small two-engine air-taxi together with a sick lady who had been to the capital for treatment and was accompanied by her husband. When they were half way into their flight and flying over dense jungle at an altitude of ten thousand feet, a propeller snapped. Fortunately, Paulo, the pilot, was able to stop the engine and steady the plane which was shuddering violently. Suddenly, beads of sweat formed on his brow as he told his four passengers he would have to turn back to the nearest town, which was Sena Madureira. Tom and Ethel prayed while Paulo piloted the stricken craft back in search of an airstrip. God took care of them and although they only had one engine, they made a safe landing in Sena Madureira. Even though James and Dorrie were not in town at the time, their house was a welcome haven for the four stranded passengers during the four days they had to wait for another plane to come and take them on the rest of their journey.

Tom's medical work continued to make a big impact on the region and greatly supplemented the work in the church. One of the early cases that first made a big impression in town was after a violent fight at a festa one Saturday evening. Each weekend these fights were a regular occurrence in Tarauacá, and were aided and abetted by ample supplies of liquor. The situation was made even worse by the use of large machetes or fish knives that were all too readily available. Their use often resulted in murder.

In the small hours of one Thursday morning, Tom was awakened to attend to a casualty of yet another brutal fight. At the front gate of his house a crowd was milling around. In the middle of the crowd, two men shouldered a long pole on which a hammock was suspended. They were waiting for the doctor to emerge. By the aid of a flashlight, Dr. Tom examined a young man lying in the hammock. His head, face and clothes were soaked with blood, and his breathing was rapid and shallow. The distraught family members told how that in a fight during a wedding party someone had struck the victim over the head with a long machete, obviously with the intent to kill him.

When the party carrying the poor victim arrived at the hospital, the seriousness of the situation became even clearer. The blow with the sharp machete had sliced open the left side of his skull, which resulted in a long wound stretching from below his left cheek bone to behind his left ear. With the skull bone penetrated, it left brain tissue damaged and exposed. The young man was very shocked, having lost a lot of blood. When Tom asked his friends to donate blood to help save the patient, they all disappeared. Tom thought that little could be done for the poor victim apart from dressing the wound.

Although Tom thought the unfortunate man would die during the night, he was surprised on the next morning to find his condition was unchanged. The case was so grave it merited treatment in a highly developed neuro-surgical unit with a team of skilled surgeons and anaesthetists. However, what does one doctor do in the heart of the forest with limited resources?

Having arranged some blood from volunteer donors and anaesthetized the patient; with a fervent prayer for help, Tom began to repair the damage.

God in His gracious mercy spared Adalberto. Following a rather stormy period during which he needed to have part of the head wound reopened to drain a blood clot from his brain, he made a very good recovery. When he left hospital about six weeks later, his only complaints were of partial loss of vision in one eye and mild epileptic seizures which were controlled with medication.

News of this operation spread around Tarauacá like wild fire, even in Rio Branco and beyond. The news gathered greater dimensions when it was reported that Tom was doing neuro-surgery in Tarauacá. For obvious reasons the victim gained the nickname of " Cabeça –aberta," which means "Open-head".

Although previously opposed to the gospel, Adalberto began to attend the church and after some months accepted Jesus Christ as his Saviour. He smiled when the comment was made that the Lord had to open his head to get the gospel in. Years later, he moved to Rio Branco and found employment as an attendant at a petrol station. Ironically, Adalberto was shot dead during a robbery at that station.

Time and space would prohibit cataloguing the hundreds of operations performed and lives saved through Tom and Ethel's ministry in Tarauacá. More importantly, hundreds came to a saving knowledge of Jesus Christ and several of these are serving God in many other parts of Brazil. In Tarauacá, Tom became even more popular than the state governor. When Tom and Ethel arrived back from their furloughs to the United Kingdom, the airport was crowded to receive the hero of the town.

The Missionary Aviation Fellowship (MAF) serviced the New Tribes (NTM) missionaries in that whole region and operated out of Erunipé, a town two days down river from Tarauacá. Frequently, the MAF flew both missionaries and Indians out from the many tribal areas for emergency treatment in Tarauacá. Often the missionary patients convalesced in Tom and Ethel's home for weeks on end.

Ethel, thrilled to see what the Lord was doing in the Tarauacá church, dedicated her time to Sunday school and children's work. Always the perfectionist, Ethel felt that if a job had to be done for the Lord, it must be done well. For that reason, Ethel sat at her desk daily and learned next week's lesson by heart so that she could speak without hesitation at Sunday school time. She also patiently taught Lucimar how to work with boys and girls.

Perhaps one of the most unusual incidents in Tom and Ethel's nineteen years in Tarauacá happened one Wednesday, when a poor lady and her husband arrived from Carauarí on a Brazilian Air Force flight. The couple had travelled down the River Juruá by canoe for a whole day to arrive at the town of Carauarí, in the hope of finding someone to help them. Back at the forest, the lady got into serious difficulties while in labour to give birth to her eighth child. The baby could not be born because of an arm presentation and subsequently died. No one in the forest could help and when they got to Carauarí, there was no medical help there either.

They felt relieved when they heard that an Air Force Buffalo plane was passing through that way on its monthly flight from Belem at the mouth of the Amazon to the most westerly town in Brazil, Cruzeiro do Sul. En route, the plane stopped at various interior towns including Carauarí and Tarauacá. On board the plane was an Air Force doctor who, after examining the woman, realized she needed urgent help. The captain of the plane consented to transport the couple to the nearest medical help which was Tarauacá, almost a two hours flight away.

When they arrived in Tarauacá, mid afternoon, the Air Force doctor called for help to transport the lady to the hospital. This was provided on the back of a truck. The Buffalo plane went on to Cruzeiro do Sul, but the doctor remained to see if he could be of any help locally. When Tom examined the lady, she was in very bad shape. The long ordeal and flight had sapped her strength, plus the fact that she had lost so much blood and was burning with fever.

Tom recognized that he would have to operate on the lady urgently but would first have to try to control the fever and also give her some blood. He immediately gave her antibiotics and then classified her blood group. In the absence of a blood bank and with some foresight, Tom had a registered number of people in Tarauacá of differing blood groups who would volunteer blood in any emergency. This certainly was an emergency and after withdrawing blood from the donors, he almost immediately transfused blood to the critically ill woman.

Tom then told Victor not to preach too long at the evening service, since they would need to operate on the lady later that night. The hospital had half a dozen local nurses but none of them were qualified beyond the training they received at the Tarauacá hospital. Some of these nurses barely knew how to count when they first donned a nurse's uniform. The Air Force doctor hoped to pick up the return flight the next morning at seven o'clock. He assisted Tom with the operation while Ethel and Victor attended to the anaesthetic machine and monitored blood pressure and pulse.

The lady was on the operating table for three hours, during which time Tom removed the dead baby and then had to do a partial hysterectomy as the uterus had been badly torn due to the efforts in Carauarí to pull the baby free. This was done with great difficulty because of the decomposing state of the baby and the mother's infected tissues. As they were suturing up, the lady took a secondary haemorrhage and in spite of frantic efforts to revive her, she died on the table.

The distraught husband came into the theatre when he heard of his wife's death. He threw himself across her dead body with loud convulsive wailing. When Tom calmed the man down and sympathized with him in the loss of his wife, the pitiful man explained another predicament that confronted him. The Air Force plane was the only flight that would take him back to Carauari, where his other seven children were waiting for him alone in their house in a lonely clearing in the forest several hours walk out of the town..

The Air Force doctor explained that without prior authorization from Belem, the plane would not be able to transport a corpse. That meant that if the man was to take advantage of the free flight to take him to his needy family, his wife would have to be buried before six o'clock in the morning and it was already past one o'clock. That gave him less than five hours to see to his wife's funeral, although he did not have any money.

The town was in total darkness when Tom and Victor left the man with his wife at the hospital and went to the home of the chief of police to wake him up to register the death. After this, they went to the homes of two deacons from the church and asked them to dig a grave. The deacons readily consented and made their way to the cemetery, while Tom and Victor went to fetch hurricane lamps to use in the graveyard. They also had to waken the man who had authority to allocate a grave and indicate the plot.

At two o'clock in the morning, it was a most eerie sight in the graveyard to see the silhouette of the two deacons digging a grave by the misty light of the hurricane lamps that were suspended from a nearby tree. The early morning dew caused two halos to encircle the lamps as the two men silently dug the grave.

After this, Victor went home to get some wood to make a coffin, while Tom went to call the carpenter. At the hospital, he measured the length of the corpse with a piece of string and within half, an hour the carpenter had a simple coffin-like box made. They wrapped the box with cloth that Tom obtained from a shopkeeper who kindly got up to attend to a sale at three o'clock in the morning.

By 4 a.m., the lady was put into the coffin and buried half an hour later. The man caught the flight at seven o'clock that morning promising to return to put up a headstone in memory of his wife. He was never heard of again. That was a night to remember.

Over the course of the nineteen years Tom and Ethel worked in the Acre, they had a succession of various missionaries who worked with them. After Victor and Audrey left Tarauacá in 1974, Peter and Joyce Logie, seconded from their church in Clydebank, Scotland, gave spiritual leadership at the church. Kathleen Elliot, a nurse and midwife from County Fermanagh, gave a lot of help at the São São Gomes hospital for several years until ill health forced her to return home. John and Hazel Matthews, former Faith Mission pilgrims from County Tyrone, did a sterling work pastoring the church and overseeing the construction of the modern church building still used today.

Raising children in some of these remote areas without medical help can present clear problems. Perhaps this was highlighted in Tarauacá in 1971, when Tom and Ethel were on furlough. God was working in the town, although one morning the Maxwells were taken aback to find that someone had placed parts of a dead chicken outside the front door of their home. Locals told the missionaries that this indicated that someone had put the spiritist curse of Macumba upon their home. That day, the couple resisted this curse in the name of the Lord Jesus and claimed the merits and power of the atoning blood of Jesus Christ.

Just after this happened, Victor, together with their elder daughter, travelled to Feijó, a smaller town twenty minutes flight from Tarauacá in the same direction as Rio Branco. For some time New Tribes missionaries, who worked with the Catukina Indians down river from Feijó, had been asking Victor to go over to this town where they had a base house. They wanted him to conduct meetings with a view of opening a work there.

After Victor arrived, he was able to rent a hall and hire the seating out of the local cinema. Without the benefit of any literature, he went from door to door inviting people to the meetings. Opposition from the priests was expected and did happen, but God blessed each night that week. On the first Sunday evening, there were thirty-five people present. Numbers increased night after night and by Thursday, almost one hundred and fifty were attending. The priest came to the hall one evening and stood at the door to see who was attending the meetings. Several people trusted the Saviour during the special effort.

While this was happening in Feijó, Audrey remained in Tarauacá with Heather but all was not well. Heather was somewhat dull and lethargic during that week and by Thursday, she was running a very high temperature. There was no way of contacting Victor. Furthermore, the nearest medical help was two hours away by airplane, and there was only one scheduled flight per week. Audrey gave Heather aspirin but on Thursday night, the temperature climbed to 104°. Audrey spent most of that night bathing the baby in cold water to try to reduce the fever.

The weekly scheduled flight came early on Friday morning. Audrey knew that it was her only chance of getting the baby out of Tarauacá to medical help in Rio Branco. After a sleepless, night she sent word at 4 a.m. to Sr. Messias, a deacon at the church, to say that Heather was very ill and needed to go to Rio Branco on the flight that was due to arrive in just over an hour. Sr. Messias kindly carried Audrey's baggage one mile from the house to the airport, while she carried her baby daughter who was still burning with fever.

The arrival of the weekly flight was a highlight of the week for people in Tarauacá. Generally, a crowd gathered at the small airport to see who might be arriving or leaving and to pick up parcels or letters that might have been sent from some relative living in the capital. When Audrey and Sr. Messias arrived at the airport with the baby, a larger crowd than usual packed into the small terminal. Several soldiers were there to meet an officer and a group of nuns was expecting another party of nuns to arrive from Cruzeiro do Sul.

Audrey placed the child into Sr. Messias' arms while she bought tickets for the flight. Just then, Heather went into convulsions and there was great panic all around. Audrey was sure the child was going to die. Panic gripped her as she dropped what she was doing to seize the baby into her arms. After a few moments, the convulsions stopped and Heather went limp and seemed lifeless in Audrey's arms. People crowded around while the distraught mother tried to give mouth to mouth resuscitation to what she thought was her dying baby. A soldier tried to feel the baby's wrist for a pulse and when he could not find a beat, he announced to all present, "She is dead. The baby's dead."

Audrey was distracted and yet was sending minute prayers to heaven for Heather. Just then, the airplane, a DC 3, landed and taxied to the apron at the front of the air terminal. When the pilot noticed the crowd, he went over to see what was happening. By this time Heather, had started to breathe normally but was in a deep sleep. The pilot cleared the crowd from around the mother and child and told a member of the crew to take Audrey and the baby to the aircraft because he was taking off for Rio Branco immediately.

Audrey settled into the seat of the plane with the baby tightly held in her arms. After take off, the pilot came down the cabin of aircraft to speak to Audrey who explained that her husband was in Feijó with their other daughter. As soon as the plane was airborne, the pilot radioed to Feijó requesting that someone find where Pastor Victor and his daughter were and to tell them to be be ready to leave the airstrip in fifteen minutes.

Victor and Sharon were located and were at the airport just as the plane came in to land. It taxied to the apron and without stopping the engines, they opened the back door of the plane for Victor and Sharon to scramble on board. As soon as the door was shut, the captain lost no time in making the DC3 airborne again.

Audrey was relieved to see Victor and Sharon. Other passengers had been comforting Audrey in her distress. The pilot bypassed Sena Madureira to avoid any delay in rushing the child to hospital. At Rio Branco, an ambulance was waiting to rush the baby and the Maxwells straight to hospital. She was given immediate attention there, and began to recover within hours.

In the aftermath of that illness and distress Victor and Audrey remembered the "curse" that had been put upon their home a few days earlier. They were reminded that they were in a battle against the powerful forces of darkness. Again, prayer and praise were lifted up to God for His deliverance. This illness interrupted the plans to start the work in Feijó, which remained dormant until Jack and June Bennett went to the town a few years later. However, it was learned later that Branca, Sr. Messias' daughter who was at the airport with her dad and Audrey, was so touched and shocked by the events that day that she went home and received Jesus Christ into her heart.

In later years, Branca went to study at the Baptist Seminary of Amazonas, after which she engaged in the work of the Mission and served the Lord in Amazonas and then in Portugal for a number of years. What seemed like tragedy at that time became triumph.

After her release from the hospital, Heather remained sick for almost another year. During most of that time, Tom and Ethel were back in Tarauacá so this gave more confidence to the anxious parents when their children became ill.

Even worse heartache was felt by Robin and Thelma at the end of 1978, when their darling baby Ruth was born in Manaus with a harelip as the result of Thelma staying with an American missionary family during her pregnancy when the daughters had rubella. Robin and Thelma took Ruth home to England for a repair operation. The operation was a success but a few weeks after being released from the hospital, little Ruth was readmitted to the Redhill Hospital near

Brighton with staphylococcal pneumonia. Baby Ruth's death a few days later broke her parents' hearts.

In spite of this setback, Robin and Thelma returned to work in Boca do Acre where the infamous Black Fever that had claimed so many lives was still rampant. The Lord gave Robin and Thelma two other lovely daughters, Rachel and Helen. When Helen was only one year old, she also fell victim to a similar unidentified pyrexia as Heather Maxwell had suffered earlier. The malady persisted and Robin and Thelma thought they were going to lose a second child.

They travelled to Manaus early in June 1971, where Tom and Ethel Geddis were seeing to the registration of Tom's medical diplomas. In a letter to Mr. McComb, Tom revealed just how serious the situation was.

> On Sunday, Robin and Thelma arrived here in Manaus with little Helen in a very sick condition. They thought she was going to die in Porto Velho, where the plane stopped overnight. The doctor there advised them to take Helen straight to Rio de Janeiro or São Paulo for treatment.
>
> On Sunday night, she looked so poorly that we feared for her life. It seemed to have been some virus infection. However, the Lord was good and we praise Him that she is much better and well on the way to recovery.

Baby Helen had a relapse, so as a result the whole family had to hastily return to the United Kingdom.

Paul and Reta, who were living in Canutama, also feared Black Fever when their little son David became seriously ill with similar symptoms that had touched the other two missionary children. They also were obliged to return home to seek medical attention. In Tarauacá, John and Hazel Matthews' daughter, Christine, had repeated bouts of a different illness that forced them to leave Tarauacá.

Doing God's will and engaging in God's work does not make the workers or their families immune from illness or trouble. On the contrary, they are frequently the targets of Satan's vilest attacks. No target is more vulnerable than the Christian's offspring. For that reason, much prayer ascends to God for these little ones. As the Acre missionaries have proved, buffeting runs parallel with blessing. Often the children who are keys to open doors, are just as frequently the vulnerable targets Satan attacks to frustrate the Christian worker.

Chapter Fourteen

HEAVENLY RESOURCES

Frequently, the missionary needs to know how to cash in on heaven's resources to meet earthly emergencies. Throughout Tom and Ethel's first term, it became apparent that he would need to revalidate his medical qualifications in Brazil. They made initial inquiries about this procedure on their way home through Rio de Janeiro late in 1970. Tom was informed that besides needing all his diplomas authenticated, he would also have to complete a two-year course at a university either in Rio de Janeiro or São Paulo and then undergo exams. It was going to be a time-consuming process, which would divert them away from their missionary work.

During furlough, they appealed to the prayer groups and friends to pray about this matter. The return journey to Brazil was a restful four week voyage on the *SS Bernard* of the Booth Line. When the five thousand ton vessel docked at the floating harbour in Manaus, the Port Authority doctor went on board to give the ship clearance. Tom talked with the fellow doctor and mentioned that he was planning on going to Rio de Janeiro to revalidate his medical qualifications. The doctor took Tom by surprise when he said, "Just last month the government in Brasilia announced that they were decentralizing the authority of the medical faculties in the South, and that the University of Amazonas will have the authority to authorize the revalidation."

The doctor invited Tom to visit his home during the following week. He then explained that although the legislation was complete, the University of Amazonas was waiting for tutors to come from Rio de Janeiro to familiarize them with the procedure.

In the meantime, Tom made the necessary application to the Medical Faculty at the University of Amazonas in Manaus. In a letter to Mr. McComb on 21st May, 1971, Tom explained what was happening.

> We are still in Manaus where things are moving very slowly, but I suppose that we can't expect everything to be sorted out overnight. All the necessary papers have been translated and are now in the hands of the University authorities. They are trying to reach a decision as to what is now necessary. The Dean told me the other day that since this was the first case of revalidation that they have treated here at this university, they were not too sure as to what all was involved. He has invited some friend of his from Rio to come up and help them. This friend is due here this week but just what he will decide, no one knows. Anyway, apparently we have a lot of exams to do but no one at the moment can tell me just when it will be possible to do these.

Another letter two weeks later contained some good news of further developments.

> We can only praise God for what He has done for us in these recent days and thank all those friends who have upheld us in prayer. The revalidation process was completed and now we just have to await the paper work from the University authorities.
>
> The two professors arrived up from Rio last week to help the faculty here get things organized. They said that the process of revalidation would probably take one year

but since the faculty was not yet geared to handle this, they would treat my case as an emergency and have my exams ready in thirty-six hours.

I could hardly believe it but it was true. Last Friday, I had the exams and was able to satisfy the examiners. Now it only remains for the paper work to be completed by the University, and then we are free to go where we please. We do appreciate the prayerful support of so many at home. It is at least part fulfillment of the Word that the Lord gave us before we left home, "The Lord will fulfill his purpose for you."

Everyone was astounded that what should have taken at least two years to complete was secured in three days. A year later an American missionary doctor in Amazonas applied for the same process and after three years, he still had not got it.

God does answer prayer. There have been many experiences whereby the missionaries have proved that like Paul, when we are in trouble, pressed out of measure and even despairing of life itself, we learn not to trust in ourselves but in God who delivers us from death. Paul also added, "Ye also helping together by prayer..." (See 2 Corinthians 1:8-11) The vast network of prayer affects God's work and enables God's servants all around the world.

In answer to the prayers of the Lord's people Robin McCready and Victor Maxwell experienced God's protection in separate incidents. At Canutama, the prewar Catalina flying boat belonging to Cruzeiro do Sul, Brazil's national airline, had already landed in the middle of the river on its weekly flight to Canutama and Labrea. Several large canoes started out from the nearby river bank and converged on the aircraft once the propellers had ceased to rotate. While the plane was still drifting downstream, the passengers disembarked from the flying boat into one large canoe while the baggage was placed into the other canoes. When the transaction had finished, the flotilla of small canoes pulled away from the plane as the men paddled towards the river bank.

When the canoes were well clear of the propellers, one engine kicked into life with a great roar as one propeller started to spin.

The din grew even greater when the other engine started. Soon the pilot was giving the full throttle as the plane surged its way through the water upstream. As it gained momentum, the aircraft began to lift out of the river while leaving in its wake great waves fanning towards either river bank. When it was clear of the water, the clumsy looking flying boat climbed above the forest. The distinctive roar of the Catalina could be heard all over town as it echoed through the forest and droned off into the distance. Locals knew that the plane would return from Labrea in two hours.

It was almost two o'clock when the unique sound of the Catalina could be heard from a distance. Friends called to each other, "Here comes the plane."

Workers, passengers and interested friends waited at the river bank for the plane to descend. Robin was waiting for a letter from Fred Orr in Labrea. Most people were familiar with the flight pattern but as the plane neared Canutama someone remarked that there was an unusual roar from the plane.

Just then, the Catalina came into view and circled the town to make its descent upstream against the current which helped slow the aircraft. As the plane hit the water, it bounced off the river's surface and into the air again. It then came down with a tremendous thud and splash, which was followed by the sound of metal fracturing. From the river bank, Robin and friends could see that the plane had broken into two parts.

Immediately, the onlookers scrambled into the waiting canoes. Soon, like a mini armada, canoes of all sizes converged on the stricken aircraft. Robin was in one of the leading canoes going out for the rescue. It seemed to take so long to reach the plane but when they did, the crew had already opened the hatch while some were already standing on top of the floating fuselage. The Catalina did not hold more than twenty people, so those who got out first, quickly scrambled into the canoes. Others were finding difficulty getting down the plane's narrow aisle so Robin climbed up the wing of the plane and from there to the fuselage as the craft continued to drift down river. From where he stood, Robin was able to pull several people clear from the plane and into the waiting canoes.

Just after Robin rescued a few people from what seemed like a floating tomb, there was sudden panic when the rear of the aircraft submerged into the river and began pulling the other part under the muddy water. Most of the waiting canoes pulled away for fear of being sucked down into the water with the plane. In the confusion, they had abandoned Robin who was still stranded on the wing of the doomed plane, which was sinking fast. He hollered at the top of his voice, "Help me. Don't leave me. I can't swim."

One man saw him and bravely turned his canoe around and headed back to the plane. When he got near the wing, he told Robin to jump. The impact of Robin frantically jumping into the canoe rocked the small craft and nearly turned it over. The man was able to steady the canoe and then started to paddle for all he was worth.

They were not far away from the Catalina, when there was a yawn-like sound as the doomed aircraft sank under the muddy flow. Eight people failed to get out of the plane, including an aunt of Zení Orr. Robin and Thelma thanked God for his safe deliverance. Robin resolved that he would learn to swim.

In 1971, the Brazilian government ordered all foreign missionary agencies in Brazil to register according to a new code they had introduced for controlling the number of foreign missions working in the country. Victor was responsible to prepare the documentation for the Acre Gospel Mission. Being in Tarauacá was a distinct disadvantage since most of the work had to be done in Manaus, which was almost two thousand miles away and involved two extremely expensive flights. Nevertheless, it had to be done so Victor arranged to travel to Rio Branco on 28th September of that year. On the following day, he caught another flight to Manaus.

Just a week prior to the planned flight, an Air Force friend in Tarauacá told Victor that there was a possibility of an Air Force DC3 coming through Tarauacá from Manaus on 21st September, and then returning to Manaus the following day. The friend promised a free ride on the Brazilian Air Force plane if there were places available, though he would not know for sure until the day the flight arrived. The offer for free rides on Brazilian Air Force planes was usual practice for interior and remote places. It was also a big saving on finances.

When the flight arrived on Wednesday afternoon, Victor received confirmation that there was a place for him on the flight early the following morning. That evening at the weekly prayer meeting, Victor led a short study on Psalm 37, which was part of the church's consecutive study programmed through the Bible Psalter. The study focused on the characteristics of a "good man" as set forth in the Psalm. Verse twenty-three was the text of the evening, "The steps of a good man are ordered by the Lord: and he delighteth in his way." Although Victor expanded on these wonderful words that evening, he did not know their full significance until a week later.

Next morning, he said another good-bye to Audrey and the two children and was at the airport in time to catch the DC 3 for the eight-hour flight to Manaus. On arrival, he set to the business at hand almost immediately. The process was drawn out and time consuming. On the following Tuesday, news came through that the flight on which Victor had originally planned to travel from Tarauacá to Rio Branco, and for which he had made a reservation, had crashed in the Acre forest. All thirty-two passengers and crew had lost their lives. Among the dead were some very good friends, which included three students whom Victor taught at the Tarauacá High School and the former mayor of Tarauacá, Sr. Tupenir, who had been such a help to Tom and Ethel when they first arrived in the town.

It was a chilling moment and caused Victor and Audrey to realize that it was of the Lord's mercy that had preserved Victor. They could not help but remember the last word spoken at prayer meeting before Victor left, "The steps of a good man are ordered by the Lord: and he delighteth in his way."

God's guidance does not always protect His children from disaster, but He does direct them to the right places. The Mission needed to have confidence in God's guidance, as many changes took place in the Mission's work during the early seventies. Because of failing health, Mr. McComb retired from the leadership at the home-end of the Mission and was replaced by Allen and Ada Loney.

Jack Bennett, from Loughall in County Armagh, was definitely guided to the work of Acre Gospel Mission just when some missionary families had to leave Brazil. Jack was a former Faith Mission Pilgrim and, like several other missionaries, benefited from the course at the Missionary School of Medicine in London. He arrived in Brazil about the same time as Olive Thompson, a nurse from Bangor, County Down, and also a Faith Mission pilgrim. Both of them did the language course at the Amazon Valley Academy in Belem. After completing their studies, Jack went to work in Sena Madureira and Olive coupled up with Hazel Miskimmin for the work in Boca do Acre.

Sadly, Olive had to retire from the Mission's work after two years. Jack Bennett filled in for James and Dorrie in Sena Madureira. After his first term, he returned to England to marry June Ruddell, a nurse who completed her Bible School training at Emmanuel Bible School in Birkenhead. Following their wedding in Coventry, Jack and June returned to Brazil to live and work in Sena Madureira and Boca do Acre.

At this time, many new missionaries were added to the ranks of the Acre Gospel Mission in Brazil and it was felt that it was neither right nor fair for so much responsibility to fall on Francisco Franco and Corina. It was therefore decided that any protracted problems should be attended to by the missionaries who visited the Mission apartment in Manaus. However, it was soon found that this arrangement often distracted the missionaries from their work and was not the best use of their time. It became obvious that the Mission in Brazil needed a full-time presence in the city and a proper base from which to conduct its operations.

Just when the Mission leadership was discussing this matter, Bill and Mary Barkley, independent missionaries who ran a book store in Manaus, announced that they were moving to a new literature ministry in São Paulo. They approached Victor Maxwell and offered their property to the Mission at a reduced price. The property, an old Portuguese colonial house, had great potential and was ideal as a headquarters in Manaus.

God's provision for the purchase of this building was exact in its timing, adequate in capacity and the price was very reasonable. However, the Acre Gospel Mission had no fund to be able to come up with big money in a short time but they did have the promises of God. The Acre missionaries lived by faith and had always proved God's faithfulness in small things as well as mammoth steps.

It was a small everyday matter which demonstrated God's provision when James and Dorrie were returning by canoe from the mouth of the River Caeté, two days after Christmas Day. Late that afternoon, they had just finished the last of a series of Christmas parties for the children who lived in or near to Sena Madureira. As they made their way up the River Iaco, the gentle breeze created by the movement of the canoe was a pleasant relief from the sweltering heat they had felt earlier in the meeting. Dorrie sat at the front of the canoe with several girls from the church. She mused over the frenzy of activities during the previous two weeks of Christmas events. Besides the children's programmes and parties, the youth also had their special night and even the school had furnished a virtual banquet. On all these occasions, there had been an abundance of cakes and sweet drinks. Every day for two weeks, James and Dorrie had been baking cakes and buns. Since they were on a tight budget, nothing was wasted so those buns that were either burned or misshaped, were consumed by James and Dorrie.

Out of her thoughts, Dorrie spoke up to James and said, "James, I'm tired of eating sweet things. I would love fish for dinner when we get home."

The words were no sooner out of her mouth when a long, five-pound, silver fish jumped up out of the water and fell into the canoe at Dorrie's feet. The stunned fish wiggled and flipped across the canoe until one of the girls banged it on the head. Although it is common to see fish jump out of the muddy water, never before had one jumped into their canoe. It almost seemed as though the Lord had heard Dorrie request. That night they had something different for dinner.

The Lord who provided a fish for James and Dorrie, had also provided a coin in a fish's mouth at Galilee to pay the tribute tax for Peter and Himself. Could He not provide money to the purchase this house in a short time? He did. After paying an initial down payment, the exact balance arrived at the Mission's Belfast office on the last day of the deadline that had been set by both parties to finalize the transaction.

After two years at home, Allen, Ada and their children, Mark and Olive, returned to Brazil while Victor and Audrey took up the vacancy they had left in Belfast, heading up the home end of the Mission. Allen and Ada moved into Ebenezer, the new Mission house, to attend to the Mission business from the city. Besides seeing to the day to day affairs of the Mission and missionaries, Allen also made a commitment to renovate, enlarge and modify the Ebenezer. He was very well suited for this job, and almost single handedly, transformed the old Portuguese colonial house to provide small apartments to accommodate missionaries and pastors passing through the capital of Amazonas.

While Mark and Olive attended a local school for missionary children, Ada gave warm hospitality to all who arrived at Ebenezer and made it a home from home for the missionaries going on furlough or returning to Brazil. Francisco Franco and Corina remained good colleagues to all the missionaries although they had bowed out of any responsibility for the Mission affairs.

In Northern Ireland, the first "Acre Weekend" took place in 1975 at Miss Eccles' Guest House in Bangor with seventy people present. In that same year, the Mission released several publications, "Into a Large Place" and "Journey to Jordan," as well as produce the first documentary film of the work in Brazil, "For My Sake."

Fred and Zení Orr, with their two children, Fredinho and Florence, moved from Labrea to Manaus after the Labrea church called a Brazilian pastor, José Salsa. Fred had caught the vision of establishing the Cruzada Amazonica, an agency set up for the training of Brazilians for evangelization of their own people and supplying interior churches and missionaries with the literature and tools to do their work.

At first the Cruzada operated from Fred and Zeni's home, which was a large apartment at the top of a five-story building. It gave an excellent view of the wide expanse of the river, but there was no elevator in the building. After several years in that apartment, it became obvious that the family needed a separate house. The Cruzada also needed other premises to accommodate their expanding literature ministry.

In an amazing way, the Lord provided the funds for the Cruzada to purchase property in the centre of the city. This building was renovated and transformed into a ground floor Bible bookstore with a classroom and an office on the upper floor. In a Mission circular, Allen Loney reported the following developments at the Cruzada.

> The rent of the present place, five floors up and without a lift, has a one hundred and thirty per cent yearly increase. Fred Orr and the Cruzada members have been on the look out for a place to buy, but they had virtually no funds to purchase such a place.

> Just recently, we found premises for sale which are close to the port and the city centre. First, the members of the Cruzada asked the Lord to indicate if this purchase was in His will. This was positively confirmed, so then they had special sessions to pray that the need would be met.

> Unknown to them, the day before this particular prayer meeting, some friends in Canada sent $2,500 to the Cruzada without knowing of their need or prayers. It was while they were at prayer, that they got word of this gift. When these friends heard what their gift was to be used for, they kindly offered to pay the balance of the property. Again the Lord's promise has been fulfilled - "Before they call I will answer."

> As they now make plans for its use, they ask for prayer that they might be led in its design so that it may be utilized in the best possible way. There is a lot of work to do to the building. They have already dug out the basement to turn the bottom floor into a street-level evangelical book shop, through which they will continue their distribution of CEF material and other literature.

> The next floor, about fifty-six feet in length, will be for the Cruzada offices. There may be a third floor where the Cruzada teaching and training ministry will eventually be conducted. Much work is before them but the young folks are keen to help with it. Praise God He has supplied all the need until now, and we know that He will go on to supply every other need as it arises.

There was great rejoicing when the Cruzada Amazonica moved into their new premises. Idemar, one of the original teachers in Labrea, led the administration of the work and bookstore. One of their first moves was to invite the Brazilian leader of the Child Evangelism Fellowship to Amazonas to give training classes to hundreds of volunteer children's workers from all different churches who were eager to reach boys and girls for Jesus Christ in Manaus and elsewhere.

Every month a team of the Cruzada workers travelled fourteen kilometres from Manaus to Aleixo, which was originally a leprosarium. For four hours, they visited leprosy patients in their homes and in the wards of the infirmary. Besides singing and conducting gospel services in the wards, they also provided radios and cassette recorders so that the Christian patients, many of whom were blind, could benefit from the Bible-reading cassettes.

If ever a man's steps were ordered by the Lord, it was those of Bill Woods, who continued to devote his life to relieve the suffering of leprosy patients. Leprosy is as much a dreaded word in Brazil as in many other places. It is the very fear of this disease that often has the worst effects on its victims. Fear of leprosy is deeply rooted in the myths of history and ignorance, and it is this fear that often isolates the afflicted person. As a result of society's ignorance and superstition about leprosy, marriages and families break up and frequently jobs are lost.

Throughout his six years of demanding studies at the university, Bill also conducted seminars to try to eradicate ignorance by explaining that leprosy could be treated. He also set up workshops to provide the suitable orthopaedic footwear for leprosy patients who suffered from deformities. Pastor Francisco Poderoso, who teamed up with Bill in the Boca do Acre, worked alongside Bill in this project. After its huge success in Manaus, they were soon invited all over Brazil to set up these same workshops.

It was a great day when Bill finally graduated from medical school. The long years of hard work and conscientious study had reaped deserved dividends. Bill topped the graduation class of 1974 and when his name was called to receive his diploma, all the students gave him a standing ovation for his great achievement. He was just sorry that none of his family could be there when they placed the diploma in Bill's hand.

To achieve his medical qualifications in a foreign language was no mean feat. A good rest and holiday would have been more than justified, but it was not for Bill to rest on the laurels of his success nor was it in his nature to take things easy. On the day after his graduation, Bill left Manaus for Rio de Janeiro to start two years of study at the "Miguel Couto General Training Hospital" to specialize in ophthalmic surgery.

Rio de Janeiro is undoubtedly one of the most beautiful cities in the world. The beautiful beaches of Copacobana, Leblom, Ipanema and Barra de Tijuca draw thousands of tourists from all over the world. The towering peaks of Pão de Açucar and Cocovado give outstanding views of the whole Guanabara Bay. However, there was little time for Bill to indulge in the splendours of the beautiful city. His application to the work for over two years really paid off and in due course, Bill obtained the experience he needed and earned his diploma as a qualified ophthalmic surgeon.

In a prayer letter at that time, Bill reported the following.

> "My time in the beautiful city of Rio has come to an end, and the purpose of my coming here has been accomplished. After graduation, I moved to Rio to take a two year residency course in ophthalmology, leading on to specialization in ophthalmic surgery. For a long time I found the surgical part of the course very difficult but many of you prayed for me. I needed those prayers because for weeks, I trained on pigs' eyes. It really was quite sickening at first, and I never want to look another pig straight in the eye. Today I am grateful for a steady hand and the confidence that comes through knowing that we can do all things through Him.
>
> The "shoe making" projects are all enjoying great progress. Last year, I was able to visit three of the four centres that are now making special shoes for the patients

with leprosy. I was thrilled to see the results as I examined over one hundred patients using these orthopaedic shoes. One man had suffered three ulcers on one foot and two on the other over a period of eleven years. As a result of the shoes, he now has no ulcers even though he walks five kilometres to work every day.

Last September, I was able to give a report on this work at the Congress of Dermatology held in the nation's capital, Brasilia. Each speaker was introduced, 'Professor So and So,' but when it came to my turn, the chairman simply said, "And now our beloved William." I am grateful to the Lord for the measure of acceptance I have with my Brazilian colleagues.

After Bill finished the course in 1977, he planned a visit to Northern Ireland to see his mother whom he had not seen for ten years. News of his mother's health was not good, but he needed to travel to Manaus to organize some matters before his planned trip to the United Kingdom. A phone call home before leaving Rio indicated that his mother was in good shape in spite of her ill health.

He called home again the following weekend from Manaus, only to hear that his mother had passed away on the Thursday of that week. It was a bitter blow and very ironic that when Bill was at last free to travel home to see his mother, he should miss her by just a few weeks.

On his way home, Bill went to visit missionaries in Guinea Bissau where he put his medical skills to good use. However, Africa gave him something more than he expected. Not for the first time, Bill picked up malaria which he was not aware of until he arrived in Northern Ireland. It took some time for him to recover, but after he recovered he spent several months representing the Mission in deputation meetings. Bill also travelled to Vellore, India, in May 1978, to attend a course in reconstructive surgery at Schieffelin Leprosy Research Sanatorium.

In November 1978, Bill returned to Brazil to administer the orthopaedic shoe making programme which was being carried on in seven centres across Brazil. Before long, this work took on greater dimensions when in 1981, he was invited by the Acre government to set up a leprosy programme in their state. Acre had the highest incidence of leprosy in the Americas.

Before long, first in Cruzeiro do Sul and then in Rio Branco, Bill devoted his time to a programme of ophthalmic surgery. Over a period of several years, Bill restored sight to more than five hundred leprosy patients who had suffered blindness from the disease. He also conducted a programme of reconstructive surgery to provide mobility to hundreds of patients who had lost the function of their limbs. Another Mission agency worked in unison with Bill and took over his programme of providing the orthopaedic footwear for his patients. This agency also employed leprosy patients to provide artificial limbs for leprosy amputees.

Added to this, the Italian government sent a team of doctors and surgeons to work with Bill in the leprosy programme in the Acre. They poured in money and equipment. In the late eighties, the revolutionary Multidrug Treatment (MDT) was introduced and made a dramatic impact on the disease all over the world. Bill's team of workers travelled extensively in the Acre diagnosing cases and administering the new MDT. After a few years, the incidence of leprosy in the Acre dropped from eleven cases every thousand people to two leprosy patients in one thousand.

This demanding mission to treat all leprosy patients in the Acre, both by medicines, surgical corrections and overseeing the work, called for a team of dedicated workers to help Bill achieve his goals. Besides a group of Brazilian nurses and visiting surgeons from other parts of Brazil, God also called Emily Gilchrist to play a major part in this work.

Emily, from Castlederg, County Tyrone, had been a missionary for almost ten years in Nigeria where she and other missionary colleagues were kidnapped during the infamous Biafran War. She was held captive for six weeks by rebels. After this, she returned to Nigeria and worked in a Mission hospital. Her vast nursing and missionary experience made her a great asset to the developing leprosy programme.

Emily's dedication was obvious to all who knew her, most of all to her patients. They loved her gentle ways and the patience she demonstrated in taking the time to listen to their fears and problems. Emily read the scriptures to them each afternoon. Her dedication may be discerned in a letter she sent home in 1982.

Both the physical and the spiritual needs of the patients are being attended to in the hospital in Rio Branco. One blind man was admitted with a terrible wound on his heel. Part of it even appeared missing, so I felt the doctor might amputate his foot. It was so bad that the big fat worms were peering out at me when I began to clean up the wound. I spent a good few days trying to remove the worms with dressing forceps. When I finished the dressing, more worms would still be found each day. Eventually after a few weeks of patient treatment, the hole was completely filled in and healed.

I praised the Lord for all His help in treating these patients. More so, for the opportunities given to witness to them in their terrible sufferings, for this is my real objective.

I work with a lovely Christian girl, Ruth, who dearly loves the Lord and wishes to serve Him. She is so happy to have me work with her in witnessing to the patients. Sometimes when the clinic isn't too busy, we do the dressings together. While doing so, we sing hymns and are able to encourage them. They enjoy this, especially those in the wards who have accepted the Saviour.

One man, after we completed his dressings, told us he was a backslider for years and would like to return to the Lord. It was a thrill to see him kneel on the floor of the dressing-room and come to the Lord. I was able to get him a Bible. I know that you will pray for these babes in Christ, that they will grow in the Lord and be witnesses to their families and friends when they return to their homes.

While a pastor was visiting one of our patients, he had the joy of leading one of our nurses to the Lord. Pray for the hospital staff, that the lives we live and the witness we bear will be used to reach them too.

Emily was only one of a group of missionaries accepted by the Mission for the work in Brazil in 1978. In the previous year, Millicent Bailie, who trained at Redcliffe Missionary Training College in London, returned from North East Brazil where she had been working with World Missions to Children that largely concentrated in providing homes for Brazil's many orphans. Because of a change of policy which transferred children out of institutionalized orphanages to adoptive families, Millicent was obliged to make a change of direction. This led her to the Acre Gospel Mission, through which she felt the Lord was calling her to reach the children of Amazonas with the gospel.

Children's work had always been a feature of the Acre's church planting ministry and had been the means of easing doors open that otherwise had been tightly closed. Children's work was the key that unlocked the door in Labrea and Tarauacá.

Millicent invested three months at the CEF Teaching Training Institute in Kilzimmer, Switzerland, before she left for Amazonas with Acre Gospel Mission. In Manaus, Millicent teamed up with her former colleague from Recife, Jovita Mesquita. Together they worked among the boys and girls in Manaus, not only in Good News Clubs and Five Day Clubs, but also teaching the Word of God at various schools, churches and the juvenile detention centre. They also conducted teacher training classes in conjunction with the Cruzada Amazonica and CEF in Brazil.

Millicent and Jovita were greatly encouraged in their work among the children by repeated visits from Millicent's dad, Jack Bailie. He not only travelled with them, but also visited the other missionaries and greatly encouraged them by his cheerful presence. Jack was also a good carpenter and gave a ready hand to help various projects.

After Millicent had to leave Brazil due to ill health, Jovita continued the work they had started. Using public transport in Manaus, which at times is dangerous, Jovita still travels to different parts of the city to conduct five-day clubs or giving training classes.

Mina Shaw, from Newtownards, trained at the Faith Mission Bible College and spent several years conducting gospel missions in various parts of Ulster. Like Millicent, Mina also went to Kilzimmer to the Teacher Training Institute in order to be equipped to reach the boys and girls in the Acre. After studying Portuguese alongside Emily and working for several years in the interior, Mina moved to Rio Branco. There she was able to establish many contacts in the local schools and teach the gospel to all age groups. For more than fifteen years Mina has continued to teach in the Rio Branco schools and conduct her teacher training classes and Daily Vacation Bible Schools in the city as well as various interior towns. Several of her boys and girls developed into fine servants of God and are in Christian work today.

John Matthews and Hazel McAteer, both from County Tyrone, also had been to the Faith Mission Bible College in Edinburgh for their missionary training. While there, they fell in love and indicated their desire to serve the Lord in Brazil. John's training was suddenly interrupted by the unexpected death of his father and as a result, he had to return to the family farm. God's call to Brazil persisted as John and Hazel were married in the summer of 1979. Later that year, they went to Brazil to join Tom and Ethel in Tarauacá. Hazel, a nurse and midwife, was able to take the place of Kathleen Elliot, who had to return to Fermanagh because of illness.

It was difficult to obtain entry visas for these new missionaries during the seventies. Millicent already had hers but the other four had to take a stand of faith that the Lord would open the door. Their faith was tested over many months until it got to an embarrassing stage where they dreaded anyone else asking, "Have you got your visa yet?"

The Lord opened the door in His good time and eventually the visas were granted. They were glad when they were able to travel to Brazil.

Just before Millicent left for Brazil in 1978, James and Dorrie arrived home in Belfast for a planned retirement with James having reached the magical age of "senior citizen." Through the kindness of the Munn family in Belfast, the Mission was able to purchase a house that became home for James and Dorrie. Later it became the home base for Acre Gospel Mission.

After eighteen months at home, James and Dorrie deeply pined for Brazil, which had been their home for thirty years. However, James felt that it was not right to return just because of their longings for the country and people. He needed to know that the Lord was opening the way for them to return. It was while he attended the Worldwide Missionary Convention in Bangor that God challenged him again. He heard a missionary speak on the text, "The children of Ephraim, being armed, and carrying bows, turned back in the day of battle." (Psalm 78:9) James, despite his age, felt convicted that he was armed with the language and years of experience and still had much to give for the Lord, so he and Dorrie returned to Brazil in 1980.

On this occasion, their role in Brazil was different from any they had known before. They replaced Allen and Ada to run the headquarters of the Mission in Manaus, while Allen and Ada again returned to Belfast to assume the leadership at home.

The Gunnings tenure in Manaus corresponded with the arrival of Millicent, Jovita, Mina and Emily. The veteran couple were ideally placed to give a lot of attention and care to these new missionaries at a formative time in their new careers.

The time James and Dorrie spent in the city also allowed them to have closer ties with Francisco and Corina, their friends from the early days in Sena Madureira. They were constant visitors at the Mission headquarters and when Francisco travelled on business, Corina came to stay with James and Dorrie just as in former times.

James and Dorrie continued in Manaus until mid 1982 when Victor and Audrey arrived to relieve them from the headquarter's work allowing them to return to Sena Madureira, their first love.

While Victor and Audrey looked after the Mission headquarters and their children were at the New Tribes boarding school, they also maintained a close relationship with Francisco Franco and Corina, as had all the Acre missionaries in the city. By this time, Francisco had given up his city office to take charge of a government sponsored river boat which was used as a floating supermarket to attend to the needs of the interior population. As a member of Gideons International, Francisco also took a good supply of New Testaments wherever he travelled.

It was another sunny and hot day in Manaus in late September 1983. That afternoon, Victor and Audrey took Francisco and Corina to the large boat docked just out of the city. Francisco usually travelled without Corina, but on this occasion he insisted that she join him for the trip. Although Corina was born in the interior, she had an apprehension about travelling in these remote regions. After they spent some time socializing with Francisco and Corina on the boat, Victor prayed with them. In a short while, the boat pulled out from the bank and headed up river. Francisco and Corina planned to return within two months.

All did not go well on the trip. Although Francisco had been able to make good sales and distribute God's Word to hospitals and schools in various riverside towns, Corina became ill. Less than two weeks into the trip she went down with a high fever and acute abdominal pains. As a result of this illness Corina was confined to her cabin.

Victor received an urgent radio phone call from Francisco who had arrived at a small town on the River Solimões. He wept as he asked for urgent prayer for his wife as she was gravely ill. Her inflamed appendix had ruptured causing peritonitis. In vain Francisco tried to arrange for a small air-taxi to transport her out of the interior. In São Antonio do Apituã, an American missionary doctor aspirated her swollen abdomen, but there was little else he could do for her. Slowly the boat made its way still farther up river as Corina's condition deteriorated.

Victor relayed Francisco's urgent message to James and Dorrie who in turn informed Corina's sisters of her critical condition. On the following day, James travelled with Corina's sister Maria on two flights from Sena Madureira to Manaus. Early on the next morning, they took another two hours' flight in a different direction to arrive in São Paulo de Olivéncia, a small town where the floating supermarket had already arrived.

When they got there, Corina had already spent twelve days at the town's hospital. Both Maria and James were shocked to see Corina's ashen complexion and sunken cheeks. She was only a faint resemblance of what they remembered she had been when they last saw her. A doctor in the town courageously operated on Corina and removed a large part of the bowel. The local priest kindly gave a lot of attention to Francisco and Corina and provided the doctor what medicines he had at the parochial house.

At first, the doctor was optimistic in Corina's prognosis and said he would operate again on Corina two weeks later. James and Maria kept vigil at her bedside and allowed Francisco to continue his trip up river to Benjamin Constant, where the boat had been expected over a week earlier.

Corina regained a little strength, but on the day after her husband left, she suddenly became very ill again. James tried in vain all that day to contact Francisco. Late that night, they finally got word to him by a Ham Radio operator, but Corina was sinking fast. She maintained a bright testimony in her dying hours. James and Maria sat by her bedside, reading the scriptures and praying with their frail friend. Quietly Corina loosed the moorings of her earthly life early on the morning of 29th October 1983 and entered into the presence of her Lord.

From Manaus, Victor arranged for a Baptist missionary pilot in Benjamin Constante to transport Francisco back to São Paulo de Olivência. The funeral was delayed until three o'clock in the afternoon allowing time for Francisco's flight to arrive. James conducted the simple service at the grave side in the lonely and remote cemetery. Only five people stood around the grave as they laid to rest the remains of a quiet, but faithful Christian friend.

Francisco had to remain with the boat until it returned to Manaus, but James and Maria travelled by plane back to Sena Madureira with the sad news to Corina's family. When Francisco returned to Manaus two weeks later, he closed up his apartment and moved into the Mission house to live with Victor and Audrey.

He continued as local representative of the Gideons International until two years later when he moved away from Manaus to another part of Brazil. It was a sad and regrettable end to an endearing couple who had maintained a long and loyal friendship with all the Acre missionaries.

Chapter Fifteen

PUSHED INTO EUROPE

In the first century, the apostle Paul proved that closed doors can be as much of God's guidance as an open door. Paul desired to go to Bithynia and attempted to go into Asia but on both occasions, God somehow closed those doors. God's plans are always better than ours and His timing is perfect even though we may not always see it at the time. Just as the Lord had a better plan for Paul in Europe so He also had better plans in the same continent for Stephen and Hetty Smith.

In 1979, most of the churches which the Acre Gospel Mission was working with in Brazil were led by Brazilian pastors. Pedro Moraes was pastor at Boca do Acre, Miquel Nogueira was leading the work in Canutama, José Salsa had replaced the missionaries in Labrea, João Marinho assumed the role of pastor at Sena Madureira and Epitácio Barros had settled in as pastor alongside the missionaries in Tarauacá. Some other national workers had pioneered new areas, such as Manoel Urbano and Feijó and planted churches in these smaller towns. The majority of the missionaries still in Brazil were engaged in support ministries to the Brazilian churches.

However, the Mission had lost a number of missionaries due to illnesses or domestic circumstances. This depleted some needy areas of the work so there was an urgent appeal for new workers both national and foreign. Two young couples responded to this challenge in Northern Ireland. They applied to the Mission in Belfast and were duly accepted.

Stephen and Hetty Smith completed their Bible School training; Hetty at Redcliffe Bible College in London and Stephen at the Bible College of Wales in Swansea. They had long been acquainted with the work of the Mission, since Stephen was Ada Loney's nephew. They were married in Belfast and were anxious to serve the Lord in the Amazon.

The other couple was Richard and Terece Dilworth, who were also accepted for the work in Brazil. Amazingly Richard had come to know the Saviour as a child through the ministry of Sam Doherty, who had been led to the Saviour by Fred Orr more than thirty years earlier. Richard, from Dungannon, and Terece from Finland, met when they were students at Moorlands Bible College in England. Following their wedding, they felt constrained to serve the Lord in Brazil.

Both of these couples were frustrated to discover that although they were ready and willing to go to the Acre, they faced great obstacles. The Brazilian government had clamped a moratorium on visas for missionaries, largely prompted by the influx of thousands of Mormon missionaries to their country.

Special prayer was requested all over the country but the situation did not seem to change. On the contrary, even existing missionaries in Brazil had to re-register their permanent status with the federal police. Some on temporary visas were forced to leave the country. Months dragged by and although both couples gained experience in church work at home, a year passed since they had been accepted for Brazil without any progress.

Two years earlier, while Hazel Miskimmin was on furlough, she made contact with various missionaries in Portugal and planned to visit the Azores Islands following the visit there by the Operation Mobilization ship, the Doulos. Hazel's plans were thwarted and, instead of reaching the islands, she ended up spending three months with a church in Feijó, a town near Lisbon. It was a profitable time and Hazel returned home to challenge the Mission and friends to consider Portugal as a needy mission field.

A subsequent visit to Portugal by Allen and Ada confirmed that Portugal was even more needy than Brazil and merited the Mission's consideration in view of the new missionaries being impeded entering Brazil.

After Allen and Ada reported about their visit at an Acre weekend in Portrush, Stephen and Hetty felt that rather than wait another indefinite period for their visas, they would prefer to follow up some contacts that Hazel had made and go to Portugal to begin language study. After five and a half months working with the church in Feijó they returned to Northern Ireland for the birth of their first baby, Joanne. At that time, there was also a desire born in their hearts to serve the Lord in Portugal instead of Brazil. Stephen takes up the story.

> During our stay in Portugal, we were deeply challenged by the tremendous need of so many who knew nothing of the Gospel of grace. How sad it is to watch the many cults and 'isms that are busily employed in spreading falsehood, while so few are serving the true cause of Jesus Christ.
>
> While returning from Portugal, we felt that should the door to Brazil close, we would willingly consider going to Portugal as an alternative field. Although visas for Brazil were not forthcoming, we had planned to leave for Brazil in August 1982.
>
> It was just then that news came through from Brazil that missionaries on temporary visas were having to leave the country. It seemed impossible for us to leave for Brazil in the immediate future, but the Lord had already prepared our hearts for this news and for His will.
>
> For us, the closed door to Brazil now points us to an open door to Portugal. The Mission has already had several favourable contacts. We plan to leave for Portugal in October. Initially, we will be occupied with further language study.

Until Portugal entered the European Union, it was one of Europe's poorest countries despite its great influence in its many colonies all around the world. Its population of ten million people are mostly Catholic, but the Roman church has lost most of its influence and power among the people. In the northern part of the country the people are more religious and still follow traditional Catholicism whereas south of Lisbon fewer people attend the Catholic church except on special days.

Stephen and Hetty returned to Portugal and spent some time near Lisbon to perfect their Portuguese. While there, they were introduced to the Alentejo Province in 1984 through Ivan Fletcher, a Brethren missionary. At first Stephen and Hetty went to work with Ivan and a small group in Sines, a picturesque fishing village where the believers had purchased an old Roman Catholic chapel.

Sines was surrounded by other towns of similar size and small villages where there was no gospel witness. In an amazing way, the Lord provided a spacious apartment for Stephen and Hetty in Santo André, a new town that had been built for the developing industries being introduced to the region. Although they travelled ten miles to Sines to help in the work there, the couple were trusting the Lord to open a door for a work in Santo André.

There are no short cuts in God's work, so Stephen and Hetty had to plod at the work. Nearly every day for one year, they engaged in door to door evangelism. Initially they were received with suspicion because they were thought to be Jehovah's Witnesses or Mormons. In a short while, Stephen discovered that nearly every one in town was as new to the region as they were. Most had been repatriated from the former Portuguese colonies of Mozambique and Angola. Some of these had escaped radical and bloody revolutions with little more than a suitcase and the clothes they wore.

To Stephen and Hetty's delight, they discovered that among these refugees were several believers who had been bright for the Lord in Africa but despaired of finding other believers in Portugal. These escapee believers formed the nucleus for the new work in Santo André.

In 1985, Stephen organized the first meeting in their apartment. Outside their own family, only two others were present. At the meeting the following week, only one turned up. Missionaries soon discover that humility generates trust in God, and Stephen and Hetty had to keep on trusting and plodding in spite of the discouragements. Gradually the numbers began to grow and within a few weeks, the congregation grew to eight people.

Izabel dos Santos, a Brazilian teacher, joined the work in Portugal and went to help in the small church in Sines. Stephen and Hetty combined with Izabel to blitz the surrounding villages with the gospel. They also started an informal young people's group on Thursday evenings in their home. This work began to pay dividends when Filimina, a young woman who had taught catechism in the Catholic church, accepted the Saviour. Another drug addict came to know the Lord. These were the first fruits of the work, although there were disappointments when some early converts drifted back to their old ways.

As the work increased, it became clear that the group needed a place of worship. Prayer was solicited from the prayer groups at home. It was a great day when the local Council in Santo André gave Stephen a site to build the church on the bottom floor of a block of apartments. He wrote about it for the Acre News.

> Since the group of believers was very small, it was with great apprehension that we accepted the town council's offer of this site. There was only enough finance to buy one hundred bricks. We would need about four thousand bricks for the project, but we made a start.
>
> How faithful God was! Each time finance was low and the bills appeared, our Heavenly Financier supplied the need. Much labour too was required to perform this mammoth task. Enthusiastic volunteers came from the churches in Azeitão and Sines, and together we served as labourers, bricklayers, plasterers, carpenters, plumbers, electricians, painters, decorators and cleaners to complete a building to the glory of God in as short a time as possible.
>
> What a day of blessing we all experienced on 15th February, 1986 as we all met with many visitors to inaugurate the building for the preaching of the Gospel. More than seventy visitors from Santo André itself attended the service. Some weeks after the inauguration,

one of these visitors was the first to be led to the Lord within the walls of the new church. He was Nelson, the local council gardener whom we had spoken to on a number of occasions. He came to us in distress one Sunday afternoon after being aware of satanic involvement in his life since he had started coming to church. Only once before, some fifteen years earlier, he had attended an evangelical service where the message left an impression on him. He told us his story. We told him yet again of the power and love of Christ and with joy, he accepted the Saviour. Since then, his wife has made a profession and his grown children have come to church a number of times. Nelson's neighbour also came to know the Saviour through his witness.

It is interesting to see the reaction of the folks who reside in the area of the church. Many wished to attend just to see what went on inside but were afraid of what the neighbours might say. However, some have overcome that fear and disregarded the ridicule. One of these was Dona Ana, who attended regularly and after many months of thought and concern, trusted the Lord.

To overcome some of this apprehension that people have about being seen entering a 'Protestant Church,' we commenced English lessons on Wednesday and Saturday mornings. Those who came were adults, who under normal circumstances, would never have darkened the church door. Through this effort attitudes have changed. One man who attended the classes finally came to a service. Another, who used to forbid his daughter to attend a church where they lived in Lisbon, has come to the lessons and has become a very good friend.

After having a summer outreach to the children of the area, we felt we should commence a Sunday school in the church. Joanne and Richard have made good friends at school and at the apartment blocks. They attract many children to our home and some come to the meetings. We were encouraged by parents who promised to send their children along. Although the promises were mostly broken, only five children came, the children didn't seem to mind. They enjoyed singing the gospel songs and learning the verses. The following week more appeared, and we were thrilled at the way they had memorized the Scriptures. One young boy appeared almost every Sunday but once we started singing, he fled! I had no idea we sounded so bad! The children themselves have become the best advertisement for the Sunday school. Of the twenty who now attend regularly, only two ever heard the Gospel before. The majority of their parents do not come to church.

The first year in the life of the church in this new building has been completed. How we praise the Lord for all that has been done. We have prayed and God has blessed. The attendance has risen and believers have grown in grace. Some time ago, we celebrated the Lord's Supper with them for the first time. What a blessed experience to remember His death in His appointed fashion.

Undaunted by the arrival of their second child, Richard, Stephen and Hetty continued to make visits to the surrounding villages and used every means possible to take the gospel to the needy people. The work was great and it became evident that this work could not be done alone. They needed reinforcements, especially since Izabel dos Santos had fallen in love with Mauro, a young man from near Lisbon. They had planned to marry and head back to Brazil.

Allen and Ada had been making summer excursions to Portugal to help Stephen and Hetty in the outreach to boys and girls in the various locations. God laid this work greatly on their hearts, and it was a big step for them when they finally decided to go and live in Portugal early in 1988. They were replaced in the Belfast office by Audrey Maxwell.

It was not an easy step and just prior to their departure, they were given a great fright when word came through that Mark Loney, Allen and Ada's son, was on the Logos ship that floundered on rocks in the Beagle Channel off the most southerly coast of Latin America. Thankfully, after a few anxious hours, word came through that he and all the crew had been rescued in that terrifying night. Prayer was requested for Mark's future. No one knew then that within a few short years, Mark would also follow his parents and work alongside his cousin Stephen in Portugal.

Allen and Ada's arrival in Portugal coincided with a visit from Pastor Francisco Poderoso, to whom Allen had taught music when he worked in Boca do Acre many years ago. Writing of those early days Allen sent this report.

> We had a great time with Francisco and Cirene. While they were here, we had meetings in Santo André, Azeitão, Melides, Sines, Milfontes and Santiago. In all the meetings we had many visitors and new contacts to build on.
>
> Since we first visited Portugal some time ago, Ada and I have been interested in a place called Melides. A meeting was arranged for Francisco in the Melides Town Hall, and the man in charge was most helpful. We visited the homes in the village and distributed invitations to our special gathering.
>
> The local men never attend church. They feel they should leave religion and knitting to the ladies. When we invited them to join us, they said they would come but we didn't believe them. However, having the meeting in the Town Hall was just the right place to meet with them. Each week, the man in charge of the Town Hall holds a gathering for the elderly folks in the village. At this gathering they weave, do tapestry, or just gather to chat and have a bit of company. In the main hall where we were to have our meeting, we found over one hundred people gathered together. A band of some sort was playing their music while some locals were up dancing.
>
> It was a great opportunity in this Roman Catholic village and later that evening, we were able to show a film which had a gospel message. Immediately afterwards,

before anyone could escape, Francisco was up at the front with his recorded music playing as he started to sing. His Brazilian accent was captivating for the Portuguese. He gave a simple gospel message and upon leaving, everyone received a gospel leaflet. We had some good contacts afterwards.

The children's meeting in Santiago is discouraging. We have been going along each week, but the children just do not attend the meeting. Please pray for us. We still have not received our residence visa and this is necessary, if we are to commence our literature work in the markets.

Although the strategic work at the markets in Alentejo was originally a challenge that Allen and Ada had embraced, they were not able to follow through on this work because of repeated denials for a licence by the local authorities. Instead they decided to go to the needy town of Santiago, which was very resistant to the gospel.

What had been a closed door for Allen and Ada became an open door for Aroldo and Emmanuelle. Not long after they arrived in Portugal, they obtained a licence to use a bookmobile at the Alentejo markets. Aroldo was raised in a Christian home in Brazil and led to the Saviour there when he was a teenager. He came to Northern Ireland to visit his brother and while there, he became acquainted with the Acre Gospel Mission. When he was studying English in Belfast, he met Emmanuelle, a French student who attended the same class at the Rupert Stanley College. While Emmanuelle was visiting a missionary couple in Dublin in November 1987, she accepted the Lord Jesus as Saviour. It was a real international saga when a French girl fell in love with a Brazilian in Northern Ireland and they went to work in Portugal. After Aroldo's training at the Irish Bible College in Tipperary, they were accepted for the work in Portugal at the end of 1991.

Aroldo still maintains the literature ministry at the various markets each week. This report appeared in the Acre News in the spring of 1996.

Aroldo and Emmanuelle are thankful to the Lord for the provision of the literature display trailer and are most grateful to all who prayerfully and financially support this project. They are accepting the challenge to cover a wide area and their goal is to attend all of the monthly markets and annual fairs. They also plan to reach into the small villages and hamlets, where there is neither market nor fair to distribute free Christian literature.

It is demanding work that requires Aroldo to travel to different areas constantly. He needs your prayers for protection while he covers about five hundred miles each week on the very narrow roads.

It was a special victory to obtain permission to work in the market in Sines. His colleagues and believers were overjoyed with the news. Aroldo had pursued the normal legitimate channels to seek this permission. Seemingly, it was granted some time ago but he wasn't informed about it. Some of the town authorities did not like the kind of books being offered. It is wonderful to see God's power at work and to know that our God is bigger than any town council.

Another report sent in August 2000 gives an insight to one of the markets.

The literature ministry is not easy, but serving the Lord at the market can be adventurous. Some take the literature just to get rid of us, while others want to retain their religious beliefs. Very few people will allow a conversation. When we do have opportunity, it is a privilege to share our personal faith in Jesus Christ.

Serving the Lord at the markets can also be dangerous at times. Some visitors to the market and even some traders, have hatred in their hearts and are on the look out for revenge. The other day I witnessed a fight between gypsies and some Chinese traders. It was not a pleasant sight but quite impressive with both sides using Kungfu kicks and knives. On another occasion, a trader beside me was beaten up because he would not allow thieves to steal from his stall.

Arriving at yet another market, I discovered the police were everywhere with guns, dogs and horsemen. They were searching for illegal drugs and merchandise.

It is not always so dramatic at the market, but in the middle of everyday-life we have to shine as lights for the glory of the Lord. I am glad to say that among the traders I am very well accepted. Please pray for Europe and especially for Portugal. This work convinces us that only a move of God's Holy Spirit can bring salvation blessing.

Elonilda do Santos from Tarauacá, better known to her friends as "Branca," was also introduced to the work in Portugal and became an associate children's evangelist alongside Allen and Ada in Santiago. Although gifted in this work, she also encountered stiff resistance to the gospel in this town. Nonetheless, she worked with Allen and Ada with the young people's meetings either on the roof top of their apartment block or in a small hall they rented on the street.

After Mark Loney returned from his time with Operation Mobilization in South America, he enrolled at the Belfast Bible College. While there he met Judith Gardiner, whose family had been long time friends of the missionaries. Judith was an accomplished musician and an extremely talented soloist. Judith and Mark soon manifested great affection for each other and after Mark had served a short while in Portugal, they were married in January 1994.

Their arrival in Portugal opened up new fields for the Mission, working in Milfontes and Cercal, two towns south of Santo André. Also, the increased number of workers on the field and the growth in the various churches, allowed Stephen and Hetty to organize summer camps at which all the missionaries helped. At first these camps were planned for children and youth. Stephen is constantly invited to preach in other areas of Portugal. It was during these visits to different parts of the country that he caught the vision for providing family camps during the summer where church groups could have their retreats. This was made a very definite matter of prayer.

In an amazing way, the Lord provided a camp site near to Milfontes in 1999. The Island Christian Centre at Porto Covo, although privately owned, has been put at the disposal of the Acre missionaries in Portugal. The camp, which is only several hundred yards from the sea, had previously been a twenty-five acre pig farm and for five years it had been dormant. The main house, cottages and many outbuildings are being renovated to provide accommodation for up to one hundred people.

Initially, the missionaries had to install an irrigation system for the dormitories, a septic tank and a meeting house with a kitchen. Stephen is master of many trades and was able do many jobs himself or give leadership to most of the manual work. Mark, a qualified horticulturist, oversaw the laying of lawns and levelling of a football field. To accomplish all this work, they not only had the help of local people, but work parties from the United Kingdom travelled to Portugal for six weeks during summer months to help develop the camp facilities. Other volunteers took care of the kitchen duties and other jobs that arose.

Mark, Judith and their baby, little Klara Lynn, moved into the house at the camp and they administer the day to day camp operation. Although they have responsibility for the camp, Mark also pastors two small churches at Cercal and Milfontes.

Besides the Acre missionaries operating in the Alentejo region, they also maintain good working relationships with other Portuguese Christian workers in various towns scattered over this southern Province of Portugal. Several young people from the Sines church were commended to training for the Lord's work at the Word of Life Bible College, near Lisbon. Among these were Sandra and Rogério Ramos, whose parents are pillars at the Sines church. After his training Rogério married Sonia whom he met at the Bible school. After a further period at a Bible School in England, they returned to Sines in 1999 where Rogério pastors his home church.

His sister Sandra married a dynamic young man who is energetically involved in the leadership of the Word of Life. Vanda is also working at the Word of Life. She was converted as a young teenager in the early days of the work in Santo André before her family moved to Lisbon.

With the inclusion of several national pastors on the Committee of the Island Christian Centre, there is great expectancy for the potential of the camp. Already several churches from Lisbon have sent teams to work at the camp and other churches have planned spiritual retreats for the various departments of their churches at the Island Christian Centre.

* * * *

Just a few years after Hetty and Stephen committed themselves to the work in Portugal, the Lord opened another door in Europe. It was not by coincidence that the Mission came into contact with Dennis and Maree Murphy and their work in Gran Canaria. Denis and Maree had been working in Spain for several years and although they were not attached to any Mission, they were doing a sterling work for the Lord. At their invitation, Allen and Victor visited the Murphy family in Las Palmas. Subsequently, Dennis and Maree applied to come in under the wing of Acre Gospel Mission.

Gran Canaria is one of the largest of the seven main islands that constitute the Canary Islands, which are located sixty miles off the North West coast of Africa. With a population of more than one million people, the beautiful archipelago is among Europe's most favourite holiday resorts. The people of these sun drenched islands are friendly and warmhearted, but the majority are staunchly Roman Catholic. Their resistance to the gospel was as hard as the volcanic rock which the islands are famous for.

Dennis and Maree had a great relationship with evangelical life on the islands and worked in cooperation with the Port Evangelical Church in Las Palmas. After several years in one interior town, they were greatly challenged by the needs of a large housing development at Jinamar, a town south of Las Palmas.

Although they had a family to raise, Dennis and Maree gave themselves unsparingly to this work. Soon the small congregation grew into a young church, as souls professed faith in Jesus Christ.

After much prayer and persuasion, Dennis was able to obtain a site for a new church building. Steps of faith were honoured as the Lord miraculously supplied the need for the construction of the church building. While keeping up a busy programme of meetings, construction work continued every day. Occasionally, friends from home visited Gran Canaria to give their expert help. The building programme was closely monitored by local authorities, but the Lord gave grace and supplied the need to meet every deadline and condition.

More importantly, the Lord was adding to the church and soon it was in need of a full time pastor. A report in the *Acre Missionary News* gave details of Dennis' induction as the first pastor of that new church on 25th February, 1989.

> It was a privilege for us to attend such an important event. As we approached the new church building, we had the impression of a building still under construction with bare concrete blocks and the entrance unfinished and blocked up. We entered by a temporary door down a concrete staircase and then into a large church worship area. Although unfinished, here was a building already in use. The platform was attractively decorated for the occasion and the sanctuary was completely full of friends from other churches on the island who had come to share in the joy of the day.
>
> Their meeting was led by Pastor José Martinez, the President of the fellowship of Independent Evangelical Churches in Spain, who gave the charge to Dennis. The service concluded with the laying on of hands and prayer, committing Dennis to the Lord for the future days in the work at Jinamar.

The Lord supplied good transport for them as they put their minibus to work, travelling far and near with a good audio system to preach the gospel where they had opportunity. Daily Vacation Bible Schools and summer camps were great arms of the work which continued to prosper and grow.

For a short while, Dennis and Maree were joined by Geoff and Jean Park from Liverpool, who mainly worked with young people at the Port church in Las Palmas.

Early in 1988, Evan and Carmen Williams went to work in Gran Canaria. Evan previously had worked for several years with Tear Fund in Honduras where he met Carmen. Their friendship blossomed into romance, and they were married in Carmen's home country. Following three years of study at the Irish Baptist College, Evan and Carmen were accepted for the work in the Canary Islands.

They settled into an apartment in Pedro Hidalgo, another housing development in Las Palmas, where there was a small congregation. Having already learned the Spanish language in Honduras, Evan was able to go to work immediately and soon became aware of the tremendous need in the area. Besides trying to encourage the believers, he engaged in door-to-door evangelism and then set up a telephone ministry. These endeavours were slow but paid off. They had the joy of leading several to the Lord and baptizing them into membership of the church.

On 1st June 1990, Dennis and Maree felt constrained to revert to their previous status as independent missionaries. After two years of sowing and reaping in Pedro Hidalgo, Evan received an invitation from the small church in Lanzarote to become their pastor. Evan, Carmen and their two children, Deborah and little Evan, transferred to this smaller island where Evan was inducted as pastor of the church on 21st. February 1991. Just at that time, Mark Loney went to work with Evan for six weeks as part the Belfast Bible College field term.

For the next nine years, Evan took responsibility for the Evangelical church in Arrecife. Lanzarote is an interesting island of contrasts. It boasts the beautiful valley of a thousand palms and yet has landscape that resembles what might be found on the moon. It has a population of nearly seventy thousand nationals and many expatriates settling in retirement or holiday homes.

During their time on Lanzarote, the congregation grew considerably as Evan conducted evangelistic outreaches to other parts of the island. Some of their choice young people went to Bible college and returned to the work. Invited teams from Northern Ireland went to Lanzarote to help construct a new church complex for which

Evan had worked for many years. The Lord wonderfully supplied the need both in material and manpower.

Among the many visitors to Lanzarote were Jim and Sandra Thompson. Theirs was not a passing interest in the work. Summer after summer, they returned to help Evan and Carmen in the work at the youth camps. They organized the monthly Acre prayer meeting in their comfortable home in Bangor. This exposure to the work and involvement in it soon resulted in the Lord calling Jim and Sandra to Lanzarote.

When God calls a man or woman, there is always a price to pay. After Jim and Sandra completed their studies at the Irish Baptist College, they were accepted for the work that the Lord had laid on their hearts. Not only were they stepping out, but their two children, Kyle and Nathan, were at a crucial stage for their education.

The family stepped out and trusted the Lord in this move and arrived in Lanzarote in August 1999. Ironically, just as they arrived to work alongside Evan and Carmen, Evan expressed his disappointment that they would have to leave the island because of the educational needs of their little boy, Evan. It was difficult news for the new couple, but they felt that God had called them to the work. Marcos, one of the young men from the Arrecife church who studied at the Belfast Bible College, was installed as the new pastor. Jim and Sandra settled down to study Spanish while their children enrolled in a local English speaking school.

In over seventy years of experience, the Acre Gospel Mission has proved that God's work is always greater than the workers, whether they be national or foreigners. With God there are no foreign workers, just members of His body who function to accomplish His purpose.

Chapter Sixteen

A GATEWAY AT THE MARKET

Changes sometimes result from conscious decisions we make, while other changes are uninvitingly thrust upon us. However, they are no less part of God's plan for us to accomplish His purpose.

Nell Shannon and Dulcie Robertson were independent missionaries who faithfully maintained a witness at the central market in Manaus for over thirty years. They were always good friends of the Acre workers and when Nell retired to Northern Ireland and Dulcie to London in 1983, they donated their house to Acre Gospel Mission. Besides the house, they also asked Victor that the Mission carry on the witness they had sustained for so long at the market.

At that time, Hazel was working in Labrea but felt that her work there was finished and she was anxious for a new challenge. During a visit to Canutama and Labrea, Victor and Audrey put the challenge of this literature ministry to Hazel. Right away she responded positively to the invitation and was on her way to Manaus within a few days.

Hazel's work at the gateway of the market made an immediate impact on many passersby. Allen Loney wrote of that work some years later.

Hazel arrived in Manaus just when Miss Dulcie Robertson was ready to hand over the ministry at the market, where she and Nell Shannon had faithfully stood with their display of gospel literature for many years.

Every morning Monday through Saturday at seven o'clock, Hazel leaves the Mission house carrying her bags of books and leaflets. She walks down the crowded streets to the big market in the centre of the city and near the waterfront in Manaus. The rough pavements are thronged with people going about their business. Hazel is conscious that she is about her Father's business.

As she approaches the market, the thoroughfare narrows. People file past hordes of street vendors who have taken over most of the footpath with their stalls, which are cluttered with all sorts of goods. Little children and their mothers try to sell shopping bags, fruit, or vegetables in the doorways.

Eventually, Hazel reaches the huge enclosed market with its grey walls and three lovely wrought iron gateways. She heads through the central gate and just inside, she unlocks a wooden chest that quickly unfolds into a Bible and tract display. A poster displayed on an adjacent pillar illustrates "The Broad and Narrow Way." Another poster announces "The Two Calls," which depicts a rich man sitting at his desk, too busy to attend to the evangelist. At the bottom of the poster are startling words, "Thou fool, this night thy soul shall be required of thee".

Hazel has tracts in her hands and starts to distribute them to all who enter through the gates. Although ignored by many and scoffed at by some, she does have opportunity to speak to many others. Once Hazel gains their attention, soon she is able to show them the way of salvation through Jesus Christ.

Through this daily witness, Hazel led hundreds of people to Jesus Christ. Many of the converts return to ask advice from Hazel or request literature to use in their witness for Jesus Christ.

Perhaps the most remarkable conversion at the gateway was that of Manuel, one of the local traders who was raised in a spiritist family but was hungry for the truth of the gospel. He was struck by Hazel's zealous approach to evangelism near to where he was trying to make a living. This enthusiasm and sincerity soon got to him and after reading the literature, he not only accepted Jesus Christ as his Saviour but also became one of her greatest supporters at the market.

When another young man named Marcos accepted the Saviour at the gateway, he wept. Like Manuel, he also came from a spiritist background but after his conversion, he went home and told his family about the Saviour. His mother, father and then his brothers and sisters came to the Saviour. Years later Marcos' brother, Alan, studied at the Bible Institute and became the pastor of the Evangelical church in Feijó.

Besides the work at the market, Hazel also visited the campuses of different schools several evenings each week to distribute gospel literature. During these outings, she recruited many young people from local churches to help in this evangelistic outreach. Through this endeavour many students came to the Saviour, and several of these young people who accompanied Hazel were called into full-time Christian ministry. Hercules was a down-and-out drug addict whom Hazel met on the street and led to Jesus Christ. She then helped sponsor him at a rehabilitation clinic. Today, he is the resident caretaker of a church in Manaus.

Hazel supported many students during their Bible school training. One such young man was Elias, to whom she taught English and supported through his studies at the Baptist Seminary. Today Elias has a degree in theology, speaks four languages, and pastors the church in Tarauacá .

These years of witness were not without mishaps and setbacks. One Wednesday, Hazel arrived home from the market brimming with enthusiasm that she had met a man who was a representative for a Publishing House and was selling Bibles at wholesale prices. She told Victor that the man would be at the house shortly with some of these Bibles, so she needed dollars from the safe.

As good as his word, the well-dressed young man arrived at the Mission house and was very courteous in showing us the range of Bibles he carried. He had zipped Bibles, small Bibles, large Bibles and was prepared to sell them to Hazel at fifty percent off the retail price. Without any hesitation, Hazel told Victor to take them all.

The total bill came to just under $500.00. The young man gave us a receipt, and then Hazel placed an order for another quantity of Bibles for when he would be in Manaus again. No deposit was needed for this order. After the salesman left, there was general thanksgiving for the fortuitous contact.

On the following Saturday, not long after lunch, several of the missionaries were taking their afternoon siestas when they were disturbed by someone knocking at the front door. Emily Gilchrist attended the door, only to be confronted with three men. They asked if this was the Mission base, to which Emily replied positively. Although they were in plain clothes, they announced that they were policemen.

Emily became a little nervous at this news, for she had been to the bank a few days previously when the manager had impounded a $100 bill that she had purchased at the Ulster Bank in Belfast. The Brazilian bank informed her it was a counterfeit note and refused to give it back to her. Besides losing the money, she believed to be perfectly valid, she now thought the police had come to arrest her.

The policeman saw Emily was taken aback and immediately declared the purpose of his visit. He said he had come to inquire about the theft of Bibles. Emily was somewhat relieved that at least the police had not come for her.

Emily called for Hazel. Instead of having a siesta, Hazel was in the basement of the house preparing a taped message to the friends at home, telling them of her great bargain in Bibles. When she heard that the police were at the door, she came immediately and wanted to know where Victor was. Emily said Victor and Audrey had gone to meet their daughters, who were up from the boarding school for the weekend.

Hazel politely confronted the three men by asking, "How do I know you are policemen?"

The leader produced his wallet and showed his police identity badge. He then produced the copy of the order Hazel had given to the young man on Mission paper and said, "That young man was a thief. He bought those Bibles at the Evangelical bookstore with a check that bounced. I know that you have nothing to do with the crime but if you still have the Bibles, we will have to take them back and nothing more will be said about it to you."

Hazel had only sold a few Bibles while the majority were still in boxes in her apartment. She lost no time in bringing the Bibles out of the store and handing them over to the men, with a mixture of relief and disappointment.

As the three men carried the boxes out to a waiting car, Hazel followed them and spied the original salesman sitting in the rear seat of a Chevette with a gun pointed into his side by another officer. The young man seemed to be in distress and was crying. He shouted to Hazel that he was sorry.

Hazel waved her arm and retreated with haste before closing the door.

"Where is Victor?" Hazel called. "Wait 'til he hears what happened."

Hazel didn't know that Audrey went on her own to meet her girls while Victor was resting in another part of the house. Later when the Maxwell girls and Audrey arrived and Hazel discovered Victor was at home, she was ready to blow a gasket.

After a while, it all settled down. About a week later, Victor met the fellow who was in charge of the bookstore and related the story to him. He was interested to hear that the police had caught the thief, so he went to the police station to find out what had happened to the stolen merchandise. On hearing the details, the police told him that the missionaries had been conned twice. The thief and the so called "police" were all part of the same gang and had probably resold the Bibles several times.

Hazel maintained the witness at the market for more than ten years, until her mother's deteriorating health forced her to retire from Brazil.

While Hazel was at the market every day, Victor and Audrey, with whom she shared the Mission house, attended to the administration of Mission business. They also worked with the General Association of Regular Baptists in Manaus, where Victor taught at the Baptist Seminary. Many of these students later became leaders in the Baptist movement in Amazonas and other parts of Brazil.

Besides the work at the Baptist Seminary, Victor and Audrey also worked alongside a Brazilian couple, Januário and Tereza, to establish a new church in a new development on the other side of Manaus. Several young people who were led to Christ in that work are serving as missionaries today, and the church, Calvary Baptist Church, is led by one of Victor's former students.

When they returned to Brazil in 1995, besides leading the work of the Mission, they also founded a Baptist Church at Nova Aleixo. This work mushroomed in a short time and many people trusted the Lord. There were other contrasting outreaches that were reported in the Acre News in the summer of 1997.

> For two years, we have been swinging between two social extremes on most Saturday afternoons. Audrey has a Good News Club in a slum area of town where the poverty is overwhelming, the squalor is unbelievable and the stink of stagnant water below the house is foul. Nevertheless, for almost two hours, boys and girls sing choruses, learn Bible verses, listen to the gospel and then eat some goodies that Audrey takes with her.
>
> After a shower and a quick change of clothes we travel to an upper-class residence in another part of town. At the side of a beautiful swimming pool and under the idyllic setting of overhanging palms, we conduct a Bible study for a group of professional people. Following the study, a substantial meal is served. Most of those present do not attend any church, so this gives great opportunity for the gospel.
>
> The meetings in the slums have been very responsive. Several children have trusted the Lord, as well as some of

their parents. The study at the side of the pool seemed to produce nothing. That is, until at a recent Saturday afternoon study, a young man, totally unchurched, secure in a good job and living life to the full, sought the Lord. Conviction of sin had taken sleep from his eyes and finally led him to repentance and faith in Jesus Christ. Now as a believer, he is concerned for his aged mother and six brothers who are not saved. Another professional man accepted the Saviour as a result of the study at the pool, and he also has an avid hunger to know more of the scriptures.

During the eighties, several missionary families were obliged to leave Brazil because of family commitments. Tom and Ethel left Tarauacá and were followed by John and Hazel Matthews. Sadly, their daughter Christine became quite ill and needed specialized treatment, which brought about their exodus from Brazil.

Jack and June Bennett, who led the work in Manaus for several years, also had to relinquish their work and return to Northern Ireland. For six years, Jack pastored Moneymore Congregational Church before taking responsibility for the home end leadership of Acre Gospel Mission in 1995.

Emily Gilchrist, who had given many dedicated years to the leprosy programme returned to Northern Ireland to marry Jim McFarland on 22nd March, 1989.

These depletions from the work in Brazil left vacancies that could not be filled by foreign missionaries. They were not forthcoming. However, the investment of time and training with young Brazilians equipped many of them to replace the foreign missionaries in the interior.

In Boca do Acre, Pastor Pedro Moraes and his wife Antonia inaugurated the "Mary Harvey Memorial School" in honour of Mollie, who had given so many years to that work. Antonio Aquino, Elias, Alan, Anotonilso, João Filho, and Eliezer are all involved in work to which the missionaries dedicated their lives years earlier.

In 1987, Lucimar went to Labrea to help in the church. After three months, the pastor left to pastor the church in Canutama. This meant that a lot more responsibility fell on her shoulders. As well as this work, with the help of the young people of the church, she initiated a series of children's meetings in strategic parts of the town. Lucimar also became very concerned for the number of deprived children who could not afford to attend the schools where uniform was compulsory. The former day-school which Fred had founded in Labrea, had ceased to function five years earlier and the building had been forfeited to the local authorities.

In view of the growing children's work and need to do more, the church's office bearers agreed to restore the day school. They soon went to work and constructed two rooms at the back of the church, plus a kitchen and toilets. Lucimar persuaded the mayor of the town to pay for the teachers who were members of the church. Within a short time, the Christian school in Labrea was up and running again.

As well as the academic work, the children were taught the scriptures each day and some pupils and their parents accepted the Lord Jesus as Saviour. Numbers at the school increased and the town's civic fathers were so impressed with the school that they made arrangements for the original church school buildings to be returned to the church. Today the school continues to function with over three hundred children attending.

A report from the *Acre Missionary News* of summer 1991 gave an insight into her work.

> It can be lonely enough in Labrea for Lucimar, but she has involved herself in the work of the church and community. The town officials have commended her for the great work she is doing with the children. Over two hundred boys and girls are taught daily by four Christian teachers at the school, which has been built as an extension behind the church.
>
> An army officer lived just across the road from Lucimar's house. He was a known spiritist and practiced all sorts of rituals in his home. He took a great interest in the young people of the town and had an evil influence on them. This gave the believers a lot of concern. In fact, they met to pray for his removal. In a recent letter Lucimar

was delighted to give us the news that the officer is to be transferred to another town. However, the other week a man arrived at Lucimar's door to say that the devil owned Labrea, and that he would be paying Lucimar a visit because of her opposition to Satan. Lucimar wrote, "God gave me the courage to tell him that my God, who lives in me, is greater than Satan. I sent him away in the name of the Lord Jesus. The devil is very busy and recently there has been a lot of violence in the town, which gives everyone a lot of concern."

Please remember Lucimar as she lives alone.

The Lord not only protected Lucimar but also greatly used her in Labrea. After six years of hard work there, Lucimar went to Boca do Acre where she repeated her dedicated work among the children of the town. To see her moving through areas of the town was like a repetition of the Pied Piper as hordes of children followed her to her meetings. Her weekly radio programme "Precious Jewels" was listened to by thousands out in the forest areas.

Lucimar still endeavours to continue her work and witness among the children in Rio Branco.

Chapter Seventeen

OUT ON A LIMB

No believer can aspire higher in his Christian experience than to be a genuine servant of Jesus Christ. In the first chapter of Romans, Paul demonstrates two principal characteristics of a servant of the Saviour; his motivation as debtor, "I am a debtor both to the Greeks and to the Barbarians, to the wise and to the unwise." The depth of that motivation is measured by what Paul was ready to do, "So, as much as in me is, I am ready to preach the gospel to you that are in Rome also." These are the words of a man who also said that he was ready to suffer and be offered for Christ.

To their colleagues in Acre Gospel Mission, no couple displays these qualities of servanthood more by their motivation and readiness to serve the Saviour and sacrifice for Him, than James and Dorrie Gunning. They have been role models for all new missionaries and are affectionately looked upon as parents by many Brazilians who have grown to respect them.

New doors and new challenges opened for James and Dorrie, even though James was at an age when most men begin to take life in a slower lane. João Marinho, although he had spent most of his adult life in Acre, always had great concern for his family and neighbourhood back in Malhada Vermelha, Rio Grande do Norte, where there was little or no gospel witness.

Every morning in Sena Madureira, James and João met for prayer at 5 a.m.. During those times together, João shared his burden with James. Nearly every day they prayed about this matter. One day, João invited James and Dorrie to consider going with him to open a gospel witness in the interior of Rio Grande do Norte. It was a stiff challenge for anyone, but James and Dorrie agreed to pray about the invitation. After a short while, they gave João a positive answer.

James and Dorrie returned to Brazil after a busy furlough in May 1985 and almost immediately went to Sena Madureira, where James presided at a farewell service for Pastor João Marinho. Shortly after this, João and his family moved three thousand miles across Brazil to set up home near Malhada Vermelha.

He prepared the way for James and Dorrie and months later, this veteran couple embarked on a completely new work that would have been very daunting for a couple forty years younger. A report of the first steps of this venture appeared in the Missionary News.

> Much has happened since 15th May, when James and Dorrie returned to Brazil with Emily for a further term of missionary service. First of all, they visited Sena Madureira where they had laboured for so many years. While there, Pastor João Marinho retired and a new pastor was installed early in June. The church was packed with many friends present, including the mayor and all the town's councillors.
>
> James then visited Labrea, Canutama and some other churches they had helped while in Manaus. Meanwhile, João Marinho, his wife and their two youngest boys travelled out to his people in North East Brazil. João, having sold his home and possessions in Sena Madureira, travelled to Campo Redondo, the town nearest to his family village.
>
> About six years ago, after some days of unusually heavy rains, three reservoirs one below the other, burst as the resultant flood swept through the town. Like a tidal

wave, the rush of water uprooted a solid sixty foot cement bridge and carried it about two hundred yards down river. Many houses in the town were swept away. After the disaster, the governor financed a new housing development to rehouse the people who had been left without a home.

With the money gained from his sale in Acre, João has been able to buy one of these houses for himself. He is rejoicing in the Lord's provision. He says that the greatest blessing is that the Lord has given him the desire of his heart, to be able, along with James and Dorrie, to preach the gospel to his parents and people.

When James and Dorrie arrived a few months later, they were accommodated in a small house on the main street of Campo Redondo. It belonged to a widow who kindly agreed for James and Dorrie to stay there while she was away. The house had no ceilings and rats ran freely at night. During the day, there were swarms of flies everywhere that were only outnumbered by the many people who came to visit the new couple.

In Campo Redondo, there was a small church just one hundred yards from the house where James and Dorrie were staying. Sr. Benjamin, an American missionary, visited the area periodically but was not able to stay for very long. João's cousin, Sr. Gabriel, was in charge of the Wednesday prayer meeting and he was pleased that missionaries had come to live in the town and help them.

Already others are coming into the meetings. A woman's meeting has also been started on Thursday evenings, the first having been held in João 's house. Five of his neighbours attended and listened well.

João had been looking for a house for James and Dorrie and finally found one in the street next to his own house. James and Dorrie purchased the house, which was little more than a basic shell. Immediately James started to renovate and enlarge their new residence.

The climate and terrain in North Eastern Brazil are in stark contrast to that of Amazonas and Acre. In Campo Redondo, which is about one hundred miles from the coast, the climate is temperate with insignificant humidity due to the insufficient rainfall. This rough and mountainous region consists mostly of scrub land and barren wastes where many people barely etch out a scant subsistence in a hostile environment.

Like Amazonas and Acre decades earlier, the people of the region are deeply steeped in superstition and Roman Catholicism. At first these people who live in tightly knit communities where most families are related to each other, were suspicious of foreign missionaries.

James and Dorrie ignored the suspicions and spoke to all in the town. Gradually, the suspicions were eroded and the zealous and friendly couple were able to breakdown any distrust and make friends with many people in Campo Redondo. They also established amicable contacts in Malhada Vermelha, where most of João Marinho's family lived. These friendships were instrumental in introducing people to the meetings where many of them were converted.

Because of the new interest generated in Malhada Vermelha, James devoted time to help João construct a Church Hall in the village. Among the new converts was João Marinho's aged father, Sr. Pedro, who came to know the Saviour during a visit from Jovita. Pedro was the first of several in the family who came to profess faith in Jesus Christ.

Another notable conversion was that of Junior, a young man who lived next door to James and Dorrie. Although his parents were not Christians, Junior attended the meetings regularly. However, they were saddened to see him abusing and wasting his life in liquor and drugs. The missionaries set to praying for their wayward neighbour and one day James was overjoyed to lead Junior to personal faith in Christ.

Right from the outset of his conversion, Junior showed great desire to serve the Lord and soon went to the Bible Seminary in Ceará. There he met Cristina and after completing his training, they were married before being accepted as members of the Mission. Besides being the Vice President of the Mission in Brazil, Junior also is the pastor of a church in Tangará, forty miles from Campo Redondo. From there he has been working at establishing a witness in Irapurú, a village adjacent to where they live.

During James and Dorrie's time in the North East, they built up many contacts and great respect with other Christian workers in the wider region. This paved the way for other workers to follow, after James and Dorrie retired from the work in 1991. As they had done many times previously, they walked out of their furnished home and left most of their belongings, including their car, for the Brazilian pastor who followed after them.

After they left, Pastor Plinho, who had been led to the Lord by Paul and Reta Mayner in Canutama many years earlier, became the pastor of the Campo Redondo Church and a coworker with João Marinho.

After a survey of the field by Victor Maxwell, it became obvious that there were many open and opportune doors for the gospel in that region. Under the local leadership and cooperation of Pastor José Soares, new missionaries entered into the area. First, Sam and Andrea Scott from Kilkeel went to work with Pastor José in Santa Cruz for a short while. They were replaced by Billy and Agnes Jones, who were given responsibility for outreach into Sao Bento and Paraiso. Billy and Agnes, from Waringstown and Ballymena respectively, met at the Belfast Bible College and after learning Portuguese in Manaus, gave themselves unreservedly to the work. They are perfectly at home in Santa Cruz and their two lovely daughters, Sarah Jayne and Rebekah, have won the hearts of many locals. Billy not only preaches at the various developing congregations but he also has weekly classes at the High School in Santa Cruz where he teaches English and the Bible to more than five hundred students.

Besides Campo Redondo, Tangará, Santa Cruz and Malhada Vermelha, still other towns beckoned and workers were needed. Trevor and Yvonne Bennett responded to the challenge and after many years working with Slavic Gospel Association, they embarked on a new mission in Brazil. Their initial months in the country were spent at language school in Belem at the mouth of the Amazon. In September 1997, they moved to Campo Redondo. After settling in to the work, they have opened a new work in Lajes Pintadas and are still planning to reach other needy areas. Trevor and Yvonne had no children and were glad to open their home and hearts in September 2000 when they adopted their little Brazilian daughter, Bethany Joy.

Meetings have started in Coronel Ezequiel while plans are afoot for a witness to be established in Jaçaná. Both towns are within a twenty mile range of Santa Cruz. Workers are needed for these needy areas. Already David and Christine Bell have arrived in Brazil with their little daughter Esther and are currently engaged in language study.

David's parents have had an Acre prayer meeting in their home for many years. Christine trained and worked with CEF for several years before meeting David. Once they complete language study they will move to an interior town in Rio Grande do Norte. Their presence will consolidate the work that the Jones and the Bennetts are already engaged in.

Chapter Eighteen

HEAVENLY TREASURES

The missionaries in Brazil needed to keep a clear vision of the spiritual nature and priority of their mission, as well as the spiritual need all around them. Yet they could not close their eyes to the social need that they frequently encountered. Perhaps these parallel aspects of the work are demonstrated best by Fred Orr's and Bill Wood's contrasting but equally important work.

Fred and Zení continued to be totally involved in the work of the Cruzada in Manaus while Fred travelled extensively to attend invitations to preach at conferences and evangelistic missions all over Brazil. Besides these meetings, Fred was also teaching at several Bible schools as well as having his weekly Bible study at the Cruzada headquarters. The whole thrust of this ministry was to equip Brazilians for the work of the gospel.

The work of the Cruzada bookstore continued to grow and became the main supplier in the region for all CEF material. Zení was provided the opportunity to teach the Bible in several schools and to better equip her for this work, she travelled to São Paulo to do the CEF Teacher's Training Course. Here is Fred's report about that trip.

Zení went to do the CEF leadership course. After leaving Manaus, the plane almost crashed into the forest. It fell more than two thousand metres. They ran into ice and rough weather. Zení said the screaming aboard was terrible. People panicked as trays of food sailed through the cabin, spilling over everybody. She was sure she was going to die. The fellow beside her shouted for her to pray! She said she could not speak. Then he yelled, "Do you not believe in God?"

Eventually she stuttered, "I'm a believer in Jesus."

Waiting for the impact on the ground was terrible. She wanted to die before that happened. Many people fainted and quite a number were hurt and taken to the hospital in Brasilia. On arrival, Zení was met at the plane by the CEF director and his wife.

Zení found the studies interesting but very demanding. Every day her first class began at seven o'clock in the morning. That meant rising very early for devotions, breakfast and chores. Every Friday they had exams and with all the "homework" each day, they certainly had to grind. Her letters show an interesting development, ranging from her doubts about being able to cope, to confidence that she would succeed. She is now back with the family in Manaus.

The work continues in the seminaries and it is a real privilege to be a part in the shaping of these young lives for the Master's service. I have promised the director of the Baptist Seminary that I will do some Bible studies for them this term.

Hazel's work was complemented by the work of the Cruzada Amazonica. On Tuesday evenings, she took many of the converts to Fred's weekly Bible study at the Cruzada headquarters. Some of those early converts also attended the meetings that Fred Orr started in the garage of his house.

The meetings in the garage began because Fred's family could not find a place of worship in their area that was faithful to the Word of God. However, the purpose of the meetings was not to attract believers from other churches to augment their numbers. Evangelism and teaching the Word of God were the main emphasis at this Sunday evening service. Mostly neighbours attended and within a short time, quite a few locals trusted the Saviour.

Further to the weekly meetings several workers of the Cruzada visited many homes in the area and had the opportunity of leading some people to faith in Christ on the doorstep. When the congregation outgrew the capacity of the garage, Fred was able to purchase a shell of a house farther down his own street. Within a short time, they had renovated that house to accommodate the increasing number of converts and people attending the meetings.

On 10th January, 1993, the Hebron Evangelical church was founded. José Cardoso, grandson of Sr. Artú in Boca do Acre and a former seminary student of Victor and Jack, became the pastor of the new church and coworker with Fred Orr. Fred's and José's families threw themselves wholeheartedly into the work and week after week, people came to know the Saviour. The original house had to be enlarged twice until it was finally knocked down. On the same site, they built a magnificent church which accommodates two hundred and fifty people.

The church has become renowned as one of the primary places for sound Bible teaching in Manaus and Fred's Tuesday night bible study is attended by believers from other churches. They are strong in evangelism and have an AWANA troop of nearly two hundred children.

Also in 1991, Fred officially retired from the Acre Gospel Mission but continued to be committed to the work God had called him to. He stimulated the Cruzada's Board to organize the Hebron Bible Institute which later was transformed into the Hebron Theological Seminary. This provided a wide spectrum of theological and practical courses for Christian workers of all denominations. Missionaries who were former students at the Institute, are being supported in different regions of Brazil.

Originally, the Hebron Institute's classes began in the Cruzada's downtown premises and then moved to the more spacious Hebron Evangelical Church, where there was more room for the increased number of students. Besides Fred and Pastor José giving lessons, Millicent Bailie and Zení offered training classes in Child Evangelism. Fredinho and Dr. Florence Orr, Fred's son and daughter, were invited to teach at the Institute as well as other pastors who were requested to lead specialized courses. Later, Victor was also part of the teaching body of the Institute.

Pastor Elias, a member of Hebron Evangelical Church, studied at the Baptist Seminary of Amazonas where Victor taught. He was invited to pastor the church in Tarauacá. During Elias' time in Tarauacá the municipal authorities recognized the great contribution that Tom and Ethel had made to the local population by naming their new maternity unit after Ethel, "A Clínica Ethel Geddis."

Alan, a brother of Marcos who trusted the Saviour at the market, had a dramatic conversion after which he trained for three years at Hebron Bible Institute. Later, he became the pastor at Feijó. Antoildson, another graduate of the Hebron Bible Institute, replaced Hazel at the market during her absence and then became the assistant pastor to João Marinho Filho, João Marinho's son in Sena Madureira. Other national graduates of the Hebron Bible Institute are involved in many other mission agencies in Brazil.

After Victor and Audrey had to leave Brazil in 1997, the Mission house that had been headquarters for the Mission for twenty-five years was no longer needed. The Hebron Theological Seminary purchased the property and transformed it into a school for more than forty students who are preparing their lives for the Lord's work.

Fred has given his life to the work in Brazil and that life is now being reproduced in the lives of other young people who are dedicating themselves to the same Lord for His work in Brazil.

* * * * *

Bill Woods pursued his goal of trying to eliminate leprosy and to alleviate the handicaps of those who suffered from many deformities caused by this dreaded disease. Besides this, Bill purchased a site on which he built a house in Rio Branco. The following report gave an update of his work.

Bill spoke on the phone, "I finally moved into my new house. I have been enjoying it since May. It is so convenient."

He added that he installed the electric himself, put the glass in the windows, made his own kitchen cupboards and fixed the ironwork across the windows to deter the entry of thieves. He commented, "At least it is only a few minutes' walk from the hospital and affords some privacy and more space."

However, two days later, he went on an hour's flight to Manoel Urbano. From there he went on to Tarauacá and later as far as Cruzeiro do Sul, before catching the long flight to Manaus.

These have been busy weeks in Rio Branco, where Bill has been sorting out the charts and reports of over four thousand patients and preparing them for visits from specialists for orthopaedic and plastic surgery.

One case gave Bill some cause for anxiety. The surgeon gave a twenty-year-old boy a face lift. Because of this leprosy, the boy was left with the appearance of an old man. After the operation, he had suffered a hemorrhage under the skin and the operation had to be repeated. Two days after the plastic surgery, the surgeon left and the patient had another hemorrhage. Bill wrote, "I had to reopen his face myself. I was sure that he was going to lose all the skin on one side of his face and be left with a burn-like scar. The Lord answered prayer and the bleeding stopped. I think I'll just keep my wrinkles after all."

Bill also told of a little lady who had been blind for fourteen years. "She was so maimed by leprosy that she even had to have food put in her mouth. Because she had no feeling in her hands, she could not locate the spoon or even the bathroom door! Now, she has sixty per cent vision and has been calling me her Angel."

Summing up a year's work Bill wrote the following:

For me, this was a year of travel. I travelled to the south of Brazil, São Paulo and Rio de Janeiro, twice to refresher courses on leprosy and three times to accompany patients who were going there for surgery or treatment. In November, I was called to Brasilia for a conference on leprosy with the Ministry of Health. I also went to Manaus with a patient who needed treatment for cancer. Besides these trips I had many visits across the state of Acre to supervise the work in the interior towns.

This was a year of toiling. The outpatients' clinic is hectic some days, with scores of patients all wanting to be attended to immediately. My morning clinic usually takes six hours. The eye clinic, which is once a week is the worst. The other doctors just say, "I cannot attend you here, come to my private consulting rooms." That means everyone wants me to attend them. We haven't tried to count the number of operations we got through last year. It seems that I get the patients and jobs that no one else wants - like the Sunday morning, I spent picking the maggots out of a woman's nose. The nurse who was helping me stopped counting at eighty. Ah well, it certainly works up an appetite for lunch!

This was also a year of triumphs. What a thrill to see folks respond in the outpatients' clinic well to treatment, their skin patches clearing up with no deformity setting in. This year, I was able to tell many patients, "You have been cured and you only need to come back for a check up." A totally blind six-month-old baby girl was brought to me. She had congenital cataracts. After surgery, it was interesting to watch her find and pick up her toys.

An old leprosy patient with one blind eye was brought in. What a blessing for him to be able to see again, especially since he has no feeling in his hands. A young boy just left the hospital after having the function of his thumb restored through a tendon transfer.

Manoel, another patient, will be returning to Cruzeiro do Sul soon. Although he is only forty-five years old, he has been in a wheel chair for twenty years. We amputated one leg and operated on the other foot. We were able to have him fitted with an artificial leg, and he is walking now unassisted.

Geraldo, a Christian patient from Labrea, was in the same condition and went home walking with hardly a limp. He also had an artificial leg fitted.

Missionary nurse Emily Gilchrist and her Brazilian colleague Ruth conducted meetings each week in the wards. The greatest triumph of the year is to see patients come to the Saviour.

Even though Emily had to leave Brazil at the end of 1988, the team of Brazilian doctors and medics under Bill's leadership and the help of the Italians devoted themselves to their goal of reaching every leprosy patient in Acre. Leprosy has not been eradicated from the region, but it is now below the World Health Organization's guideline of high risk region.

Bill Woods has come a long way since the night in Canutama, when he heard the young man's voice echo through the night air, "Do something. I want you to do something." Bill has done all that he could and more than any one could have ever dreamed of. He was even admitted to a Leprosy Hospital and classified as a suspect patient. God has richly blessed His child, gifted him, guided him and protected him. Today, thousands of people in Brazil would rise up to call him blessed.

Bill's expertise is now much sought after in other parts of Brazil and beyond. Invitations come regularly from many other Brazilian states, requesting his counsel or inviting him to lead a seminar. Many of these states covet his presence for their local leprosy programmes. In the summer of 1997, the Minister of Health for Brazil, Dr. Abib Jatene, was in Rio Branco to pay an official visit to the Leprosy Unit at the hospital and publicly applaud the fine work the team had done.

The Bolivian government's health department has solicited the services of Bill's Rio Branco team to train their workers in the technique of introducing the Multi Drug Therapy to their frontier areas, where they border with the Acre. Bill has been invited by the same government to give seminars in several large Bolivian cities.

Testimony of Bill's work is best told by those who work with him. Nurse Ruth Rodriques, a great friend to Emily and a long term member of the Leprosy team, says, "The patients say that under God in heaven, Dr. Bill Woods is their father. He is dedicated and untiring in his work for his patients. We thank God for Dr. Bill."

His close coworker, Dr. Léia Borges, says, "I cannot find words to describe the work of this man. He is so human and down to earth, yet he is so dedicated and resolute in his drive to help his patients. He is greatly respected by all his professional colleagues and throughout the state he is greatly esteemed by the governor, the senators and members of the State Legislator."

In August 1981, the City Council of Cruzeiro do Sul made Bill an honorary citizen of their municipality. Likewise, in November 1990, the City Council of Rio Branco conferred an honorary citizenship to Bill. At the Congress for Leprosy in Endemic Countries, convened at the famous Iguaçú Falls on 5th June, 1997, the Brazilian College of Dermatologists conferred an honorary award on Bill in recognition of his excellent work in Acre.

Bill is unaffected, spontaneous, and genuine in combining his social concern and surgical skills with his love for souls and dedication to his Lord. Undoubtedly, the attention he gives to the dying body is because of his compassion for the never-dying souls of his patients.

On 1st January 1997, Dr. Bill's work was recognized by her Majesty Queen Elizabeth II, who awarded him an OBE (Officer of the British Empire). An invitation was given, or better still, a summons was issued, to receive the award at Buckingham Palace. The investiture took place on the 4th November, 1997.

Following the news of Her Majesty conferring this honour on Bill, Brazilian Senator Flaviano Melo addressed the President of Brazil and fellow senators on 5th June, 1997 with the following speech.

> Mr. President and Senators, I wish to put on record in this house the honour that is being awarded to Dr. William John Woods by the Queen of England for humanitarian service. You may ask what has that to do with us? It so

happens that Dr. Woods has performed his work in the state of Acre which I represent as senator.

Dr. William Woods arrived in Acre for the first time in 1963, working as a missionary. He visited the Leprosarium, "Colonia Asilo Souza Araujo" in Rio Branco, Acre, and was deeply impressed by what he saw. This led him to take a leave of absence from his mission and go to Manaus to study medicine.

In 1979, fully qualified as a doctor, he returned to Acre to commence his unceasing battle against leprosy. In 1986, the Ministry of Health decided to introduce the new treatment/therapy recommended by the World Health Organization in the states of Amazonas, Rio de Janeiro, Federal District (Brasilia) and Rondonia. Dr. Woods immediately approached the Ministry of Health and was successful in getting the state of Acre included in this project, thus making this modern therapy available to the Acre people.

Making excellent use of this new treatment and counting on the professional help and expertise of nurses such as Ruth Barbosa, Ursula Mihlam, Vania Barros and doctors José Furtado, Roberto Couta, Léia Borges, Dr. William commenced the mammoth task of reaching those in need. Wherever there was a carrier of this disease, Dr. William and his team got to work. Often in my political journeys across the state and in isolated regions, I heard of and saw the evidence of this noble work.

Please consider the very interesting results of his endeavour - the incidence of leprosy across the state has been reduced from 105 cases per 10,000 in 1985 to only 15 cases per 10,000 in 1996. It is important to emphasize the help that these professionals have received; - the many small boats equipped and manned to reach the headwaters of the many rivers and the financial help from non-governmental sources, all to facilitate Dr. Woods and his team.

Acre is still a needy state - the disease is endemic but according to Ministry of Health analysis, we are on track to reduce the incidence to one per 10,000 by the year 2000.

All this is due to the untiring commitment and complete dedication of this doctor from Ireland whose vision is to see leprosy eradicated in our state. He is doing a great service to the people of Acre.

This is all I have to say, Mr. President.

Enough has been said.

Chapter Nineteen

A ROYAL AUDIENCE

Tuesday, 16th May, 2000, was a beautiful sunny spring morning in central London. At ten o'clock Lucimar, Audrey and Victor stepped out from the crowd of onlookers who lined the railings outside Buckingham Palace and walked across the pebbled courtyard. Lead-like soldiers, dressed in their red tunics and black trousers, stood motionless outside their sentry boxes with automatic weapons resting on their right shoulders and the famous tall black busbies almost obscuring their faces.

From the courtyard, the three friends proceeded through a short tunnel that emerged into a large rectangular enclosure. At the other side, men in top hats, tails and neat pin-stripe trousers ushered the three colleagues under a large canopy and into a magnificent, plush reception area.

Lining each side of the hallway members of the Household Cavalry stood at attention with gleaming swords held upright in their hands and their bright breastplates and helmets reflecting a galaxy of sparkling light from several majestic chandeliers. A polite courtier checked the credentials of the three friends and ushered them up several steps into a long and lavishly decorated corridor. Delicate but elegant tapestries and huge oil paintings adorned the high walls on either side of the corridor. The deep pile of the red carpet gave Lucimar the feeling that she was treading on air.

A high ranking airman received the three into the resplendent ballroom of Buckingham Palace. The band of the Grenadier Guards was almost hidden from view in the minstrel gallery, at the rear of the ballroom from where their beautiful music set the mood for the opulent surroundings.

Other guests filed into the large ballroom as Lucimar, Audrey and Victor were shown to their red velvet seats in the first row, just fifteen feet from the rostrum where Her Majesty Queen Elizabeth II would soon stand.

Apart from gasps and exclamations of surprise and wonder, little had been spoken in the few minutes it took to reach the ballroom. Finally, Lucimar could not contain herself and exclaimed, "Dona Audrey, this is like a dream come true. Who would have ever thought that a cabocla (a hillbilly) from Tarauacá would ever sit in the front row of the main ballroom in Buckingham Palace?"

It was truly unbelievable and it took a while for it all to sink in. On one side of the room, a double door opened to another room where those who were about to receive awards assembled in an orderly line. On the other right hand side of the room, the three colleagues could see quite a distance down a long and wide corridor where tall marble pillars and a series of mirrors led to an area where their curiosity could only speculate.

When the ballroom was full with guests, a sudden sharp crash on the floor interrupted the sound of music and buzz of a hundred people chattering. It was the leader of the traditional Beefeaters thumping the floor with his rod, announcing his and his three colleagues' arrival. Ceremoniously, they progressed down the aisle, flanked on either side by wide eyed guests admiring their unusual dress. Each step was accompanied by another thump of a rod, until they took their place at the front.

A tall gentleman dressed in Royal Air Force uniform commanded those assembled to rise for the arrival of Her Majesty the Queen. An entourage of neat Gurka soldiers and other well-dressed service men and courtiers accompanied Her Majesty, who led the way into the ballroom. When the diminutive figure of the Sovereign, elegantly dressed in blue, took her place at the front, the band started up the National Anthem.

With everyone in place, the guests seated and the band still playing softly in the background, the ceremony began. From behind the Queen, the first person was called, "Elizabeth Taylor, is made a Dame of the British Empire for her services to the arts."

The world famous movie star, wearing her renowned diamonds, emerged from the open doorway on the left. She shuffled along somewhat unsteadily on her feet but aided by a uniformed Naval officer. Although she appeared to be ill, she declined assistance as she curtsied before Queen Elizabeth. The celebrated star stepped forward to receive her Damehood. After the Queen presented the award, a few moments of conversation followed before the new Dame retreated and filed out through the door to the right.

Again, a voice from behind the Queen announced, "Julie Andrews is made a Dame of the British Empire for her services to the Arts."

As the famous singer elegantly stepped up to make her way in front of the Queen, the band struck into a medley of bright tunes from "Mary Poppins", for which Julie Andrews won an Oscar. Gracefully, she bowed to Her Majesty and then stepped forward for the Queen to pin her award on the jacket of the star's beautiful peach suit. The Queen smiled as the two ladies talked together. Dame Julie Andrews stepped backwards, curtsied and proudly retired from the room.

Another few honoured subjects were announced and appropriately decorated by the Queen, who took time to speak to each one. Each person entered the ballroom as if it was the proudest moment of their lives.

The anonymous voice from behind the Queen clearly announced the moment for which Lucimar, Audrey and Victor had been invited and were waiting, "Dr. Thomas Henry Geddis is awarded the Officer of the British Empire for humanitarian services in Brazil and to the Northern Ireland Office."

Tom stepped out to meet the Queen. Like those who had gone before, he walked a few paces to stand in front of Her Majesty. Courteously, he bowed his head and then stepped forward to receive his investiture from the Sovereign's hand. Although Tom is forever the epitome of modesty, it was a proud and deserved moment. His three friends sitting only feet away and other colleagues who could not be present, knew that Her Majesty was only giving recognition to something that they had known for a long time.

As Tom retreated after his short conversation with Her Majesty, he appeared a little forlorn and lonely in the grandeur of the Palace, in spite of the presence of so many celebrities around him. Lucimar, Audrey and Victor wanted to congratulate their friend but had to wait to the end of the ceremony. Nevertheless, his three colleagues were tuned into his thoughts, "If only Ethel could have been here."

Tom and Ethel had been inseparable until death cruelly separated the devoted couple in their fortieth year of married life on 22nd January, 1999.

Later Tom recognized that Ethel could not be in Buckingham Palace to see the Queen, because she had a greater appointment with the King of Kings in a sanctuary not made with hands. She went to be with Christ on 22nd Janaury, 1999. There she will receive the Crown of Righteousness, which the Lord shall give to all those who love His appearing.

Besides meeting her Saviour, Ethel has met her family, converts from Tarauacá and her colleagues who served with her in the Acre Gospel Mission.

Ina Orr finished her course in Labrea on 4th. June 1954.

Margaret McComb triumphantly entered into heaven on 3rd April 1982.

Corina departed to be with Christ, which is far better, in October 1984.

Willie McComb went to his Saviour and reward in May 1985.

Mollie Harvey was promoted to glory on 24th August 1995.

João Marinho fought a good fight, finished his race in triumph, kept the faith and entered into the presence of his Saviour and his colleagues, three months after Ethel in April 1999.

Emily McFarland, always gracious and obliging, also slipped into the presence of her Lord in 29th July, 1999.

When Paul wrote to the fellowship in Philippi, his thoughts were clearly filled with his first entrance to that Macedonian city. He wrote, "I thank my God upon every remembrance of you, always in every prayer of mine for you all making request with joy, for your fellowship in the gospel from the first day until now; being confident of this very thing, that He which hath begun a good work in you will perform it until the day of Jesus Christ." (Philippians 1:3-6)

Closer examination of these encouraging words from Paul show that he mentioned three days that were important to the Philippian church and to all who know and serve the Lord Jesus.

Paul recalled the first day.

When Paul mentioned the first day, he undoubtedly was recalling the vision of the man of Macedonia by whom he received a message that sent him to Philippi. The early converts of the church, the public persecutions, the praises in prison and the conversion of the jailor and his household filled his thoughts.

In this volume we have been recalling the first days of Acre Gospel Mission and we employ the words of Paul to say "I thank my God upon every remembrance of you." Thank God for the work and monumental sacrifice of Willie and Margaret McComb and Mollie Harvey. They were the pioneers of this work who did not go out to found a Mission. They stepped out to obey God and when Mollie returned alone in 1947, she was the Acre Gospel Mission. We salute these valiant servants of God.

Paul alluded to the present day.

Paul wrote of the first day until "now" - this present day. A lot of water has flowed down the Amazon in sixty-five years and it still flows as mighty as ever. Who can measure the work and sacrifice of missionaries who have given the best years of their lives to this work? Who can calculate the value and faithfulness of hundreds of supporters who have stood by those who have served on the various fields?

The Acre Gospel Mission and its missionaries have no laurels to rest on. There is yet much to do and there is still time to take off our coats, roll up our sleeves and go to work in Portugal, the Canary

Islands and Brazil. For those who cannot go, the continuing work today calls out for those who are willing stand where others stood to support this work over many years.

We thank God for the work and workers today.

Paul anticipated the Day of Jesus Christ.

What a day that will be. It is the day in which Jesus will come again. It is the day for which all Christians should be living. It is the day for which all who have been involved in Acre Gospel Mission, missionaries, support workers and supporters have been labouring. What a great day of reunion that will be when friends greet friends in the everlasting habitations of heaven. Only then will the full story of Acre Gospel Mission ever be told.